Administering SAP™ R/3: The HR-Human Resources Module

Administering SAP™ R/3: The HR-Human Resources Module

ASAP World Consultancy
Jonathan Blain and Bernard Dodd
with contribution from Max Nyiri

201 West 103rd Street, Indianapolis, Indiana 46290

Administering SAP™ R/3:
The HR-Human Resources Module

Copyright© 1999 by Que

International Standard Book Number: 0-7897-1756-5

Library of Congress Catalog Card Number: 97-89573

Printed in the United States of America

First Printing: March 1999

00   99   98   4   3   2   1

Trademarks

Warning and Disclaimer

EXECUTIVE EDITOR
Bryan Gambrel

ACQUISITIONS EDITOR
Angela Kozlowski

DEVELOPMENT EDITOR
Susan Dunn

MANAGING EDITOR
Lisa Wilson

PROJECT EDITOR
Rebecca Mounts

COPY EDITOR
Tonya Maddox

INDEXER
Joy Dean Lee

PROOFREADER
Gene Redding

TECHNICAL EDITOR
David Knittle

INTERIOR DESIGN
Ruth Harvey

COVER DESIGN
Dan Armstrong

LAYOUT TECHNICIANS
Brandon Allen
Mark Walchle

Contents at a Glance

Table of Contents

8 Planning for Personnel Development 231

9 Recruiting, Changing Jobs, and Leaving 243

About the Author

ASAP World Consultancy is an international SAP consulting company and is part of the ASAP International Group. The ASAP International Group comprises the following:

- ASAP World Consultancy—SAP/Enterprise Transformation Consultancy
- ASAP Worldwide—Recruitment and Resourcing
- ASAP Institute—Education, Training, and Research
- ASAP Standards and Assessment Board—Quality Standards and Assessment Services

ASAP World Consultancy is in the business of selling high-quality products and services related to SAP and other enterprise applications, computing systems, and implementations. The company specializes in enterprise transformation management, delivering integrated business solutions.

ASAP International Group operates globally and its activities include the following:

- Introductory SAP courses for corporate clients globally
- SAP implementation consultancy
- SAP permanent, temporary, and contract recruitment
- Business process reengineering, renewal, change management, and transformation consultancy
- SAP human issues consultancy
- SAP internal and external communications consultancy
- SAP project and resource planning consultancy
- SAP skills transfer to your employees
- SAP education and training
- SAP system testing consultancy and resourcing
- SAP documentation consultancy
- SAP procurement consultancy
- SAP access and security consultancy
- Hardware and Installation Consultancy
- Development of SAP complementary solutions
- SAP market research
- SAP product and services acquisitions, mergers, and joint ventures

The company is known for the following:

- Accelerated skills transfer
- Maximizing retained value
- Transformation management
- ASAP World Consultancy implementation methodology
- ASAP Institute—comprehensive education and training

The company prides itself on the quality of its people. It uses a combination of its own employees, international sovereigns, and associates, who bring a wealth of experience and skills to meet the needs of its customers.

ASAP has a commitment to quality and is focused on meeting the business objectives of its clients through a number of highly specialized divisions and companies.

ASAP International Group can be contacted at the following address:

ASAP House
P.O. Box 4463
Henley on Thames
Oxfordshire
RG9 1YW
U.K.

Tel: +44 (0)1491 414411
Fax: +44 (0)1491 414412
Email: **enquiry@asap-consultancy.co.uk**
Author comments: **info@asap-consultancy.co.uk**
Web site: **http://www.asap-consultancy.co.uk/**

ASAP 24-Hour Virtual Office, New York, NY, U.S.
Tel: 212-253-4180
Fax: 212-253-4180

See the advertisements at the back of this book for more details.

Jonathan Blain is the founder of the ASAP group of companies. He has been working with SAP products since 1991. He has a strong business background, having spent 10 years in the oil industry working in various roles in the downstream sector for the Mobil Corporation. He has specialist knowledge of large-scale SAP implementations, project management, human issues, planning, communications, security, training, documentation, and SAP recruitment. He has benefited from professional business training with the Henley Management College and other institutions.

As a management consultant, he has specialized in matching corporate business strategies to IT strategies. He has a special interest in business engineering and the effective management of change when implementing large-scale IT systems.

Coming from a business rather than systems background, he focuses on providing business solutions. He believes that the implementation of SAP can improve the way companies do business and that, provided common sense and logical thinking are applied, SAP implementations need not be daunting.

Bernard Dodd, after graduating in psychology at Aberdeen University, built and directed an industrial training research unit over a period of nine years at the Department of Psychology, University of Sheffield. Two years with an international business consultancy led to an open competition direct entry to the specialist Civil Service, where he served the Royal Navy for 17 years to become the senior psychological advisor to the Second Sea Lord.

Since 1990, he has specialized in technical interviewing of experts and the writing of system documentation and user handbooks for the computer-intensive industries.

Max Nyiri holds doctorates in psychology and computer science. An IT business strategist, he has extensive experience in the determination and evaluation of enterprise application-management information requirements, as well as the recommendation and implementation of IT business solutions. He uses project management and strategy implementation experience to ensure strategic alignment of information technology with business requirements.

Max was a senior executive consultant to various multinational companies. He worked for the division of Coopers & Lybrand Consulting. His success was marked by being the youngest IT senior executive worldwide for Volkswagen. He consulted for Arthur Andersen as a senior executive to set up the SAP and Baan practice. The senior executive position in a prestigious international operating bank is part of his knowledge base. He is now a managing board member of Mercedes Benz Finance, representing the Systems department.

Dedication

I dedicate this book to my dear wife, Jennifer, and our beautiful daughter, Kezia.

—*Jonathan Blain*

Acknowledgments

In writing this book, we have benefited from the help and support of many people. There isn't space here to acknowledge everyone. They have each given their time and effort freely to make this book thorough, accurate, and useful to readers. Equally, many companies have given us much of their valuable time and shared their thoughts and opinions.

Our heartfelt thanks go to everyone who has helped. The writing of this book has been a team effort, and just praise should go to each and every team member.

Tell Us What You Think!

As the reader of this book, *you* are our most important critic and commentator. We value your opinion and want to know what we're doing right, what we could do better, what areas you'd like to see us publish in, and any other words of wisdom you're willing to pass our way.

As the Executive Editor for the Client/Server Database team at Macmillan Computer Publishing, I welcome your comments. You can fax, email, or write me directly to let me know what you did or didn't like about this book—as well as what we can do to make our books stronger.

Please note that I cannot help you with technical problems related to the topic of this book, and that due to the high volume of mail I receive, I might not be able to reply to every message.

When you write, please be sure to include this bookís title and author as well as your name and phone or fax number. I will carefully review your comments and share them with the author and editors who worked on the book.

Fax: [317-817-7070]

Email: cs_db@mcp.com

Mail: Executive Editor
          Client/Server Database
          Macmillan Computer Publishing
          201 West 103rd Street
          Indianapolis, IN 46290 USA

Introduction

The Scope of This Book

The process of administering the HR-Human Resources module for an SAP R/3 system is conducted by many people who aren't computer experts in each of the thousands of specialties—nor do they need to be. The module comes complete with the most advanced computer-assisted tools for guiding you through the implementation process from first analysis to customizing to performance evaluation of the working installation. There are clearly two aspects to customizing: preparing R/3 to integrate with the HR application and adjusting the standard HR system to suit your company.

The parts and chapters in this book are as follows:

Part I, "Administering the Personnel Administration and Payroll Accounting Modules," contains these chapters:

- Chapter 1, "Building a Global Integrated Human Resource System"
- Chapter 2, "Preparing the Fundamentals of HR Management"
- Chapter 3, "Managing Personnel Time"
- Chapter 4, "Administering Benefits"
- Chapter 5, "Administering Payroll"
- Chapter 6, "Managing Business Trips"

Part II, "Administering the Personnel Planning and Development Modules," focuses on the following:

- Chapter 7, "Planning Human Resource Requirements"
- Chapter 8, "Planning for Personnel Development"
- Chapter 9, "Recruiting, Changing Jobs, and Leaving"
- Chapter 10, "Managing Business Events"
- Chapter 11, "Using the HR Information System"
- Chapter 12, "Setting Up the Control Mechanisms in HR"
- Chapter 13, "Developing HR Strategy for IT Divisions"
- Chapter 14, "Seeing HR from a Consultant's Viewpoint"

At the end of the book, you'll find a glossary of SAP and HR terms.

What You Will Gain from This Book

The administering of the R/3 Human Resources system is a matter of using its many parts. This book points out what these parts are and how they depend on each other.

This book is amenable to a focused search because it refers to the concepts used by HR specialists and SAP HR practitioners. The most satisfied readers will find that they have acquired the concepts and the language with which to ask questions of the SAP specialists.

Thoughtful readers can expect to gain a thorough understanding of the changes that will need to take place in each department. This book provides the explanations for why the changes have to take place and the benefits gained by having them done well.

It isn't an unreasonable outcome if a serious reader saves the cost of the volume by deciding that the SAP system isn't what his particular company should have at the top of its shopping list.

Intended Readers

The authors have three groups of readers in mind:

- Those close to an HR system
- Those who are thinking about an HR system
- Those who would like to inform themselves about what's entailed in running a modern, comprehensive business data processing system

Two aspects to the installation of any system deserve equal attention: the technical details of the system and the effect it's likely to have on the staff and their conduct of your business. This book reflects these two concerns.

Consultants and Advisory Staff

The intended readers close to an HR system are consultants, programmers, launchers, and managers, as well as emergency service providers in the data and personnel categories. They're likely to be

- People involved in an HR implementation
- People interested in implementing an HR system
- People interested in working with HR

One task that could fall on anyone close to an HR system is to explain why the programs are arranged as they are and why the users have to interact with a standard interface. Such explanations will be required at all levels—to the chief executive officer as well as to the recruiting consultant. The content for such explanations is available in this book.

Similarly, a company's HR and payroll specialists will want to know why their current methods won't be exactly replicated in the new SAP system.

Managers at all levels will find that this book goes into considerable detail about the data processing functions provided by the HR application; that way, they can recognize aspects of their own work that could be facilitated by having the system at their command. On the other hand, they will see that a complex system does require a disciplined approach, for instance, to the maintenance of uniform data records in standard formats.

Consultants will see that SAP system designers have made provisions for them to build for their client an HR system that's unique yet assembled from standard business programs that have been thoroughly tested and refined. This book prepares consultants to ask clients the right questions and to make proper allowances for the work involved in customizing a system to fit the client's specific circumstances and requirements.

If you want to become an SAP consultant, you will see that an extensive body of technical expertise is built into SAP programs because they have been developed in partnerships with specific industries. You will also recognize that the SAP systems' computer technology is in continuous development so as to maintain a position in the forefront. Experienced consultants will have come to grips with the necessity of maintaining a continuous schedule of self-education. They need to be in position for the next technical and perhaps geopolitical development.

Prospective HR Users

If you're thinking about installing an HR application, this book will be of interest because it maps out the various possibilities. You will see what's available and what it can achieve; you will also see what will have to be done if these kinds of results are to be realized in your situation. You won't find the costs of SAP HR programs in this volume, but you will get a good idea of the magnitude of work and expense entailed if you should proceed with an installation.

As a person seriously thinking about an SAP installation, you may find that this book draws your attention to the possibilities of achieving results that weren't at the top of your list of priorities but nevertheless would be well worthwhile in themselves and as investments in expertise for the future.

If you will potentially make decisions concerning a new computer installation, you should be careful about setting the standards and parameters by which your decision will be made. You won't want to put your entire business in the hands of an unreliable and inflexible system. You don't, however, want to specify a grossly over-elaborate system for the job you want it to do. This book tells you what the SAP R/3 system and its applications can do; it may become the standard against which you judge competitors' proposals.

General Readers

You can consider yourself a general reader if you're neither a consultant nor a manager about to purchase a computer system.

Perhaps you are familiar with computing but not with industry and business. You will find that this book gives you the key concepts used by the Payroll and Personnel Development departments. The net result could be that you develop a way of thinking about human resource data processing in the context of integrated business applications. This book points you toward the human resources concepts that should be given the highest priority.

On the other hand, you may be a general reader who is familiar with one or more sectors of industry but not fully conversant with the way business computing is developing. You will recognize many business ideas in this book. What might intrigue you is the way they're supported by standard business functions and, for example, a system of master data records. Often, the best way of processing and storing business data is quite different from the way these operations are carried out in a people-and-paper system, where the main retrieval mechanism is in the mind of the person who put the data into storage.

Whether you are a general reader with neither business experience nor computer experience, this book gives you a comprehensive road map of the territory.

Intended Outcomes of Publishing

There will be a significant increase in the number of successful SAP HR implementations because of the many ways in which the HR modules can be linked to the R/3 Financial and Controlling modules. In particular, this book is intended to increase the productivity and the reputation of the following groups of people:

- The implementation team for delivering an effective system on time, within budget, and with confidence
- The project research team for preparing the decisions
- The sponsor for making the decision
- SAP AG for making available efficient tools to do the job

Human resource management is a developing arena in which advances in business data processing and networked communications systems are sometimes seen as threats to the privacy of personal data. On the other hand, the exclusive accessibility of an employee's salary and time-keeping and benefits information to the individual employee and a strictly controlled subset of managers can be regarded as an amenity as well as a method of saving on personnel staff contact time.

The Business Territory

A good businessperson usually possesses a very good knowledge of the geographical and technical territory in which the business operates. Much is known about who buys what and how these purchases can be obtained or manufactured at a good price. The needs of individual customers are appreciated. The operating problems of the warehouses and manufacturing plants are taken into account when making plans. All this is the business territory.

A good human resources specialist knows two things in depth: how to find and recruit suitable employees, and how to avoid losing good employees by faulty administrative and managerial actions. The SAP R/3 HR system excels in supporting accurate and timely personnel management, particularly in relation to the control of working time and the various forms of compensation and remuneration.

Mechanization of business processes has been controlled largely by the equipment available: its cost and its capability. As capabilities have increased, so the cost of programming the equipment has become an ever-larger proportion of the total cost of reengineering. Complexity can be costly.

This line of reasoning has been followed in the manufacturing sectors of industry and in commerce. But in the personnel area, many companies have tended to keep a separate system for what could be very sensitive information—the capabilities and remuneration packages of the employees.

The decision-maker has to set out the pros and cons of providing office automation and communications to assist in each element of the business. To reengineer everything might be costly yet fruitful, although the time it takes to achieve this may entail an unacceptable risk—the market may have changed too much in the interim. What's needed is a software tool that allows the chosen design to be up and running quickly, yet which is easy to tune to new circumstances as they arise.

Making a complex decision isn't easy; some decision-makers may be prone to several errors.

Some Procedures for Using This Book

You could begin at the end of this book or, if you must, at the beginning. The table of contents is be a good place to start your reading.

A sensible approach to intensive study is to first make up your mind about what you want to find and then look until you find it. If you have a particular type of business in mind—your own or one you would like to be a part of—you might find it interesting to cull for information directly relevant to your business and skip anything that doesn't seem relevant at this stage.

The world of computing is paved with clusters of capital letters that mean something to those who use them as technical terms. If you know what the acronym stands for, you may be able to work out what the whole term refers to. A good way of sampling this book is to think of an acronym and see if this book mentions it. Why not begin with the glossary? It is surely as good a read as a comprehensive dictionary.

Delegation is a possibility. You could place a Post-It note in each part that seems difficult and ask a junior colleague to give you a report by the end of the work week.

Errors in Decision-Making

You may be under pressure to choose between making a high-quality decision based on careful consideration of a great deal of information or a fast choice between a few obvious possibilities. More information may give extra accuracy and confidence, but the response will be delayed if more input is required. There is a right moment for most decisions—maybe when costs are low, or maybe as a matter of cornering the market by spending now to profit later. The right moment might be when you know you can lay your hands on the expertise to get it right.

Reluctance is resistance to change. Timidity may be passed off as prudence, but it may also allow the best moment for a decision to pass by. The research team shouldn't be allowed to look indefinitely. Lack of data isn't necessarily an excuse for avoiding a decision. A slow movement in the problem may have taken place if analysis takes too long, which renders the solution invalid.

Hunches may have to be the basis for impossible decisions. There may be no rational means of arriving at a choice in the circumstances. In diagnosis, there may not be enough information to come to a single conclusion. A decision may have to be based on a hunch, an unsupported prediction of what might be in the future. With luck, at least one course of action can be adapted to circumstances if they should change as implementation proceeds. SAP is an example.

Extra information may be sought by decision-makers beyond that necessary for logical choice, particularly if a choice has been made and declared already. This isn't the same as finding out more about the option chosen to make better use of it. Comforting it may be, but redundant verification of a decision can be costly in time and resources.

Tunnel vision or rigid thinking can afflict decision-makers. The risk of a bad decision can be high if no options or alternatives are presented or if the variety of choice is too narrow—and it's not good enough for researchers to dig out some options that are clearly out of the question. Genuine alternatives must be considered before making a choice. Despite what may be said about timidity, doing nothing should always be a carefully considered option.

A bad decision might occur if the dominant attribute is used without evidence to justify the choice. The sales force for a certain product might seem very knowledgeable because they're always displaying their knowledge. This knowledge could be erroneous, however, and the product may be unsuitable for the job in mind.

The Orientation of the SAP R/3 System

SAP R/3's designers have worked with thousands of companies, effecting the transition from legacy data processing methods based on mechanization of traditional manual procedures. They have seen how difficult a process can be if you start with the existing procedures and try to stitch on a computer.

The designers have therefore started at the other end. They have built and tested all the standard business programs needed to put together a modern system for just about every type and structure of business, whether the throughput is mainly material objects or mainly information, or even if the throughput is people. Each standard program has been specialized to perform to the highest possible level in the work it's designed for. There are no compromises.

Because these standard programs are so highly polished, users aren't allowed to alter them in any way. They are sacrosanct.

These highly efficient programs are amenable to only one form of control. They're designed to consult tables. You can place into these tables the words and numbers that will make each program your own. You can tell it what to do without tinkering with its internal mechanisms. The process is called *customizing* because it tailors the programs to suit customers.

The customizing procedure is controlled by an implementation management guide (IMG) that contains a section for the core R/3 system and a further section for each application module integrated with the core. The HR system is customized under control of a section of the IMG.

The Enterprise Data Model

Inside the R/3 system is a complete description of the programs available. You can inspect this description from various viewpoints. When you find a part that looks like something in your existing company or in your target concept of how you would like your company to be, you can have the system save a copy of that part and build it into your model.

If you have a piece of your enterprise modeled this way, you can command the system to show just which standard business functions would be needed to implement it. There can be a seamless transition from modeling to designing the implementation.

Business Process Orientation

At one time, businesses, like military armies, were described in terms of the number of people at each rank in the hierarchy. You modeled the business like a stack of bricks.

A more modern and fruitful approach is to think and model in terms of processes. Particularly, the logistics processes are modeled as value-adding chains of subprocesses, not according to the division of labor. It's but a small step to conceive of the entire corporation as the subject to which should be applied the event-driven process chain method as part of business workflow management. Watch for this kind of language in order to acquire the status of technical terminology. Try "system-controlled, industry-specific, and company-specific modification procedures applied to standard software components" as a working definition of what the SAP implementation activity entails.

Because quantities and values are invariably posted simultaneously, synchronized logistics management and financial accounting is normal and results in improved quality through efficient logistics.

With the rapidly widening possibilities afforded by improved communications, including the Internet, the business model for the immediate future will take for granted an efficient logistics system and a closely coupled manufacturing organization. The SAP model looks toward customer-driven enterprises that take orders for and deliver goods and services globally.

The role of R/3 Human Resources is to ensure that the employees needed to run the enterprise are recruited, rewarded, and retained. The processes needed are treated to as much design attention as any of the industrial production processes.

The extensive array of SAP products includes many different examples of standard business programs that can be configured and customized to suit individual user corporations.

Administering the Personnel Administration and Payroll Accounting Modules

Building a Global Integrated Human Resource System

In this chapter

Introducing the HR Components

The SAP R/3 HR-Human Resources application brings together an extensive family of components fully integrated with the SAP R/3 system. These components are divided between two personnel modules:

- PA-Personnel Administration and Payroll Accounting
- PD-Personnel Planning and Development

Each module may be installed without the other, though if both are to be installed, they should be installed together to take advantage of the integration of the PA and PD databases.

The benefit of creating a global HR data structure accessible to all the entities in your organization is that data can be accurately maintained without duplicate entries. Facilities are provided for fast entry of employee master data, both online and in the background. Original documents, including employee photographs, can be scanned into optical storage by using SAP ArchiveLink.

Personnel in an integrated system can be managed seamlessly from the status of applicant, through organizational assignment and reassignment, to leaving and retirement.

Salary and benefits are also managed through the HR database, as is the processing of travel expenses. As a result, the total costs of any group of employees can be analyzed and planned.

The HR Information System (HRIS) and Executive Information System (EIS) can display personnel data in graphical format such as organization charts or as employee data using the reporting facilities.

Integrating the Management of Employees

Most components of the HR-Human Resources application can be progressively implemented as required. Some can be configured as standalone systems, perhaps in a transitional stage in the progress toward a fully integrated SAP installation.

The HR-Human Resources application's constituent modules are designed to serve two themes—one financial and one concerned with workers' skills:

- PA-Personnel Administration and Payroll Accounting emphasizes payroll and associated procedures. This module is also referred to as PA-Personnel Administration.
- PD-Personal Planning and Development seeks to add value to the personnel resource by career management, beginning at first recruitment and with continuity across extended absences.

The components of PA-Personnel Administration are as follows:

- PA-EMP Employee Management
- PA-BEN Benefits Administration
- PA-COM Compensation Administration

- PA-APP Applicant Management
- PA-TIM Time Management
- PA-INW Incentive Wages
- PA-TRV Travel Expenses
- PA-PAY Payroll

The components of HR-PD Personnel Planning and Development are as follows:

- PD-OM Organizational Management
- PD-SCM Seminar and Convention Management
- PD-PD Personnel Development
- PD-WFP Workforce Planning
- PD-RPL Room Reservations Planning

The HR-Human Resources system can stand alone or be fully integrated with the following SAP applications:

- FI-AM Asset Management—To reference the fixed asset master records, the asset of a specific company car, for example.
- FI-Financial Accounting—To relate to payroll accounting and posting, for example.
- CO-Controlling and CO-OM Overhead Cost Control—To analyze wages and salary costs, for example.
- PM-Plant Maintenance—To transfer completion confirmations to the plants concerned and subsequently release the employees for other work, for example.
- PP-Production Planning and Control—To transfer completion confirmations to the production departments and to assign employees to other activities, for example.

The comprehensive system of access protection is applied to all of the HR-Human Resources application's interactions with any other SAP or non-SAP application.

Understanding the Fundamentals of the HR-Human Resources Application

Certain concepts and procedures are part of the SAP R/3 system and are available for all applications integrated with it. However, eight operational concepts have been particularly developed and exploited to good effect by many users of the HR-Human Resources application:

- Real-time operation of personnel functions
- Infotypes to manage and control access to sensitive areas of personal data
- Personnel events, in which several infotypes are presented on the same screen, information is entered, and the system is called on to update the relevant infotypes automatically
- Dynamic events, which are initiated by the system when users start to enter the information that indicates what they want to achieve

- Fast entry screens that allow you to deal with many individual personal records and transactions at once

- Automatic date monitoring, which is continuous for all dates of significance to the personnel functions

- Interactive Voice Response (IVR), which can be used in personnel departments to deal with the typically large volume of routine inquiries

- Automatic sifting of résumé submissions in preparation for a recruiting or job reassignment interview

Operating PA in Real Time

The SAP R/3 HR-Human Resources application is designed to run and use the database in real time. This method has many important advantages, of which the following is but a selection:

- Although all processing can be performed online under the control of dialogs, it's also possible to set up batch processing, which is the normal procedure for writing to storage media and for reorganizing the database.

- If you've installed and configured the CO-CCA Cost Center Accounting component, checks can be made against the cost center master data when an employee is assigned to a cost center. If this installation hasn't been effected, the HR-Human Resources application will check with its own table of records.

- The system checks fresh data for validity immediately upon entry, and there's less risk of making errors.

- Valid data is stored directly, with a time and date stamp, on a uniform database available immediately to all authorized users. The data also is automatically subject to change control management that will cause all modifications to be logged.

HR Infotypes

Personal data is stored in *information groups*, each of which can be controlled for scope and access authorization. These information groups are referred to as *infotypes*. Not every personal record need be assigned every infotype. The particular use of infotypes in your implementation will be specified during customizing.

The SAP R/3 HR-Human Resources application provides more than 100 standard infotypes:

- Organizational assignment (position, organizational unit, job)

- Personal data (current name, name at birth)

- Payroll status (last payroll, date for recalculation)

- Disability (The categories used in this infotype may be subject to specific national regulation.)

- Leave entitlement (negotiated leave, disability leave, additional leave)

- Leave compensation

- Address (permanent residence, temporary residence, home address)

- Work schedule (shift, time recording, work hours)
- Contract elements (hourly paid terms, fixed price terms, chargeable expenses)
- Base pay (change in classification, pay scale increase, change in pay)
- Garnishment of wages (child support or alimony, garnishment of property, cession of wages)
- Bank connection to receive the paycheck (main bank connection, additional bank connection)
- External transfer
- Recurring benefits and deductions (health insurance, 401(k) savings plans, commuter's allowance, rent withheld, company housing)
- Additional payments (Christmas bonus, service anniversary)

Personnel Events

The infotypes used to manage personal data in the HR-Human Resources system can be combined to form data-entry screens. Within the scope of your authorization, you can have any infotypes displayed together. When the screen data is entered, the system automatically updates all the relevant infotypes. This sequence is referred to as a *personnel event*.

Dynamic Events

When you've responded to a personnel event by entering some data, the system evaluates that data and responds accordingly to generate a *dynamic event*. For instance, if you take on a new employee, the system creates a new personnel master record. At the same time, it calculates the end date of the probationary period and creates an appointment record. This dynamic event, in turn, generates another personnel event because you have to confirm that you accept the proposed appointment for someone to interview the new employee at the end of the probationary period.

A standard consequence of a personnel event is the system's generation of a series of electronic mail messages informing all those who should be told what changes have been made as a result of the personnel event.

Fast Entry Screens

If you need to deal with several employees in the same way—the staff of a particular cost center, for example—the system will select the employees for you and display their relevant records onscreen, where you can make individual or group adjustments before you commit the screen for processing.

If you are unfamiliar with any field on any screen, you can point to it and call for online help, which takes the form of the name of the field and then, if you require it, a longer explanation of how you can use it. On the first press of the help key, a brief explanation of the field is given, from which you may display technical details or request extended help, which will often show you how the field can be used in the larger context.

Automatic Date Monitoring

It's characteristic of personnel departments that many events recur on a calendar basis—for example, renewal of work permits and scheduled performance appraisals. The HR-Human Resources system monitors all such dates and lets everybody concerned know the details; if necessary, the system updates their diaries automatically.

Using Interactive Voice Response

A large part of a personnel department staff's time is taken up by answering routine inquiries from employees, such as "How many vacation days can I have this year?" SAP has set up a system of digitized recordings of all the phrases commonly used in answering personnel queries. These phrases are used to guide callers through an automated telephone response system with a recorded message.

Processing Résumés

The Resumix System, of Resumix, Inc., is integrated with the SAP HR-Human Resources application to provide a completely automatic method of handling resumes. Applicants for an advertised position, or people who might be suitable for a job expected to become vacant, can be identified through the HR-Human Resources application.

If the job specification has been written via standard terms that accurately express the attributes needed for the position, and if the applicants have drafted their résumés with the same vocabulary, a ranking of the applicants can be made based on the comparison between job specification and résumé. A more precise matching is possible if an application form is used.

If the suitability of an existing employee is being considered, facilities are available for building up a profile of qualifications based on existing data in the HR-Human Resources application. This includes job history, assessment reports, and textual material written by employee and management.

Administering Benefits

The SAP R/3 system of benefits and salary administration is supported by the following components from the PA-Personnel Administration module of the HR-Human Resources system:

- PA-EMP Employee Management
- PA-BEN Benefits
- PA-COM Compensation Administration

The system is driven by a series of tables that you can alter to provide for whatever system of benefits and salary your company uses.

Enrolling for Benefits and Insurance Coverage

A standard screen is provided to manage the enrollment of each employee individually. The PA-BEN Benefits administration component recognizes the following types of benefits and insurance coverage:

- Health, including medical, dental, vision, and so on
- Spending and dependent care accounts
- Insurance, including life, AD&D, and dependent life
- Defined benefits and pensions
- Defined contributions, 401(k), RRSP, ESOP, and so on

Insurance coverage is specified by a system of tables that allows you to set out the method of premiums calculation and benefits, and how the associated costs are to be settled. There are facilities by which employees can purchase additional coverage.

A flexible system enables you to particularize deferred compensation plans as part of a benefits package. The following details can be specified in this process:

- Eligibility requirements
- Contribution levels by employee
- Contribution levels by employer
- Vesting schedules
- Investment options
- Stock purchases and options

Administering Salary

The aim of salary administration is to relate the organization's salary structure to the aims of providing rewards for good performance identified during the review process and removing any imbalances within the current salary structure.

The PA-COM Compensation Administration functions provide facilities to achieve the following results:

- Apply standard pay changes across organizational units.
- Override the standard pay change for any individual as an exception.
- Analyze the impact of any proposed salary changes on the organizational units and subunits.
- Assign future salary records and calculations automatically to the changed structure.

One method used to assign salary changes to employees is to use matrices to compare performance appraisal information and current salary across employees in similar jobs.

Introducing the HR Enhancements of Release 4.0

The Human Resources components are integral to the R/3 system and are updated by successive releases. Thus, HR release 4.0 is delivered with R/3 release 4.0.

One dominant theme of HR development is the emphasis on global networks of HR resources linked by intranet and Internet pathways. The justification is to improve the quality of HR information and the speed with which it can be delivered. Under this theme, various services are designed to focus on particular aspects of HR management.

Advertising Vacancies and Personnel Marketing

The Internet notifies potential applicants worldwide of vacancies in the enterprise. Anyone interested can log on to a self-service bureau and indicate the ways in which their interest can be particularized—by including or excluding a geographical region, for instance.

An application form can be presented, completed, and returned as email. The R/3 HR system can then begin processing the application automatically. For example, the system will send applicants personal IDs and passwords so that they can subsequently monitor the progress of their application—again, automatically.

Locating Internal Contacts

No matter how large the company, an integrated R/3 HR system can access every employee directory. This provides access to such information as name, position, department, telephone number, and possibly even a photo. Most of these elements can be used for selective searching and reporting.

Applying Workflow in HR

Although the SAP R/3 Workflow components have been well developed for some time, their use in HR has become widespread only recently. In particular, business workflow can be arranged to allocate tasks to the most suitable people available and with sufficient capacity at the time when the tasks are to be carried out.

The result is that all users automatically receive a list of their tasks in their R/3 Mail System inboxes. When they complete a task, R/3 Business Workflow automatically starts the next predefined work step and sends the relevant messages. This provides a straightforward arrangement for monitoring the progress of tasks step by step, if necessary. For example, the following recruiting processes can be automated:

- Submission of application forms
- Planning and holding interviews
- Drawing up contract offers
- Preparing new appointments
- Monitoring rejected applications
- Performing company-specific processes

Automated processing and extended networking can be combined to provide a comprehensive employee self-service system. Employees may be authorized to access their own personnel records and update some of them. Predesigned software packages, known as *Internet scenarios*, are available to support the following self-service functions in the HR application:

- Addresses and dependents' data can be updated to include new family members and change the information on next of kin.

- Leave entitlement can be checked and requests for leave submitted. SAP R/3 Business Workflow can be configured to forward a leave request to the person responsible for authorizing leave.

- Employees can find their own benefits data online.

- Expense account regulations can be consulted online. Expense account data can be entered online and employees can check the processing status of their submissions.

- Where Certificates of Employment are required (by banks, for example), employees can call for them online and print them in a format suitable for presentation.

Control over the employee self-service functions is managed by requiring a user ID and personal password and by restricting access to the personnel data of the user alone. Changed data can be submitted to authorized members of the Human Resources department for checking and confirmation.

Preparing the Fundamentals of HR Management

In this chapter

Introducing the Structures in Which HR Data Is Stored

Employee master data is held in data structures called infotypes (information types). A wide range of standard infotypes is provided to which you can add your own by copying and modifying existing structures.

Infotypes also can hold other data types used in the management of human resources. Three types of data structure are needed for HR operations:

- Organizational structures that define the company organization, the deployment of personnel, the pay scales, and the wage types
- HR data structures that hold information about particular individuals
- Master information that specifies the formats for recording the significant HR events that require changes to the personal data and the payroll status of individuals

Interpreting the Personnel Structure

Two aspects of a person's identity at work can be considered independently:

- The administrative arrangements, used mainly for payroll purposes
- The organizational arrangements that determine how the individual's work is managed

The HR system requires you to assign each employee a code for each of the following administrative entities:

- Client
- Company
- Employee group
- Employee subgroup
- Payroll accounting area
- Organizational key

N O T E The organizational key can be derived from the company structure and the personnel structure. The employee group and employee subgroup can also be identified in the organizational key. ■

A standard hiring event is initiated to accept the details of an employee and store them in a specific format defined by the infotype 0001, which is referred to as *organizational assignment*. The organizational arrangements made for each employee are specified by the following entities:

- Job
- Position
- Organizational unit

If your system is integrated with the HR Planning (PD) component, an additional link must be established with the PD elements.

Interpreting the Company Structure Infotypes

Each instance of SAP R/3 is installed with the capability to support several clients. Each client's transactions are identified by a client code. This is done because, for example, one client may be used for testing parts of the system, whereas another client is running the productive operational system.

A small company may not differentiate between the client and the company code. However, many corporations compose an association of individual companies that each prepare their own financial documents, which are then consolidated to report the financial situation of the group as a whole. Thus, the client may have one or more affiliates that use separate company codes to allow the system to differentiate their transactions and thus compile separate financial documents.

For accounting purposes, the *company code* is defined as the level at which the statutory balance sheet and profit-and-loss accounts are produced.

A *personnel area* is defined solely in PA and must be assigned to a particular company code. It is therefore associated with a particular client. The personnel subarea is also used only in PA and must be referred to a particular personnel area.

The organizational key builds a convenient aggregated structure for your particular company. It's built from elements already defined in the organizational and personnel structures.

Exploring the SAP Concept of Client

When your system is customized, the clients are each assigned a three-digit alphanumeric identification. Client 000 contains the SAP original system, and this can't be changed. An identical client 001 is delivered as well.

The system tracks which elements are used in all clients, and which are active only in a particular client. The following elements are defined as client independent:

- Data structures such as field definitions, table structures, and file setups
- Client-independent tables
- Transactions
- Programs
- Standard reporting
- Authorization objects
- Help documentation

The following elements are defined as client specific, although they may be used without alteration:

- Client-specific tables that must be copied from the original client
- Personnel data records
- Authorization records
- Authorization profiles

Customer-specific programs can be used in any client. Data can't be exchanged between clients, and all reporting activities are necessarily confined to a single client. Any customizing alterations to the standard structures are confined to the client in which they were established.

Personnel data is held separately in each client, which protects against unauthorized access. If an employee is moved from one client to another, however, a separate set of records has to be created under a new personnel number.

Defining a Company Code

If two or more legally independent companies are affiliated to the client organization, they will each have a different company code so that their accounting can be independent. Each firm will be assigned a four-digit alphanumeric identification during the customizing process. The company codes used in PA will be the same as those used in any other applications also in the R/3 implementation, such as Controlling, Financial Accounting, Materials Management, or Sales and Distribution.

The PA component uses the company code to identify various default values that are suggested when new data is entered or reports are prepared. Also, the company code is used in the following circumstances:

- As an element in authorization checks
- To propose a default value for the country key for an employee's personal data, address, and banking data
- To select a default value for the currency key for an employee's basic pay
- To select a language code for text output, such as employee remuneration information

N O T E The output language need not be the same as the logon language that is used for dialog at the terminal. ▨

Using Personnel Area and Subareas

A *personnel area* is a unit defined within PA for convenience in managing personnel data. It's a subunit of a company code. A *personnel subarea* is a division of a personnel area. Personnel area and subarea are each designated by a four-digit code. These units are used to refine and particularize accounting data, reports, and authorization checks.

Work schedule planning and the management of pay scale and wage type structures normally refer to personnel subareas. The control features needed for specific countries are stored at the personnel subarea level.

The personnel subarea has to identify the legal entity via a valid company code. All personnel assigned to the subarea belong to the same company code. The country grouping parameter determines country-specific features for personnel data, wage types, and pay scale groups for accounting. Work schedules, holiday calendars, substitution arrangements, absence, and leave types are set up for each personnel subarea.

Understanding the Organizational Personnel Structure

The personnel structure that represents a person's job is necessarily associated with the parent organization's management structure. If your implementation doesn't have the HR Planning and Development (PD) module installed and configured, you have to define the details of each job in the form of control tables under the guidance of the customizing process. If you have the PD module integrated, these tables will be set up and maintained in the PD module.

Defining a Job

A *job* is defined by the standard description of the function to be performed and the tasks to be dealt with by an individual person.

Defining a Position

A *position* is defined as an organizational grouping of work that can be performed by one person. It can comprise one or more jobs.

Defining an Organizational Unit

An *organizational unit* is defined as an organizational grouping of employees, such as a department. However, an organizational unit may be larger than a department. The status and perhaps title of an organization unit depends on its position in the company hierarchy.

Integrating PA with HR Planning and Development

If you're operating with an integrated PA and PD system, you will be transferred to an HR Planning transaction when you assign an employee to a job, a position, and an organizational unit. The system automatically links the position data to the employee group, employee subgroup, personnel area, personnel subarea, company code, business area, cost center, job, and organizational unit data.

The benefits of this integration can be seen when you hire employees or reassign them to other parts of the organization. For example, if the position to which an employee is to be assigned has been established as a possible outcome of the hiring or organizational reassignment events, the system will automatically suggest the appropriate field values for the personnel area, employee group, and employee subgroup. You can enter these items manually, but the system will verify them against the data stored for the position.

The PD module will also take account of the staffing percentage and the planned working hours for each position. When you assign employees to positions, the system will report to you if this assignment will leave any percentage of their planned working hours unassigned. If so, you may be able to assign the employees to additional positions, if they have been defined in the PD module.

Using the Administrative Personnel Structure

The following structures are used to locate personnel data:

- Employee group
- Employee subgroup
- Payroll accounting area or payroll area
- Organizational key

Defining the Employee Group

The employee group is indicated by a single-digit code established in customizing by reference to a catalog to which client-specific categories can be added. The main employee groups in PA are as follows:

- Active work force
- Retirees
- Early retirees

If the system knows the employee group, it will suggest default values for payroll area and basic pay, for example. The employee group ID can be used in reporting and as part of an authorization check.

Defining the Employee Subgroup

An *employee subgroup* indicates the status of employees within their employee groups. Your company may define subgroups of the active workforce according to whether they are pay scale or non-pay scale employees, for example. All control features for the personnel structure are defined at employee subgroup level.

For example, the employee subgroup ID can be consulted to determine whether an employee's pay is to be calculated on a monthly or hourly basis. The subgroup may determine whether a standard payroll with personnel calculation rules is to be used and whether exceptions are allowed. Collective pay agreements can be managed by this means.

The employee subgroup is also used to determine the validity of time management entries like the following:

- Work schedules
- Attendance/absence quota types
- Time quotypes

Defining the Payroll Accounting Area

The payroll accounting area, often referred to as the *payroll area*, is an organizational unit for performing a payroll accounting run. By using their organizational assignments, payroll areas identify a set of employees and the exact dates of the accounting period to be used. The employee payroll accounting data is assembled according to when their payroll is to be run.

A payroll area can be changed only at the end of a period, even though an employee might change status during the period. For example, an industrial worker may become a salaried employee in a different payroll area.

Building the Organizational Key

The organizational key is used as part of the authorization concept in the PA and PD modules. It's made up of 14 characters that can be interpreted in whatever manner is established in customizing. The organizational key isn't necessarily related to the organizational unit.

Exploring the Wage Type Structure

Primary wage types are used when maintaining personnel data and may be referred to as *dialog wage types*. The group, primary wage types, also includes automatically generated wage and salary types.

A *wage type model* is a structure of wage types that's consulted when determining basic pay. The default pay is chosen according to company code, personnel area, employee group, and employee subgroup.

Wage and salary types are subject to permissibility checks that depend on the employee's organizational assignment. Checks can also be specified to control how often a wage type is authorized in a given period.

A wage type's operation indicator controls whether it's applied as a payment or a deduction. The entry combination parameter controls whether wage types are entered with or without amounts, and with volume specifications or a unit of time or measurement.

Secondary wage types use indirect wage type valuation by indicating a module name or variant as well as the corresponding rounding off preference. The amount is then calculated using tables.

Using Pay Scale Elements

A pay scale structure is made up of the following elements:

- Pay scale type
- Pay scale area
- Employee subgroup grouping for the collective agreement provision
- Pay scale group
- Pay scale level

Pay scale information is stored in infotypes that define how the data shall be interpreted. For example, basic pay is recorded in infotype 0008, one for each employee. Recurring payments and deductions are stored in infotype 0014, additional payments in infotype 0015. Wage maintenance is stored in infotype 0052.

The pay scale type defines the area in which a pay scale or collective agreement is valid. This pay scale or agreement may be determined at company or trade union level. It may apply throughout a whole industry.

Pay scale types are given a two-digit code and confined to a specific personnel country grouping in customizing.

The geographical area over which a pay scale or a collective agreement is valid is defined as the pay scale area and assigned a two-digit code. It's associated with a specific personnel country grouping in customizing. Default values for pay scale types and groups linked to the personnel subarea are suggested when you create a basic pay record for an employee in infotype 0008.

Using Infotypes in Personnel Administration

Infotypes are used in personnel administration and recruitment to associate stored information with a specific personnel number of an employee or the applicant number of an applicant. Each infotype has a unique ID in the form of a four-digit number. Customer-specific infotypes are between 9000 and 9999.

The following key master data infotypes have to be created before a personnel number can exist in the system:

- Events (0000)
- Organizational Assignment (0001)
- Personal Data (0002)
- Payroll Status (0003)

Users will mainly see infotypes as screens or parts of screens displaying information or offering it for editing. In a database, the infotype can be a data structure or a set of data records.

Every infotype has to be assigned a validity period in the form of a start date and an end date. This life span must not extend beyond the validity period of the object represented by the infotype, nor can it begin before the object itself exists. Thus, a job and a work center will each have a validity period. Any infotypes associated with them must have validity periods that are shorter or the same.

The status of an infotype record has to correspond to the status of the object it refers to. Thus, a planned object will have only infotypes with the status of planned. However, an object that has the status active can have planned and active status infotypes assigned to it.

Storing Personal Data

Infotype 0002 (Personal Data) stores data for identifying an employee. The Personal Data infotype has time constraint 1, which requires that an infotype record must exist in the system from the date the employee is hired. The data is divided into sets:

- Form of address, first name, last name, second name (if necessary), and name at birth. The name by which the employee is known, initials, employee's academic title, name prefixes, and name suffixes are also in set 1.
- Date of birth, place of birth, nationality, and language.
- Number of children, marital status, and (in some countries) the employee's religious denomination.

Optical Archiving

Companies may be required by law to hold archived documents for a certain length of time. Optical archiving servers can store documents more cheaply and in less space than paper or microfilm storage systems. SAP ArchiveLink is an interface system that allows R/3 users parallel and direct access to optically archived documents from their work center, without the need for time-consuming searches.

ArchiveLink includes a user interface and an application interface comprising function modules that have to be integrated with the applications they serve. Application data objects are linked with archive objects. SAP Business Workflow includes object methods that can process the data and archive objects.

Each document stored in an archive has a unique key, and each archive has a unique optical archive ID. Each SAP object that uses a particular object type and object key has a unique identifier.

A link table is constructed to associate the identifiers for each document using the optical archive ID. An entry in a link table can associate an SAP object with any number of documents. References to an archived document exist only as entries in link tables.

The application interface has the function of linking application objects with archive objects so that these objects can be displayed, retrieved, or saved. For example, an FI-Financial Accounting invoice document can be linked to scanned copies of the original invoices that have been optically archived. The application interface can also link application documents with archived outbound SAP documents.

In addition to the direct links between R/3 and its main applications, SAP ArchiveLink is fully integrated with the DMS-Document Management System. This allows any application with links to DMS to be linked to the optical archiving systems.

Inbound faxes can be processed directly in SAPoffice, optically archived, and linked with application objects without having to be printed.

Personnel Administration can use SAP ArchiveLink to store and retrieve copies of original documents such as contracts of employment, personnel appraisals, and employee photographs.

If you're archiving, each scanned document is assigned a document type that, for example, identifies the appropriate personnel administrator, who then receives it as an inbox item. The document type may also identify an organizational unit, job, position, or work center. The administrator can confirm these assignments.

If more than one record is generated for the infotype to which a scanned document is assigned, the system will present them all so that the personnel administrator can link the document to an employee and just one infotype.

Managing Personnel Time

In this chapter

Managing Time with the PA-TIM Component

There are various ways of recording or inferring the time an employee has spent at work. There are also various ways of comparing this data to some form of work schedule. The outcome of this comparison is a valuation of the time data for the individual. Therefore, three aspects of time management can be differentiated:

- How time data is collected
- How time data is stored
- How time data is valuated

The instrumentation and hardware of time measurement and recording are under continuous development. Where necessary, SAP updates the standard interface modules as new hardware is introduced to provide a comprehensive interface support system.

Controlling Time Valuation

The Personnel Administration module's PA-TIM Time Management component provides the standard software for recording, assigning values to, and evaluating all employee data relevant to time management. This component stores all its control logic in tables, which you can adjust to yield a precisely tailored system suited to your requirements.

Each day for each employee, the attendance or absence time is analyzed in relation to the preset values of the relevant shift schedule. The first result is a series of time pairs that signal when something began and when it finished—work, absence, and so on. Each time pair is then classified. By referring to the rules for overtime and so on, the system can refine the classification until each unit of time is identified by its type, which is used to choose the wage type and eventually to compute the compensation. All the logical rules for performing this classification and calculation procedure are stored in the form of tables, which you can access if you want to change the way the process is to be performed or any rates or base values.

If a new type of work time or absence category is created, you can set up the logic for identifying it and computing the appropriate compensation.

All time management data is stored in the form of time pairs and time types. When these are evaluated, you may find that there has been an error in time recording or in the way the time types have been generated based on the work schedule and plant calendar.

If you decide to make a change in retrospect (a *retroactive change*) and have the authority to do so, you can alter the original data, and the system will recalculate the time data automatically and hence the consequent compensation due. For example, you may decide that a new scheme should be backdated. As you redefine the dates for the validity of the scheme, the system will recognize that a recalculation is needed and will carry it out automatically.

Understanding the Concepts Underpinning Time Management

To take advantage of an integrated business system's benefits, it's necessary to translate many business concepts and working practices into precise yet flexible operational definitions that can, in turn, be represented in a computer program.

Plant Calendar

The calendar that shows the possible working days of a particular plant is the *plant calendar*. This calendar must show the days of the working week, together with the days observed as general and regional holidays.

Day Program

The significant moments for measuring time at work are defined as the *day program*. A series or pattern of day programs can repeat itself over the course of a plant calendar, taking into account only the working days in that calendar.

Time Model

The pattern of day programs that repeats in a plant calendar is known as a *time model*. You can define as many different time models as you require, and they can have any duration you want.

Shift Scheduling

If you roll a time model over the plant calendar, you get a *shift schedule*. You can intervene, for example, to allow extra days before and after a planned plant shutdown. Common features, such as reduced working hours before holidays, also can be taken into the time model in the form of special day programs that have the shorter working hours.

Work Time

If your company has flexible work times (*flextime*), you have to specify the components of a working day in terms of a *time frame* and *core times*. Tolerance zones in the working day are usually designated to account for the short periods of irrelevant time before work officially begins and after it officially ends. You may want to allow a tolerance zone for people coming late to work.

The system allows you to define as many breaks in the day as you want. You can designate them as paid, unpaid, or paid at a special rate. Breaks can be defined as fixed, variable, or dynamic, in which case the length of the break depends on how long an employee has worked or how much work has been completed. You can allocate part of the day for orientation or "warming up," and you can record whether people are working extra hours to save up for time off later.

Any decisions you make on the rules attached to time measurement have to be given a period of validity, and the system will automatically record the time and date of any changes that you make to the tables that store this information. If necessary, the system can be called on to deliver a history of the changes that have been made to a set of master data records.

Time-Recording Variants

There are two common variants and several hybrid forms:

- Negative time recording
- Positive time recording

The base assumption of *negative time recording* is that everyone is at work all the time unless recorded as absent. You can ignore brief absences of a few minutes, and you will have a range of good reasons for deviating from the official work schedule:

- Absence, such as vacation, work incapacity, or stipulated day off
- Special work attendance, such as attending a seminar
- On-call duty
- Overtime
- Work time substitution

The recording methods at your disposal are as follows:

- Enter data on an individual record.
- Enter data for a group of people on a fast entry screen, such as overtime for the whole work center.
- Enter data using a special recording screen, such as an absence calendar.

Positive time recording entails recording the deviations from the work schedule and the actual work times. This method is becoming more prevalent as a result of the following factors:

- Flexibility of work time is increasing, which calls for using formal and informal methods of time management.
- Flextime using time recording is more widespread.
- Workers more often determine their own work times.

As a consequence, the role of the shift schedule may often be restricted to providing a time frame and serving as the basis for the valuation of absences.

Preparing the PA-TIM Time Management Component

Many different personnel procedures are supported by the PA-TIM component so that most companies can use the standard software to record and evaluate employee time data. When collected and evaluated, time data such as absence and attendance records can be transferred to other applications.

The calendar is the fundamental structure on which all other time structures are built. For example, the following time structures can be represented with standard software modules:

- Working time models such as flextime, normal working time, and shift operation
- Planned working times, break schedules, and compensation times for each working time model
- Recognized exceptions such as substitutions, availability or stand-by, business trips
- Regulations for the payment of attendance and absences, breaks, and work on Sundays and public holidays

At the customizing stage, you can accept standard time models or edit them to suit your company. You can also create unique company-specific working time models.

The standard SAP system of infotypes is used to organize the time data of the HR-Human Resources system. The following infotypes are recognized:

- Absences—for example, vacation, illness, or temporary layoff
- Special work attendance—for example, different work center, errand, business trip, or seminar
- Overtime—for example, overtime compensated by payment or time off
- Substitutions—for example, shift or workplace substitution
- On-call duty—for example, on-call duty or standby duty
- Absence quotas—for example, sabbatical or time off
- Attendance approvals—for example, overtime approval
- Actual work times—for example, with additional account assignment, differing payment, or premium work time
- Time events—for example, clock-in/clock-out messages or work order confirmations
- Balance corrections—for example, rebooking overtime to flextime or paying out time-off credits

You can manage time data directly with the PA-TIM Time Management system. Alternatively, you can assign employees to time data agents, which can be cost centers, departments, or some other organizational entity created for this purpose. The time data agent is assigned only some personnel infotypes—just those needed to manage time locally. In the central system, a second person is responsible for unlocking time data collected by the time data agent only when the central "personnel clerk" authorizes its release.

Integrating with Work Schedules

The Time Management component has to refer to an organizational assignment infotype (0001) record for each employee. This infotype allows you to group employees by subgroups or personnel *subareas* and then define special processing rules so that all the employees performing the same task can be time-managed in the same way. You can use this facility to speed the process of entering data for work schedule arrangements. The size of a personnel subarea can be as small as an individual.

Each employee subgroup or personnel subarea can be assigned a different work schedule and can be allowed to operate under special rules for availability and substitutions. One or more of these personnel groupings could be restricted to certain attendance and absence types and be assigned special processing rules for time data evaluation and payroll accounting. Particular groups can be associated with a specific pattern of time-management rules, which can then be modified for individual subgroups if necessary. For example, employee subgroups can be defined for the management of the following:

- Time quota types
- Work schedules
- Personnel calculation rules

Personnel subarea groups can be defined for the management of the following:

- Attendance/absence types
- Time quota types
- Work schedules
- Daily work schedules
- Substitution and availability types
- Attendance/absence counting
- Time recording
- Leave
- Premiums

N O T E   An employee can't be assigned a time-management rule, such as a particular work schedule, unless the rule is assigned to the personnel subarea to which that employee belongs. ■

Representing Time Structures

One fundamental time structure is the work schedule. This data structure defines a planned duration of working time and how this time is distributed as a pattern of working days over a specific calendar period. Time structures can also be defined as working time models and as time-management infotypes.

All the work groups in your company don't have to operate on the same working pattern—you can customize the system to operate a set of working time variants, such as different public holiday calendars in different regions. Some variants also could be applied only to certain employee subgroup and personnel subarea groupings.

Although a regional public holiday calendar may be in operation, you may want to define how employees work on weekdays and public holidays in order to arrange a fair allocation of working on the preferred days for public and individual holidays. The public holiday calendar records employee attendance and absences because the payroll accounting program must take account of the different rates applicable to Sunday and public holiday working.

Personnel areas and subareas have to be assigned the specific calendar. If your organization has company-specific days off, they can also be entered in the calendar.

Defining Exceptions to the Work Schedule

A person might not complete a defined work pattern for valid reasons. Absence and sickness are predefined exceptions, but you can specify additional categories during customizing. For example, you can define special absence types such as extra leave for people who are coping with a particular difficulty or time off in exchange for overtime. (What counts as a particular difficulty will be a matter of company policy and perhaps legal definition.) Maternity leave and absence resulting from an industrial accident are example of work schedule exceptions that may have to be represented as special infotypes, to ensure that the system carries out further processing at a later date, as well as deal with the standard payroll processes.

When an attendance or permitted exception is entered, the system can carry out specific plausibility checks. You can also specify which types of absences and attendance types are permitted between specific times of the day, on which days of the week, and whether on Sundays or public holidays.

The leave quota is a standard facility, but you can also define quotas for particular attendance and absence types and assign them to employees. The system will automatically set up absence quotas and maintain them if you're operating such procedures as automatic leave accrual for flextime models and time off for overtime.

Overtime can be managed by using attendance quotas to control the amount of overtime employees can work. The quota facility can also regulate when employees are permitted to work overtime. Indicators can be set in time data so that payroll accounting can arrange the correct compensation for exceptions to the normal work schedule.

Understanding the Purpose of Time Data Evaluation

The process of evaluating time data prepares the time values used in payroll accounting. For example, evaluation determines how the planned working schedule has been matched by the actual times worked, having taken account of the permitted exceptions and other adjustments such as flextime calculations.

Although the HR time evaluation process is largely automatic, you can discern the following phases:

- Acquire the recorded time data
- Consult the planned specifications
- Perform error checks and carry out corrections
- Calculate overtime and determine the appropriate compensation

A reporting program is available; it can accept the time evaluation parameters and process the rules accordingly. (See "Using the Time Evaluation Driver RPTIME00" later in this chapter.) The time evaluation program identifies time wage types such as bonus wage types and overtime by referring to the defined rules as it processes the attendance and absence times in relation to the specified calendar.

Time balances are maintained for leave and flextime on a daily basis and for longer periods. Any quotas in operation are reduced or accumulated as the time data is processed according to the recognized time wage types. Overtime approval and leave entitlement are handled in this way.

If any working time rules are infringed, the reporting program will issue the corresponding messages.

Using Evaluated Time Data in R/3 Applications

Infotypes sometimes provide for adding data that can be interpreted by other applications with which the HR system is integrated. For example, specific activity types can be recognized and the time data can be used to report the way in which activities are allocated. This information is used in the FI-Financial Accounting and CO-Controlling modules to carry out cost assignment of personnel costs. External services can be identified and reported to the MM-Material Management module for recording and accounting.

Using Time Data from Front-End Systems

A standardized interface will upload the time events automatically. It can also download the results of time evaluation and the relevant master data. If you don't have a standardized interface, you can use a sequential file to transfer the data.

Recording Time Data

You record time data so that you can collate the information and compile details and summaries of such personnel activities as working time, leave, business trips, and various types of substitution. The data can be captured as clock times or hours, and may also be associated with account assignment specifications (needed if the information is sent to R/3 applications outside HR).

How the time data is entered can be defined. You can record exceptions to a specified work schedule and also record an employee's actual attendance times.

Automatic recording entails each employee having a time recording ID card to trigger the recording of actual clock-in and clock-out times at a front-end recording terminal from which it's uploaded to the R/3 system.

Manual entry of hours attended or clock times can be used to update records in attendances infotype 2002. Infotypes can also be used to record absences. One option allows you to enter long periods of time in a calendar format.

Time infotypes often allow the entry of a list of many records for one employee. The fast entry facility allows you to enter a range of infotype records for several different employees.

The time recording apparatus may be provided by any supplier that uses an SAP-certified interface. This uses the R/3 communication channel CC1 and operates by using the ALE (Application Link Enabling) technology.

Linking to Recording Equipment with a Mini-Master

Time-recording systems are installed to establish the time facts and collect the data. They shouldn't be treated as the method of evaluating the time data, which is the province of the HR-TIM Time Management system.

The usual method is for the central system to dispatch to the time-recording system a record known as a *mini-master* data record. This carries just enough data to accomplish what's required—to collect the time data for a given individual at a specified work center in relation to the time schedule that has been assigned.

Some companies combine time recording with admittance control. Depending on the equipment fitted in the workplace, the people admitted to a particular work center may be defined in terms of their assignment to that work center and perhaps also their authorization to enter locations elsewhere in the plant.

The front-end time-recording system must be supplied with current information that the employees who use it can consult. This data comprises individual data such as leave and overtime balances. The system also needs to know control data such as access control group codes. Thus, a download to a time-recording terminal could include the following classes of information:

- Time evaluation results
- HR master data records of employees likely to clock in or out
- Master data such as recognized attendance and absence reasons that an employee might enter

A download is performed by a single transmission of what's referred to as an *HR mini-master record*. This comprises all the data necessary for all the employees who might access the time-recording terminal.

An upload comprises all the data recorded at the terminal, such as clock-in and clock-out times and other entries made by employees. The frequency and timing of uploads and downloads are controlled by the communication parameters.

Sharing Tasks Between the Subsystem and the HR System

The tasks of the external time recording system are as follows:

- Record time events
- Validate the time events against the HR mini-master for the day
- Confirm the validity of each attendance and absence reason entered against the master data for the day
- Confirm the validity of each external wage type entered against the master data for the day
- Transfer validated time events to the subsystem interface for upload
- Transfer HR mini-master records from the subsystem interface to the time-recording terminals

The R/3 system has the following duties:

- Read time events from subsystem interface
- Upload time events via communication channel CC1
- Store time events in the R/3 table RUECK

- Download mini-master records and balances via communication channel CC1
- Download master data via communication channel 1

The HR system has the following duties:

- Read time events from the R/3 table RUECK
- Process time events
- Maintain attendance status
- Correct and supplement time events
- Transfer mini-master records and balances to communication channel CC1
- Transfer master data to communication channel 1

The external subsystem isn't required to process time events because only the HR database will have the information necessary to interpret time events such as planned working times and substitutions. Furthermore, the external recording system can't keep proper track of an employee's attendance status because there may well be several terminals at which clock in and clock out can take place. Only the central HR system can deal with problems such as missing time events.

Transferring Time Records Between Applications

The standard time recording functionality implemented as of R/3 release 3.0D consists of various mechanisms that allow time data to be collected and evaluated in one application and then sent to another.

The PM-Plant Maintenance, PP-Production Planning, and PS-Project System applications can collect data that records which tasks and activities are completed and the time taken by each employee assigned. A confirmation is posted when an activity is completed. The system then refers to the stored activity prices of the activity types involved and calculates the actual costs of the completed activity. These costs are posted synchronously to the CO-Controlling application. An activity often uses materials that have to be withdrawn from inventory. When confirmation that the task or activity is completed has been posted, the materials used can be posted automatically to MM-Materials Management, where they will be entered as an unplanned withdrawal, a retrograde withdrawal, or a non-retrograde withdrawal, according to the planning status of the completed activity. A backflush of surplus materials can also be handled in this way in response to the posting of a task completion notification.

As of R/3 release 3.0C, the PM-Plant Maintenance and PS-Project System applications also can accept a personnel number with the entry of a completion confirmation. These personnel numbers are stored in a table that provides an interface to HR, where they can be used to compute incentive wages. As of release 3.0E, the personnel number table can be consulted by the HR system's time-leveling and time-evaluation functions. These functions contribute to the input for the PA-Payroll Accounting module.

As of release 3.0D, it's possible to use the PM or PS completion confirmation posting to record attendance and absences with cost allocation in HR.

If work is being done in connection with a service order, you can arrange for the order to be the account assignment object in the MM-SRV component. Similarly, an account assignment object can be maintained in the CO-Controlling module that stores the planned hours for a particular activity. If both modules are in action, an interface table is set up for each to accumulate batches of activity completion data.

Actual data on work completion, personnel, and times can be collected by a Plant Data Collection system (PDC) or a personal computer used for manual entry. The SAP system then collects the data from the PDCs or PCs and distributes it as required. For example, the times of arrival and departure from the work center will be sent to HR for each employee. The activity completion documents will go to PM, PP, or PS according to the configuration.

Activity allocations are cost values sent by a cost center in CO to receivers, which will be account assignment objects in the various applications.

This diverse functionality for manipulating time data is being supplemented and integrated to make it easier to use, even by those who aren't familiar with R/3. Since release 3.0D, the R/3 Cross Application Timesheet (CATS) has been implemented as an add-on feature. The HR system, release 4.0, includes these functions fully integrated in the system on delivery.

Using the R/3 Cross Application Time Sheet

The idea behind the development of the CATS is to provide a non-specialist user interface for entering time data. Internal employees will probably access a terminal; external contractor employees may have to compile a time sheet. Both user types will have their data collected in a CATS database table to be subsequently processed by the relevant modules. The employees will also receive their work lists from the screen or printed time sheets.

One function of the CATS database is to support the verification of time and task data. For example, the time data has to be checked for validity, and there has to have been appropriate authorization for an activity to be assigned to a specific employee. Your company may have customized the system to ensure that an authorized supervisor has to approve and release time data before payroll action is initiated.

The key advantages of the CATS technology are seen as the following:

- The actual times of individual employees can be entered by using a uniform data-entry screen for all applications.
- Templates and default field values will minimize the keystrokes needed.
- Inexperienced users can operate the data-entry functions.
- Approval procedures will be integrated across all applications.
- Data corrections are possible in the CATS database.
- CATS will accept *user exits*, which are customized procedures for authorization checks, validations, and default value generation.

Although CATS enters data only against particular personnel numbers, there are two variants:

- Each employee enters his own hours against activities.
- Several employee numbers are identified against which the actual times worked are entered centrally.

To use the CATS system, external employees have to be assigned individual personnel numbers.

You can customize the CATS screen to show any combination of the available fields. For example, you could display the employee's planned hours taken from the work schedules and a work list with target times.

Time data can be accepted in periods from hours to months and distributed across working days in various ways. The form of entry can be actual times or numbers of hours worked. Attendance or absence data may be input.

The employee using a CATS screen can hide or display the basic constituents of the screen as designed. Some variations of layout are also possible.

A navigation link to the travel expense data entry screen can be taken, and the HR system will be called to allow references to trip numbers. Goods issue from the MM application is also accessible from the CATS screen. The goods issue document number is stored in the CATS database for reference.

If CATS is used in an implementation where the HR application isn't available, the work schedule functions won't be available and it won't be possible to access the Travel Expense screen.

Processing Time Data

A timed event can be recorded by a specialized subsystem or entered manually in time events infotype 2011. A work period or an absence can be defined by a pair of time events. The data as collected by hardware or entered manually has to be formed into time pairs before it can be used in time management.

An employee's attendance times can be recorded in attendances infotype 2002. Another method is to record only exceptions to a standard work schedule that has been assigned to the employee.

The process of time data evaluation has the task of evaluating and comparing the planned and actual specifications of the work to be accomplished. For this to happen, it may be necessary to perform some or all of the following operations:

- Import the actual information in the form of the recorded time data such as attendance and absences or time pairs.
- Evaluate the data and make any adjustments based on the recorded reasons for attendance or absence.

- Read the planned specifications of the work to be done, such as a personal work schedule.
- Consult any relevant substitution data that affects the personal work schedule.
- Consult the employee availability records.

The process of time data evaluation may well detect some errors. For instance, it may not be possible to match each clock-in time with a corresponding clock-out time (the system might find a clock-out time that lacks a corresponding clock-in). These cases constitute open time pairs and can sometimes be completed automatically. For example, the system may be able to assume that the scheduled end of a working day should be taken as the clock-out time for certain open pairs. Such automatic completion can be conducted in the form of a dialog box with the employee, who has the option of accepting the prompted default or entering a more accurate value.

A time evaluation system should notify users of any errors and save the relevant data so that corrections may be made later.

As soon as the relevant data is available, the system can calculate time balances for the day and for the period. This supports the maintenance of a data history and the continuous monitoring of time credits, absence quotas, and leave entitlements. These calculations are facilitated by a system of time types that signify what a particular period of time should be counted as. There is a time type for productive hours, another for planned breaks, and so on. The assignment of a time type allows the accumulation of time periods to form balances that can be assigned time wage types that are interpreted in payroll accounting.

If flextime is in operation, a time-evaluation system can transfer specified time type values to other time types such as the overtime balance, which is used to calculate and compensate overtime. If a retrospective change is made to time data, the system can be configured to respond by recalculating the balances.

A time evaluation system's final task is to display the results.

Setting Up for Time Evaluation

Two basic ways to handle time data are as follows:

- The Payroll Accounting system itself can evaluate time data. This is discussed later in this chapter's "Evaluating Time Data" section.
- The evaluation of time data can be processed by a specialized component designed for this task. This method is discussed later in this chapter's "Using the Time Evaluation Driver RPTIME00" section.

The time evaluation driver offers the most versatile facilities and is discussed as the primary method. Both methods depend on certain master data being available in the system.

You have to customize certain settings concerning work schedules, employee data, and wage types before your system can carry out accounting processes on time data.

Preparing for Time Management

Your system must contain at least one standard work schedule that can answer the following questions:

- On which days should an employee be present for work?
- At what time should the employee attend and for how many hours?

The implication for time recording is that you must have determined a public holiday calendar and generated monthly work schedules suitable for each employee.

Employees can work in various contexts and may be absent for various reasons. Therefore, you must have a system of codes that the time-recording system can use to record attendance and absences.

Each employee must be uniquely identified by data in at least the following master infotypes:

- Organizational assignment (infotype 0001)
- Personal data (infotype 0002)
- Planned working time (infotype 0007)

These infotypes are defined in the standard R/3 system. The HR system holds additional infotypes used to interpret the information needed for time management.

Interpreting Infotype 0050 (Time-Recording Information)

Data is stored in the time recording information infotype (0050) for each employee. One item is the employee's time-recording ID number. The ID is first checked as soon as an employee enters it manually to ensure that it's unique. At a time-recording device, the ID is used to locate the correct time-recording card. The ID number is later converted to the employee's personnel number after the time events are uploaded to the HR system and infotype 0050 can be consulted.

Another data element in each employee's infotype 0050 is a grouping code that ensures that any data downloaded to a subsystem will concern only those likely to use it. Each time recording terminal can be sent an individual package of information if necessary. Alternatively, terminals can be assigned in groups that share the same download specification. The download can include such items as the following:

- HR master data
- Valid attendance and absences reasons for the employees likely to use the terminals in the group
- Work center identification
- Operations data used to support any plant data collection facilities
- Details of any external wage types—for example, canteen or gas station accounting transactions—that might have to be recognized at terminals in the group

- Types of time-recording system that also can operate an access control group that specifies which employees have been assigned to the time-recording system for a specified time period

- Systems that can accept data for a mail indicator that signals to an employee at the time-recording terminal and then display a message text

- Systems that can challenge personal codes to implement a strict access control

If an employee is working offsite, the start of offsite work can be recorded as a manual entry when a suitable terminal is available.

The organizational assignment infotype (0001) shows how the employee has been allocated to an area, subarea, or some other employee subgroup. For example, you can work with a personnel subarea grouping for absence and attendance types. Employees assigned to this subarea are expected to use only the absence and attendance type codes assigned to that grouping. No other codes are valid at clock in and clock out.

A personnel area is usually assigned a country grouping. This identifies the valid external wage types. Employees can also be assigned a subgroup because they share a work schedule. This is needed to determine, for instance, whether a particular day is a normal working day.

If your system is conducting time evaluation, the mail indicator can be triggered by any errors detected there, such as a missing time event. The employee can be sent a reminder message.

Ten information fields are available for downloading information from a time-evaluation system:

- Date of the last day evaluated
- Selected balances from time evaluation, such as overtime
- Remaining leave (entitlement minus leave taken or compensated up to the key date)
- Remaining leave unrequested (entitlement minus leave requested)
- The result of an individual incentive wages scheme calculation
- The result of a group incentive wages scheme calculation

The details of what's displayed at a terminal are specified during Plant Data Collection (PDC) master record customization.

It may happen that master data is changed during the period over which data is being collated ready for a download. This may create several records for individual employees. In such cases, the relevant fields are filled in all the records. The download is controlled by specifying the valid from and to dates for all master data fields.

Assigning Employees for Planned Working Time

Infotype 0007, planned working time, includes a field interpreted as the status for time management. This indicator must be set to have an employee take part in time evaluation. It also determines which method is to be used according to the following:

- No time evaluation
- Evaluation of actual times
- Evaluation of actual times and PDC
- External services
- Evaluation of planned times (recording of exceptions to the work schedule)

If an employee is assigned status 2, the time recording information infotype (0050) must be maintained with the master data needed to control the device on which actual times are to be recorded. This infotype also includes fields for the employee's time recording ID number, the interface data, and master data for this employee.

In installations where absence and attendance reasons can be recorded, the time events P10 (clock in) and P20 (clock out) can interpret valid reason codes. The system confirms that the codes are valid for the current date and then generates either an attendance or absence of less than one workday for the current day or a full-day record for the previous or subsequent day.

Evaluating Time Data

The time evaluation driver RPTIME00 is the most comprehensive method of evaluating time data. However, employee time data can also be evaluated in the gross part of payroll accounting. The relevant payroll driver is RPCALCX0, as discussed later in the "Running Time Evaluation in HR Payroll Accounting" section.

The time evaluation driver RPTIME00 is the preferred method:

- Data can be collected for evaluation from external time-recording terminals.
- Time balances for flextime and time off may be formed and stored.
- Messages may be stored in connection with error processing.
- The time evaluation driver can adjust leave accounts and absence quotas by updating leave entitlement infotype 0005 and absence quota infotype 2006.

Modifying Customizing Tables and Process Control Features

The detailed calculations carried out in time evaluation can be controlled by parameters adjusted in customizing. For example, you can arrange flextime hours to be handled differently for each employee subgroup. You can determine that a flextime balance in excess of five hours should be converted to an overtime balance, and a flextime balance of less than five hours should be transferred to the subsequent monthly balance. For some groupings you might want to allow employees to exchange excess flextime hours for time off. You could set an upper limit for the flextime excess at month's end.

There are two methods of setting up the time evaluation driver:

- Adjust the process control tables during customization following the implementation guide
- Customize the rule processing used in time evaluation schemas

Providing the Inputs for Time Evaluation

The time evaluation driver needs general information from tables relevant to all employees and information specific to individual personnel. In particular, the following information is required for each personnel number:

- Data from Personnel Administration
- Time data
- Information on the payroll status
- Status from the previous time evaluation run
- Previous evaluation results

The data from PA is obtained by consulting the following infotypes:

Events	0000
Basic pay	0008
Organizational assignment	0001
Date specifications	0041
Personal data	0002
Reduced hrs/bad weather	0049
Planned working time	0007
Time recording information	0050

The following infotypes are consulted when processing an employee's time data:

Leave entitlement	0005
Overtime	2005
Leave compensation	0083
Absence quotas	2006
Absences	2001
Attendance quotas	2007
Attendance	2002
Time events	2011
Substitutions	2003
Time balance revisions	2012
Availability	2004

Which infotypes are necessary depends on the particular time-recording subsystem in use and the extent to which the relevant infotypes have been maintained for the employees concerned.

Payroll status infotype 0003 stores the recalculation date for PDC (Plant Data Collection). This date is the first to be included in the next run of the time evaluation driver.

The status of the last evaluation run includes the recalculation date for pair formation and records of any time events that haven't been processed. If notes and information messages were generated in the previous time evaluation run, they're also stored in the status infotype.

The results of the previous time evaluation include the interim balances, wage types used, and a log of quota deductions. This data is needed to complete the current evaluation, and in case it's necessary to recalculate a previous result after correcting an error.

Understanding Time Event Types

When a time recording device or manual input system accepts a time event, it must store the event so that it can be matched or paired with another time and thus allow the calculation of the time interval between these events. A time event type is a useful category when seeking to form time pairs. For example, the following time event types are determined by the time-recording system and recorded times tagged by these codes can be uploaded to the HR system via communication channel 1:

P10	Clock in
P15	Start of break
P20	Clock out
P25	End of break
P30	Start of offsite work
P40	End of offsite work

Two time event types can't be generated at the time-recording terminal. These events have to be entered manually in time events infotype 2011:

P35	Manual start of offsite work
P45	Manual end of offsite work

These time events allow an employee to begin and end work without the corresponding clock-in or clock-out entry.

The time event infotype also accepts manual entries that correspond to the time event types normally entered by a time-recording system. In these instances, the time event types aren't carried as communication channel 1:

01	Clock-in (identical to P10)
02	Clock-out (identical to P20)
03	Clock-in or clock-out
04	Start of offsite work (identical to P30)
05	End of offsite work (identical to P40)
06	Start or end of offsite work
07	Manual start of offsite work (identical to P35)
08	Manual end of offsite work (identical to P45)
09	Manual start or end of offsite work

Delimiting Time Events

There are three distinct groups of time events:

- Time events that open a pair, such as P10 clock-in and P35 manual start of offsite work
- Time events that close one pair and open another, such as P15 start of break, P25 end of break, P30 start of offsite work, and P40 end of offsite work
- Time events that close one pair but don't open another, such as P20 clock-out and P45 manual end of offsite work

If there is another P10 clock-in entry after a P20 clock-out entry, no pair is formed for the time interval between them.

A time pair can be completed by the time evaluation driver via processing rule TE30, which completes any missing entries if possible. The status of the time pair is recorded at the same time. For example, a pair comprising clock-in and clock-out on the same day for a particular employee is assigned a status of BLANK because the pair is complete. An empty status field is interpreted as an indicator that no special processing has been necessary. The term BLANK is used in programming the calculation rule. If another clock-in has been entered without a corresponding clock-out, the pair can be completed by automatically entering the next scheduled end of work following the clock-in. The status of this pair is then recorded as A to signify that the pair has been automatically delimited.

If the time-evaluation program is being run some specified time later than the unmatched entry, you can configure the system to generate an error message. For example, an employee may record a time event P30, end of offsite work. The time-evaluation program searches for an event that marks the start of offsite work. If none is found, there is an error message to the supervisor, who could make a manual entry of event P35, manual start of offsite work, and thus complete the formation of a valid pair.

Interpreting Attendance and Absence Status in Pair Formation

Infotypes 2002 (attendances) and 2001 (absences) compile aggregated statistics. However, the process of pair formation uses an employee's relevant attendance/absence status to determine entry validity. Attendance as a status indicator implies that the employee is working for the company because the most recent time event for that employee was a clock-in, offsite work entry, or the manual entry equivalents. A similar logic defines absence as a status indicator.

It's part of the definition of a time event that only certain status indicators of attendance or absence are permitted. For example, an absent employee can't enter a clock-out code. In other words, the valid precursors of clock-out are specified as clock-in, end of break, or manual start of offsite work. The definition of a time event also includes a specification of the employee's attendance/absence status that will necessarily arise as the consequence of posting that time event.

These definitions of status before and after each time event are logically necessary if the system is to form time pairs correctly. The before and after attendance/absence status can change as follows:

- Absent>Clock-In>At Work
- At Work>Clock-Out>Absent
- At Work>Start of Offsite Work>Offsite

Understanding Pair Formation

The process of pair formation is largely automatic and takes place before the data is passed to the time evaluation driver. The outcome is a stream of time pairs from which time wage types can be generated by the time evaluation processes. You can customize these processes.

1. Each time event is assigned to the current or previous day. A time event doesn't need to apply to the day on which it was entered. For example, if a night shift is operating, the time pair that ends it is normally assigned to the day on which it began. However, the time associated with the clock-out has to be incremented by 24 hours so that the length of time worked is correctly calculated.

2. The pairs for each day are formed.

3. Time tickets are generated if you're using plant data collection (PDC) for incentive wages.

The pair formation process is triggered for any day when a new time event is recorded, or for days that follow a time event that generates a time pair formation error. Pair formation can start as soon as fresh time events are uploaded or as part of a scheduled run of the time evaluation driver, according to the arrangements made in customizing. If the supervisor has made manual or back-dated changes to the data, a repeat of pair formation can be initiated.

Pair formation takes account of all time events uploaded to the HR system from a time-recording subsystem, plus any time events that have to be recorded in time events infotype 2001 as a result of dialog at a terminal in which the employee or a supervisor has entered time data.

New time events are inserted in table TEVEN, which stores all the time events ever entered or uploaded. All recorded, processed, unprocessed, and deleted time events are stored in this table.

As the HR system table TEVEN is loaded with new time events, they're also copied to table NT1, which identifies the time events that aren't yet processed. When a time pair is formed, it's inserted in the pair table PT, and the time events composing this pair are deleted from the list of unprocessed events (table NT1). Any time event that can't be processed because an error has been detected is logged in table NT2.

Interpreting the Pair Type and Status of a Time Pair

The following codes are used to classify pair types according to the employee's attendance or absence status:

0	Unrecorded absence or break
1	Employee is at work
2	Employee is absent (This pair type isn't assigned during pair formation.)
3	Employee working offsite

The status of a time pair is recorded when it's formed and indicates whether further rule processing is required by the time evaluation driver. The status of a time pair is indicated as follows:

BLANK	Pair is complete
2	No clock-in
3	No clock-out
4	No break end time
7	No start time for offsite work
8	No end time for offsite work
E	Order confirmation missing from PDC

As each day's time event is processed, the system updates the employee's attendance status.

A time pair assigned any status other than BLANK is an *open time pair*. The time evaluation driver's rule-processing logic can be set up to process open pairs in whatever way your company requires. For example, the normal start and end of the working day may be used as default time events. If no rule is provided for a particular type of open pair, an error message can be generated so that a manual entry can be made to complete the data.

Dealing with Open Pairs

The system will recognize certain logical possibilities as each new time event is processed, and you can arrange what should be done in certain circumstances. For example, if an employee is absent and then enters a clock-in at work, an open pair is formed with status 3 to signify that no clock-out has yet been found to allow the generation of a complete pair. In this instance, no customizing action is necessary. The time-recording system is simply waiting for the employee to finish work.

An employee with the recorded status of absent could enter a start of break first pair at work. This would generate an open pair with the pair status of 3, which signifies that a clock-out is missing. There are two possibilities in this situation:

- Record an error
- Record an open paid work time event and assign the normal starting time for work on that day

It's a matter of policy which choice should be set up in customizing. Similar decisions can be set up as processing rules for the situations that can appear as open pairs because a necessary time event isn't entered.

Using Dynamic Daily Work Schedule Assignment in Pair Formation

Employees can work outside the hours stipulated in their daily work schedule—for example, when some substitutions are made in which the work schedule is temporarily updated on a prearranged basis.

The HR system allows for dynamic daily work scheduling so that employees can work flexibly if necessary. Some adjustment can be made by assigning a time event to a previous day to complete a time pair, but sometimes this method doesn't produce an accurate result. Dynamic daily work schedule assignment is a suite of facilities for controlling previous day assignment in pair formation according to rules and parameters previously established. If the first time event of the day falls within a predefined time frame, the tolerance interval, the dynamic day procedure is applied in preference to the normal pair formation logic.

Skeleton times are time periods defined for the purpose of allowing the time-evaluation system to recognize occasions when dynamic assignment of daily work schedule should be applied. For example, skeleton times can be defined for early working, late working, or night working.

Selecting Time Wage Types

Gross wages are calculated in payroll accounting on the basis of the time pairs and the time wage types assigned to them. These assignments are made according to the entries in table T510S, which contains the time wage type selection rules. These rules define the time wage type to be assigned according to the employee, the day, and the time. In particular, the time wage type selection rules must take account of the following factors:

- Wage types are assigned to the planned working times of hourly wage earners, not salaried employees.
- Public holidays are paid as different wage types than normal working days.
- Overtime may have to be divided into different wage types according to how many overtime hours are worked on a particular day.

The time wage type selection rule table T510S provides two grouping indicators that can be used to control how the time wage types are to be selected for employees according to their organizational assignments:

- Indicator that signifies which customized personnel calculation rule should be used to define the time wage type selection group to be read from table T510S
- Day grouping indicator that specifies which wage type selection rule should be applied according to the type of day being worked

The day grouping for time wage type selection can control rules for such types of working days as normal working days, Sundays, and public holidays.

The internal work table TIP stores the daily input for time evaluation. Each TIP entry includes an indicator of this entry's processing class. Processing class S signifies a time entry for planned working time. Processing class M signifies that the entry is to be processed as overtime. Class A is used for absence. You can therefore maintain separate tables of valid time wage types temporarily for the S, M, and A processing classes. These time wage types precisely define the compensation calculations.

By this arrangement, the calculations of compensation can be carried out separately for planned working time and overtime. It's also possible to define whether an employee is to be compensated for overtime by time off, full payment, or proportional payment.

Uploading and Updating Time Events

You can initiate an upload of recorded time events into the SAP system in three ways:

- By a transaction using PT44 (Upload Request)
- By the menu path Human Resources>Time Management>Environment> Subsystem>Upload Request
- By scheduling when and how often to run a background job comprising report SAPCDT44, which triggers the transaction upload request, perhaps overnight when system resources are available

When the time recording system uploads all the recorded time events to SAP table RUECK, the connection is dismantled.

An uploaded time event can be updated by any of three methods:

- By a transaction using CC1 (Update PDC Messages PT45)
- By the menu path Human Resources>Time Management>Environment> Subsystem>Update Time Events
- By scheduling when and how often to run a background job comprising report SAPCDT45, which triggers transaction Update PDC Messages PT45

When a time event is successfully processed, it's deleted from table RUECK. It can then be displayed and changed manually in time events infotype 2011.

Controlling Time Event Uploads with Communication Parameters

Each communication channel can be assigned a parameter value that specifies that time events should be updated, if necessary, immediately after they're uploaded. A time event can remain unprocessed when the employee's personnel number is locked because another application is processing the employee's data. In this case, the entry remains in table RUECK and processing is postponed until the next updating run.

A validation error is logged if the personnel number can't be determined from the time record-ing ID number or if the necessary authorizations can't be confirmed. The unprocessed time event is copied to a pool.

The Subsystem pushbutton becomes active in the Time Management menu if any time events pools remain unprocessed from previous updates. You can't change an individual time event, but you can attempt to reduce the error pool by initiating a further update, which takes into account any causes of error that no longer are justified. You can also delete the entire error pool.

In addition to controlling time event updating, the communication parameters for each channel can be used as follows:

- Display the times of the last transfers
- Set the validity period of the HR mini-master records in the time-recording system

- Specify whether the absence/attendance reasons, the external wage types, or both should be downloaded
- Indicate who is to receive a mail message if errors occur
- Determine whether pairs are formed immediately when time events are updated or later in time evaluation

There are two methods of setting up the communication parameters:

- Use transaction PT41 (Communication Parameters)
- Follow the menu path Implementation Guide>Cross-Application Functions>Plant Data Collection>Subsystem Configuration (for all communication channels)

You can overwrite the default communication parameters only if the download is triggered manually.

The communication parameters control the following functions:

- Validity period of HR master records in the time-recording system, which is used to ensure that the system accepts only time-recording ID numbers valid for each day
- Transfer attendance/absence reasons, external wage types, or both with each download
- Update the stored time events immediately after they are uploaded—so that an accurate attendance check can always be available, for example
- Form time pairs immediately when time events are updated or wait until the (nightly) time evaluation run
- Nominate a time event error message receiver who can call the time-management error pool directly from the message to review and perhaps correct the error

Connecting Time Recording Systems via Sequential Files

It's possible to send time data from an external system in the form of a sequential file. However, this method doesn't use a certified SAP interface, so some other arrangement for data security must be in place.

A download can be prepared by calling the Download Mini-Master to Sequential File (RPTEDO00) report. This report reads the master data of selected employees and writes the mini-master records to a sequential file, using the format defined as the dictionary structure DWN01.

If you have the necessary authorization, you can arrange for the Sequential File Report function to generate a log that displays organizational assignment infotype 0001 for each employee.

RPTEUP10 is the Upload Time Events from Sequential File report. The following fields are expected and the data is assembled in table RUECK as used by the standard interface:

Personnel number	Entry time
Time recording ID number	Time event type
Date	Terminal ID

Time   Absence/attendance reason

Entry date

A time event error pool is generated, if necessary.

Using the Time Evaluation Driver RPTIME00

RPTIME00, a report function known as the *time evaluation driver*, is used to evaluate employee time data. The data can be collected from time-recording systems or recorded directly in time infotypes under control of a dialog box.

The time evaluation driver is normally run once daily—usually at night and for large groups, although it can be initiated for individual employees or selected groups. The following tasks are built into the driver:

- Forming time balances, such as the flextime balance or compensation (time off in lieu) account, which can be cumulated periodically or daily
- Generating time wage types, such as overtime wage types and bonus wage types, which are passed on to payroll accounting for further processing
- Generating and reducing quotas such as overtime approval and leave accrual
- Checking adherence to working time regulations and generating messages

The RPTIME00 time evaluation driver automatically takes account of any changes to the data for a previously evaluated period.

Setting RPTIME00 Parameters

When RPTIME00 is initiated, the report selection screen offers users control over the following features:

- The employees to be selected for time evaluation
- The settings of specific parameters for time evaluation

Variants can be created if the same parameter settings are needed frequently or if you want to save a variant for test purposes.

Selecting Personnel

Employee personnel numbers can be identified by matchcodes, by ranges, or individually. The standard matchcodes for selecting time evaluation personnel are as follows:

B   PDC error indicator assigned to employee personnel numbers associated with an error in a previous run

L   Time data administrator identifying employees based on their administrator for time recording as recorded in their organizational assignment infotype 0001

Z   PDC time recording ID card, which allows employees to be selected according to their time recording ID numbers

Specifying a Schema

A *processing schema* is a plan of the steps to be performed in time evaluation. A schema must be specified before the time evaluation driver is started.

Printing Time Statements

Standard form TF00 is a format in which a time statement can be printed for test purposes. You can create variants of this form or create your own. The form identification must be supplied as a default or arranged as a default for the time evaluation driver. RPTEDT00, the Time Statement Form report, is used if a large number of time statements need to be printed.

Forcing Recalculation

The normal procedure recalculates up to the first day that hasn't been evaluated completely, or for which there are errors. However, a starting date can be entered in the time evaluation driver parameter known as Forced Recalculation As Of. You may want to use this facility to reevaluate days that have already been accounted without errors. A forced recalculation has no effect on the accounting result.

Controlling the Last Date for Time Evaluation

The Evaluation Up To parameter accepts an alternative to the current system date—today's date. Without this setting, time evaluation will run up to the current system date unless there are errors.

Forming New Time Pairs

Pair formation is normally triggered automatically. However, the New Time Pair Formation parameter can be used to control the formation of new pairs each day up to the forced recalculation date.

Using Test Switches to Control RPTIME00 Program Options

The following standard test switches are provided:

Standard setting	No log of processing steps.
Display log	Processing steps are logged, with the personnel calculation rules called while logging is in force. You can control where the specified internal tables are printed by inserting PRINT XXX in the schema.
Test run	No update. The evaluation results aren't saved or exported.
Stop at function/operation BREAK	Display ABAP/4 coding. This reveals how individual functions and operations are working at the break point you've placed in a schema or personnel calculation rule. Users normally have an ABAP/4 prefix authorized for use in these circumstances. Alternatively, the report can be set to stop at all break points.

Stop at fixed positions   Used for test purposes and in the setting up of a system.
in time evaluation

The fixed positions for stopping RPTIME00 are as follows:

- After the start of selection
- After the personnel numbers are identified
- After each period, if there is more than one
- Before any infotype or cluster table is updated

Logging RPTIME00 Processing Steps

The time evaluation driver RPTIME00 generates by default a short processing log that doesn't detail individual processing steps. If there are no errors, RPTIME00 prints the most important results. If there are any errors, a short text note is displayed during online processing to indicate where the error occurred. For example, the message HR internal error while locking. Rejected person 000XXXXX appears if an infotype bearing this personnel number is being maintained at the time.

The final line of a short processing log includes the following fields:

- How many employees you've selected
- How many of these have been accounted
- How many were accounted with errors
- The number of employees for whom processing was canceled prematurely
- How many employees were rejected

If you flag the program options parameter Logging On, the individual processing steps are displayed in addition to the information given by the short logging report. You can insert various functions in a time-evaluation schema to print the working tables in order to trace an error. The following are examples:

- PRINT TIP
- PRINT TES
- PRINT SALD
- PRINT DZL

You can shorten the processing log by inserting a * in the Log Control field for any processing step in the schema under test. This will leave out the log entries for this step.

Controlling the Download of the HR Mini-Master Record

Downloading information to a time-recording system allows it to perform certain checks and to allow the employees to consult evaluation results such as their overtime situation. A *mini-master* is a selection of data fields from the HR master records assembled for the employees likely to use the time-recording system to which it's being downloaded. For each employee, time recording information infotype 0050 must contain a time recording ID number and may also indicate a version number. The time recording ID number isn't the same as the personnel number, but the system must be able to convert one to the other by consulting the relevant infotype 0050.

A time-recording system can be used to control access to the premises. An employee who has left may be granted access, so the relevant record has to be included in the download.

There are three methods of initiating mini-master downloads:

- By transaction PT42 (Transfer HR Master Record to PDC Subsystems)
- By the menu path Human Resources>Time Management>Environment> Subsystem>Download Pers.Data
- By scheduling when and how often to run a background job comprising report SAPCDT42, which triggers transaction PT42 (Transfer HR Master Record to PDC Subsystems)

A download is performed to cover the validity period of HR mini-master records, which is defined as a number of relevant days beginning with the date of the download. The default length of the validity period is defined during customization. If you initiate a manual download, you can overwrite the number of days of the validity.

An HR mini-master record is compiled from the data of all employees for whom there is a time recording information record (infotype 0050) on at least one day within the period.

At least one record has to be selected for download for each employee. If there are relevant changes to the employee's master data during the download validity period, extra records— each with its limited validity defined—have to be selected for download.

The HR mini-master record contains the following fields:

Field Name	Type	Length	Description
ZAUSW	NUMC	8	Time recording ID number
BEGDA	NUMC	8	Start of validity
ENDDA	DATE	8	End of validity
ZAUVE	NUMC	1	Version number of ID card
PERNR	NUMC	8	Personnel number
ENAME	CHAR	40	Edited name of employee
SNAME	CHAR	40	Sortable name of employee
INFO1	CHAR	8	Info field 1
INFO2	CHAR	8	Info field 2
INFO3	CHAR	8	Info field 3
INFO4	CHAR	8	Info field 4

INFO5	CHAR	8	Info field 5
INFO6	CHAR	8	Info field 6
INFO7	CHAR	8	Info field 7
INFO8	CHAR	8	Info field 8
INFO9	CHAR	8	Info field 9
IMAIL	CHAR	1	Mail indicator of error in time evaluation
MOABW	CHAR	2	Personnel subarea grouping for attendance/absence types
MOLGA	CHAR	2	Country grouping
BDEGR	CHAR	3	Grouping for subsystem connection
ZEITY	CHAR	1	Employee subgroup grouping for work schedules
ZDGBE	CHAR	1	Offsite work authorization
ZANBE	CHAR	2	Access control group
ZPINC	CHAR	4	Personal code
ZMAIL	CHAR	1	Mail indicator from time recording information infotype

Updating Infotypes in Time Evaluation

The time evaluation driver's activities result in a number of changes to infotype records. For example, infotype 0003, payroll status, is updated with the date on which the next run should start. This date may have been determined by the detection of an error in time evaluation. The next run should be started as of the date that remains processed because of the error.

The following infotypes are updated with new values when a time evaluation run is finished, if necessary:

- Leave entitlement (0005) stores the entitlement and amount used of a quota.
- Absence quotas (2006).
- Attendance quotas (2007).
- Absence and attendance reasons collected at the terminal and processed in time evaluation are stored as locked records; they are generated for infotypes absences (2001) and attendances (2002).

General status data, such as the last day processed and the last time error processing was performed, is entered in table QT, cluster B1, at the end of the time evaluation run. Time events table TEVEN is updated if pair formation is taking place in the time evaluation run, or if the previous day assignment of a time event is changed. Interface table COIFT is updated if the time evaluation driver is evaluating the time data of external employees.

Controlling the Time Evaluation Driver

The calculations carried out in time evaluation are executed via hard-coded processing steps that are called by functions available from function pool SAPFP51T. The driver uses these functions to select employees for time evaluation, retrieve the necessary data, determine the evaluation period, and save the evaluation results.

Time data processing is executed according to rules specified when the system is customized. Also, certain steps and global settings are determined by entries in customizing tables, independent of rule processing. The time types table defines the types of time balances formed.

A *schema* is an ordered list of the function calls that control the individual substeps or operations. Each function's execution is specified and hardcoded as a module of the function pool SAPFP51T. For example, there are functions for the following purposes:

- Time wage type formation
- Cumulating balances
- Overtime calculation

The functions are processed in a specific sequence that can be specified during customizing and stored as a schema.

A standard SAP time evaluation schema can be nominated as a reference schema for processing. For example, the following schemas are standard:

- Schema TM01 evaluates the time data of employees for whom only exceptions to the work schedule are recorded.
- Schema TM00 evaluates time data that has been recorded at time-recording systems.
- Schema TM04 evaluates time data that has been recorded with or without clock times.
- Schema TM02 evaluates the time data of external employees.

The time evaluation driver's processing steps are customized mainly by manipulating the processing rules to suit the individual company. For example, there may be company rules for overtime calculation to require that flextime hours be converted to overtime wage types if they exceed specified limits.

Processing rules are also used to set up different procedures according to such factors as the following:

- The type of day being evaluated, such as weekday or public holiday
- The employee's organizational assignment, such as hourly or salary
- The nature of the time data recorded

The results of time evaluation include cumulated balances, time wage types, and messages. These results are stored in cluster B2 for individual employees and periods. A history of time data is also maintained in cluster B2.

Cluster B1 holds the time balances in preparation for downloading to the time-recording system. The menu path for viewing clusters B1 and B2 is Time Management>Tools>Tool Selection.

Running Time Evaluation in HR Payroll Accounting

An employee's gross wage is calculated in a payroll accounting system by using the time wage types determined in time evaluation. This can be a third-party payroll accounting system or the HR Payroll Accounting module.

Time data must be evaluated when it reaches an accounting system. In HR, the evaluation takes place in the gross part of payroll where there's a block of functions defined as a *subschema*. There will be a different subschema for each country grouping for which the system processes payroll.

The main tasks of the payroll subschema are as follows:

- Creating personal work schedules
- Forming partial period factors and valuation bases
- Day processing of time data by using schema TC00 (the international schema for time wage type selection)
- Processing time wage types
- Valuating absences

Daily evaluation of time data may be necessary when the payroll run is carried out before the end of the period. In such circumstances, the time evaluation process can't generate time wage types for the days between the payroll run and the end of the period. You can specify that these day are to be paid based on a projection of planned working times and planned attendances or absences. Any differences are rectified by a retroactive payroll accounting run in the following month.

Time evaluation in payroll accounting is used when time balances aren't maintained, when quotas aren't changed by time evaluation, or if there's no time-recording system.

Table ZL, used as the interface to payroll, contains the time wage types for each day of the accounting period. This data is transferred to work table IT or to a third-party accounting system.

Report RPTEZL00 (Supply Third-Party Payroll Accounting System) downloads data for a required period from table ZL, cluster B2, into a sequential data set comprising the time wage types.

Managing Time Evaluation for External Service Providers

The time evaluation driver RPTIME00 using schema TM02 can evaluate external services. The service providers' details are stored by the R/3 Materials Management component MM-SRV, a purchasing application designed for services management. The time data is associated with the MM-SRV records.

Managing Leave Entitlement in Infotypes

An employee's leave entitlement can be maintained by manual entries in leave entitlement infotype 0005. If a large number of employees are to have similar entitlements, the Batch Input: Annual Leave report (RPTLEA30) can be run to generate the leave quotas for the selected employees on the basis of parameters determined during customization.

Another technique is to calculate leave entitlement for a leave year based on the previous year's time data. There's also a method of updating an employee's leave entitlement according to his attendance times.

A combination of methods can be arranged by establishing different leave types.

The Leave Cumulation report (RPILVA00) generates leave entitlement for a leave year by taking account of the following factors:

- Length of service with the company
- Organizational assignment
- Cumulated attendance hours from the previous calendar year

A guideline value can be used to arrive at an entitlement. For example, a record of 2,000 hours per year may attract a leave entitlement of 20 days for the following year. Attendance hours above or below the guideline value attract leave in proportion.

Another approach is to use programmed features to calculate the entitlement from a defined deduction period, employees' leave remaining, defined rounding and reduction methods, and upper limits for leave entitlement.

Managing Leave Entitlement in Time Evaluation

If a leave entitlement record exists for an employee in infotype 0005, time evaluation rule processing can update the total entitlement for the leave type and leave year by an increment or decrement at the end of each accounting period. The Leave Remaining field shows the result of deducting leave requested and leave compensated.

The following sample update rules are available for customizing as necessary:

- Update the leave entitlement periodically based on the employee's attendance days by using personnel calculation rule TS11.
- Update the leave entitlement periodically based on the employee's attendance hours by using personnel calculation rule TS15.
- Increase the leave entitlement by a constant value at the end of an accounting period by using personnel calculation rule TS14.

TS11 assumes that employees are entitled to a full leave year only if their attendance days reach a certain total number in the leave year. Entitlement is proportional to their actual attendance days in relation to the number required for the full entitlement. This rule is appropriate for temporary personnel working irregular hours. Their leave entitlement is recalculated at the end of each accounting period and their leave entitlement infotype 0005 is updated.

TS15 awards leave in proportion to the ratio of actual attendance hours to stipulated annual working hours recorded in planned working time infotype 0007.

TS14 increases an employee's leave entitlement at the end of each accounting period by the value stored as constant LVACR in payroll constants table T511K.

Using Time Evaluation Periods and Payroll Accounting Periods

How often payroll accounting is run depends on the payroll area. For example, salaried employees assigned to payroll area D1 are paid monthly; hourly paid employees assigned to payroll area D2 are paid weekly.

Data for payroll runs is supplied in the form of time wage types that have been generated for the current payroll accounting period and for the previous period. The time wage types are stored in cluster B2, which is part of file PCL2.

Time evaluation is carried out for a period determined at customizing for the whole system, without reference to any payroll areas. The following procedures are available to establish the time evaluation period:

- From the time management implementation guide, first select Define Accounting Period and then select the date specifications for the time evaluation period.
- Run the RP_DEF_TIME_PERIOD macro if the standard period isn't suitable and you want to define your own time evaluation period.

The payroll accounting period is defined for each payroll area when it's created. The period of time evaluation should equal the longest of any payroll accounting period assigned to a payroll area.

Differences in accounting periods can be handled in time evaluation by establishing rules to detect the end of the payroll or time evaluation period. For example, the ABAP/4 statement IF EOM will detect the end of the time evaluation period, and IF EOP will detect the end of the payroll accounting period.

Controlling Recalculation

The time evaluation driver RPTIME00 automatically checks which day is the first to be evaluated for each employee. If employee master data has changed, the new data may have to be applied retroactively from the effective date of the change. There will have to be a recalculation of the previous time evaluation results for this employee.

The starting date for time evaluation is normally the day that follows the last day evaluated without errors. If time evaluation is terminated because of an error, payroll status infotype 0003 shows this date in the field Recalculation for PDC.

If retroactive changes are made to infotypes, periods already evaluated without errors may have to be evaluated again. This recalculation can be triggered automatically or manually. From the view V_Tr82A, Infotypes, you can flag each infotype if changes to it ought to trigger a recalculation. You can indicate which fields are relevant from the view V_T588G, Field-Specific Recalculation Indicators.

The earliest recalculation date can be set for individual or all employees taking part in time evaluation. This limits excessive recalculation. A warning is issued if changes to infotypes are made that apply to periods before the earliest recalculation date.

The payroll status infotype 0003 has a date field named Earliest Personal Recalculation Date, which can be maintained for individual employees.

To set up the recalculation limit date for all employees, use the menu path Time Management> Tools>Current Settings>Set Earliest Recalculation Date For Pair Formation/Time Evaluation.

If any employee has also been assigned an earliest personal recalculation date for time evaluation individually, the system chooses whatever date is later as the limit for recalculation.

Selecting Personnel Numbers for Time Evaluation

Time evaluation is normally run overnight as a background job for either a group of employees or all employees. A special variant of the time evaluation driver is created for this purpose when the system is customized.

You can also select personnel numbers on the logical database's selection screen. The Further Selections and Matchcodes pushbuttons can be used to select only those employees assigned to a particular time recording administrator, for example. You can also specify individual employees on the report selection screen.

If some corrections are made to employees' time data in error processing, the time evaluation driver automatically selects the corresponding personnel numbers. Employees with corrected periods are automatically included in the next run of RPTIME00 for recalculation.

The time evaluation driver selects employees for time evaluation only if certain preconditions are met:

- The personnel number must not be locked for the maintenance of infotypes at the time of the evaluation.
- The employee must be actively employed with the company for at least one day within the evaluation period. The time evaluation driver checks in events infotype 0000 whether the employee is allocated employment status 3 (active).
- The employee must be assigned a Time Management status other than 0 in planned working time infotype 0007 (1, 2, 8, or 9).
- A time-evaluation schema can specify which Time Management status should be assigned to an employee for his/her data to be evaluated by using this schema.

Tasking the Time Evaluation Driver

Overall control is managed by the time evaluation driver RPTIME00. For example, the time evaluation schema determines what must be accomplished by specifying a sequence of function calls to function pool SAPFP51T. Where rule processing is required, it's called by RPTIME00. The following operations are standard:

- Selecting the employees to be processed.
- Locking the personnel numbers of the selected personnel so that their master data cannot be altered until the time evaluation run is finished.
- Determining the evaluation period or periods per person by consulting the first date to be evaluated for each employee. The system automatically initiates recalculation if any retroactive changes or error corrections need to be taken into account.
- Importing data from the database, such as the employee's infotype records, time events, and previous time evaluation results. If time pairs are formed, they're also imported.
- Triggering rule processing for time data evaluation.
- Determining the starting date for the next run as the day following the last day evaluated without errors. Record this date in the field Recalculation Date for PDC in payroll status infotype 0003.
- Exporting the results data to the database.
- Logging processing steps and displaying results.

Arranging Personnel Calculation Rules and Operations in Time Evaluation

A personnel calculation rule is an If...Then structure used to perform individual actions only if the prescribed conditions are satisfied. These rules are accessed for maintenance through the menu path Time Management>Tools>Maintain Personnel Calculation Rules.

The data used to test the conditions for a rule can be transferred by the function that called the rule if it's not already available as part of the general status data for the employee. The individual processing steps controlled by a rule are operations that can change data in tables and control the processing course.

Decision operations depend on the answers to queries that identify a time type, provide the name of the daily work schedule, or yield the answer Yes or No. A rule may include up to six operations. For example, operation OUTWP imports work center data, whereas operation VARST imports general fields.

Using Time Evaluation Schemas

A *schema* is a sequence of rule processing steps. Some steps may produce results used to control which additional steps should be taken. The HR system contains three standard schemas covering a wide range of functions. Details of the schemas can be customized, and functions may be copied from a standard schema to build customized variants.

The following factors may need to be taken into account when adopting a standard time evaluation schema or building a customized variant:

- How time data is entered in the system and form of this data
- The volume of time data
- Which time evaluation results are required
- How the planned specifications in the daily work schedule are checked
- How overtime is calculated and approved

Using Schema TM00: Time Evaluation Using Time Events

The standard time evaluation schemas provide useful basic rule constellations from which more elaborate variants can be built. If employees have recorded their actual times at time recording terminals, at PDC systems, or in time events infotype 2011, schema TM00 is likely to be suitable for evaluating the time data.

Schema TM00 is controlled by the time evaluation driver RPTIME00. It forms time balances, time wage types, and time quotas. The inputs for TM00 are personnel time events recorded at the terminals and the time pairs formed from them. This schema can also import and process time data that has been entered online.

The time data for TM00 must be actual working times entered as clock times and comprise full-day records.

TM00 compares the recorded actual times with the planned working time data in the daily work schedule. The working time data comprises the planned begin and end times, core times, and break times.

If overtime approval is granted, TM00 takes account of time entries before or after the planned working time. Otherwise, these times are ignored in favor of the planned working times.

Schema TM00 can seek attendance approval from the following selectable sources:

- Attendance approval entered in attendance quotas infotype 2007
- Overtime approval entered in time recording info infotype 0050
- Overtime approval stipulated in the daily work schedule

The schema can also be set up to calculate overtime without overtime approval. In all cases, overtime on any day isn't counted until the employee has worked the number of planned working hours specified in the daily work schedule. Overtime may not exceed the daily maximum working time. Schema TM00 can calculate daily or weekly overtime.

Using Schema TM01: Time Evaluation for Exceptions to the Work Schedule

TM01 evaluates time data that has been entered as clock times to record only exceptions to the work schedule. These entries are made online as full-day records and imported by TM01 for processing under control of the time evaluation driver RPTIME00.

Planned time pairs corresponding to actual working times are used to generate time pairs for the time evaluation driver unless they are modifying entries in absences infotype 2001 or attendances infotype 2002. TM01 automatically generates overtime for all attendance times outside the planned working times. If overtime is defined in overtime infotype 2005, the overtime hours can be approved, having taken account of overtime breaks.

Using Schema TM02: Time Evaluation for External Services Providers

External service providers can be given access to the time evaluation system and their hours recorded in the Materials Management application MM-SRV where service contracts are managed. Schema TM02 is designed to support external service time evaluation.

For each external employee, attendances infotype 2002 specifies how time data is to be collected and managed. The following additional data is normally maintained:

- Number of the relevant purchasing document with item number, which identifies the service for which time data is being collected
- Service number from which the nature of the service can be inferred
- Job key if there is more than one job in the contract

Before the time evaluation driver can process data for external services, the following prerequisite conditions must be satisfied:

- A signed service contract must exist between the receiver company (A) and the external service provider company (E).
- The contract must stipulate that the company E employees should provide the services at a plant/location that belongs to company A.
- The amount that company A has to pay for an hour of work performed by company E must be stipulated in the contract.

The hourly rate for a service is specified in the MM-SRV module in the form of service numbers. For example, service numbers can be stored as MM-SRV records of the following types:

- Foreman hour
- Apprentice hour
- Painter hour
- Bonuses for hours after 10 p.m., over the weekend, as overtime hours, for each skill or trade group

Preparing a System to Manage Time Evaluation of External Service Providers

Some preconditions must be satisfied if a system is to valuate an external service provider's time data. The principal requirements are as follows:

- The system must be customized to support the integration of Time Management and Materials Management.
- The external employee must be recorded in the HR system and be allocated a unique personnel number.

- The organizational assignment (0001) and planned working time (0007) infotypes must be maintained. An event defined for the hiring of external employees is normally created in events infotype 0000, using the standard event mini-master. This ensures that employees are assigned infotypes 0001 and 0007 with suitable data. External employees can be assigned to separate organizational units for external employees if these are established in customizing.

- The personnel numbers of external employees must be assigned to a payroll area that's not accounted by the HR payroll accounting program.

- External employees must be assigned time management status 8 (external services) in planned working time infotype 0007.

- A work schedule rule must be assigned to the employee in planned working time infotype 0007; that way overtime, night work, Sunday work, and public holiday work can be recognized.

- A job key can be used to store information on the employee's qualifications if this facility was set up in customizing.

External services are recorded in attendances infotype 2002. The absences (2001) and attendance quotas (2007) infotypes can also be maintained for external employees. Schemas can call on several variants of the overtime calculation. Overtime wage type specifications can be inspected in processing class 17.

The time evaluation driver RPTIME00 uses schema TM02 to evaluate external services by using the essential functions. Additional functions can be copied from schemas TM00 and TM04 to create customized personnel calculation rules for the evaluation of external services.

The CHECK-SRV function ensures that only employees assigned Time Management status 8 (external services) in planned working time (0007) infotype are accounted.

TM02 forms wage types for transfer to MM-SRV. If time balances are required, they can be added by copying the relevant functions from standard schemas TM00 and TM01.

The function Types is available for evaluating external employee attendance hours where actual clock times aren't recorded. TM04 contains the necessary component.

If external employees record their times in attendances infotype 2002 via a dialog box rather than at an external time recording system, these records are liable to be accounted unless the function CHECK-NOTR (No Time Recording) is set, which ensures that the Time Recording Information in infotype 0050 isn't used.

The time data on external employees is evaluated by function MMSRV, which refers to table ASMD to determine rates and the accounting object to which the values are to be assigned, such as the purchase order for the service. If the type of work as represented by a service number isn't already in use, a new service number may have to be determined. The data is then exported to the interface table COIFT.

Each time payroll accounting is run, the time wage types from the previous run are automatically compared to the new ones. If there are any differences, they're evaluated by consulting table ASMD and the results entered in the interface table COIFT.

Importing Service Data from HR into Materials Management

Use the following menu paths to inspect the HR time data containing purchase order information that has been stored in interface table COIFT by the time evaluation driver:

- Logistics>Materials Management
- Activity Recording>Environment>Display HR Data

Use the following steps to import the HR data into Materials Management in the form of time wage types with account assignment:

1. Select Logistics>Materials Management.
2. Select Activity Recording>Service Entry>Maintain.
3. Access the Maintain Service Entry Overview screen by entering your purchase order.

At this stage you can display an existing service entry sheet. If you want to add data to the existing service entry sheet, select Copy Entry Sheet. Select Create Entry Sheet if you need to generate a new service number for this purchase order and maintain its corresponding service entry sheet.

After you indicate the posting date up to which you want to import data from the time management component, the system automatically fetches all the entered data into the service overview for this purchase order. This data is now stored in Materials Management.

Integrating Plant Data Collection and Personnel Administration

Plant Data Collection (PDC) is primarily associated with managing production plant or recording the maintenance of it. PDC is part of Logistics. However, the PDC system may be linked with HR to collect data on the work done by individual employees, which in turn can be used to compute their compensation.

There are two ways of integrating Logistics and HR Time Management:

- Work confirmation documents are recorded for specific times and used to generate time tickets or entries in attendances infotype 2002.
- Work confirmations are integrated in the PA Incentive Wages component.

When a work confirmation is timed and recorded, it's referred to as a *work time event* and can be assigned an identification number. This ID can be used to access the work time event for processing in Logistics and in HR. PDC usually records these work time events in a plant data collection subsystem, although the information can be collected or corrected by manual entries under control of a dialog box at a terminal.

The processing in Logistics can include a check of the work confirmations by reference to the duration of the relevant production order, plant maintenance order, or activity network. If a work confirmation is transferred to HR, it can be used to associate a personnel number with the number of hours worked.

Defining Work Time Events in PDC

Three types of time events can be recorded in PDC:

- Personnel time events that always record a time management identification number, a date, and a time. Examples are clock-in, clock-out, and offsite work begin.

- Work time events that always record an order or network number, a date, and a time. They may also include an identification number that can be used in HR. Examples are begin set up, work start, and work finish.

- Work time events recorded without an identification number. These can be processed in Logistics but not in HR.

Time events belong to only one application; they can't be recorded and changed anywhere else. However, because HR and Logistics share the same database, time events can be inspected on a read-only basis from either application.

All time events for an employee can be inspected as time events infotype 2011. Personnel time events can be recorded, changed, or deleted from HR. Changes to personnel time events don't affect Logistics. Work time events can be displayed in HR, but they can be recorded, changed, or deleted only from Logistics.

Processing Time Events in PDC

Time events are processed the same whether they were entered via a dialog box or recorded by a subsystem. Personnel time events are uploaded from the subsystem along communication channel 1. Work time events are also uploaded from the subsystem but will be assigned to other communication channels. Personnel time events and work time events are stored together in table RUECK.

Each time event is assigned a sequential number as it's stored. This number is selected from the number range defined as object PD_SEQ_NR. Field PDSNR then stores this plant data sequence number for each time event. The source of a time event is recorded as the communication channel number from which it was uploaded.

Time events from the storage table RUECK are read by function module PLANT_DATA_ANALYZE, one channel at a time, for transfer to other function modules for processing. Time events can be uploaded by a manual request or as a batch job. Updating can be as a periodic batch job or as a consequence of an upload. These options are controlled through the PDC time management communication parameters.

Work time events can be processed in HR by the function modules HR_EVENT_CHECK and HR_EVENT_PROCESS. These functions combine existing work time events and personnel time events to form time pairs and generate time tickets:

- A *time pair* is used by comparing the two work times in relation to the employee's daily work schedule and the employee's breaks. The outcome is stored in the last work time event.

■ A *time ticket* associates a time pair with a work time event and an order number or other account assignment taken from cost distribution table C1. The time event table TIP also indicates the account assignment split taken from C1.

If incentive wages are to be calculated, plan data is read from Logistics and stored in the time ticket. Valuation can then be carried out in payroll accounting based on the activities performed. This, in turn, is used to produce production completion confirmations.

The HR_PAIR_UPDATE function locates the formed pairs in the pair table PT, the time tickets in table WST, and the links in table AT. These tables are in cluster B2 in database PCL2.

Because the time tickets store actual times, this information can be used to update Logistics files. For example, function module PLANT_DATA_ANALYZE stores the time events in two tables. Table TEVEN has the following fields:

■ Personnel number

■ Date

■ Time

■ Time event type

■ Previous day indicator

Table AFRU stores work time events in the following fields relevant to Logistics:

■ Order

■ Transaction

■ Amount

■ Actual time

■ Work center

Linkage between these tables is via the Plant Data Sequence Number (PDSNR) assigned when a time event is recorded.

As a time event is successfully processed, it's deleted from table RUECK. Locked personnel numbers, for instance, prevent a time event being processed and therefore remain in table RUECK until the next processing run. A time event that contains an error is stored as part of a work list for each communication channel and processing run. It is deleted from table RUECK.

HR personnel time events and work time events are normally processed together via the same function modules. Pair formation for work time events takes place when the entries in table RUECK are processed. However, pair formation of personnel time events can be postponed until time evaluation takes place by deactivating a switch in the communication parameters. To access the parameters, use the menu path Cross-Application Components>Plant Data Collection and then define communication parameters in the implementation guide.

Updating Time Tickets in Incentive Wages

Incentive wages are most often associated with PP-Production Planning or PM-Plant Mainte-nance time events. The data is stored as incentive wage time tickets and updated based on daily time evaluation results.

Each work time event is processed immediately. Time tickets rely on completion confirma-tions. A PP completion confirmation can have entries for labor, setup time, and teardown time. A PM completion confirmation refers only to work time. PS-Project System completion confir-mations also record simply the working time.

Using Schema TM04: Time Evaluation for Data Recorded in Hours

TM04 is designed to evaluate time data that has been entered online, either in hours or in pairs of actual times. It evaluates actual working hours and exceptions to the work schedule. The time evaluation driver RPTIME00 can use schema TM04 to import online data and form bal-ances, time wage types, and time quotas. It records employee working time in attendances infotype 2002.

TM04 works only with hours such as planned working hours or minimum daily working time in hours. Checks of the maximum daily working time specified in the daily work schedule aren't carried out when planned working time and overtime are calculated.

If exceptions to the work schedule are entered, the planned working hours are generated from the daily work schedule. Recorded absences and certain attendance times are deducted.

The following overtime rules are applied with suitable values assigned:

- Overtime begins after x number of hours per day.
- Overtime begins after y number of hours per week.
- Overtime begins after z number of consecutive workdays.

Using Schema TC00: Wage Type Generation (International)

It may be necessary to process time data that hasn't passed through the time evaluation pro-cess. For example, some employees and some time events may not have been processed for the days between the previous time evaluation run and the payroll run.

The PA-Payroll Accounting module uses the payroll driver RPCALCx0 during the payroll run to call schema TC00, which specifies the rules for day processing of time data. (The x in the pay-roll driver is the country indicator, so a variant of the driver may be used as appropriate.) TC00 can't be processed by time evaluation driver RPTIME00.

Schema TC00 evaluates clock times entered as full-day records representing exceptions to the work schedule. PA uses planned time pairs generated from the specifications in the daily work schedule. However, there may be some differences between planned and actual values if atten-dances infotype 2002 and absences infotype 2001 are updated.

If overtime has been entered in overtime infotype 2005, overtime hours will take into account overtime breaks and can be approved. TC00 automatically generates overtime for all recorded attendance times outside the planned working times specified in the daily work schedule.

Tracing the Stages of Rule Processing in a Schema

The data flow in time evaluation comprises input, processing with internal tables, and output. The parts of time evaluation open to customizing are largely confined to a processing schema of which there are several standard variants. Processing steps may be copied from one schema to another to create additional variants.

A schema is made up of three blocks of processing steps. A schema may be customized, provided that any additional steps are located in the correct blocks. The blocks are identified as follows:

■ Before day processing (initializing)

■ Day processing (evaluate data each day)

■ After day processing (final processing)

Initializing

The first schema block is before day processing, which comprises the block markers BINI and EINI to indicate the beginning and ending of the initialization sequence. This is processed once for each employee per evaluation run, unless the employee's cost center or personnel area is reassigned in the organization assignment infotype within the period under evaluation. In such cases, the time period is divided at the date of the reassignment, if necessary, into periods of one day each.

Initialization for each employee identifies the employee in one or more groupings that are subsequently used to filter the data table entries assembled for time evaluation processing.

The standard function MOD is called during initialization, and it calls personnel calculation rule MODT if clock times are recorded. If time data is recorded as a number of hours, the personnel calculation rule TMON is applied.

Day Processing

The begin and end of a day processing block is marked by BDAY and EDAY. The block of steps is traversed once for each employee for each day. The following operations have to be specified in the day processing block:

1. Access data for the day being evaluated.
2. Initiate planned-actual comparison of working hours.
3. Calculate overtime.
4. Select the time wage types for planned work and overtime hours.
5. Cumulate daily results.
6. Determine flextime balances.
7. Update monthly balances.

Final Processing

The after day processing or final processing is marked as a block by BEND and EEND. It performs only the two following tasks:

- Update leave balance.
- Export evaluation results.

The after day processing block is used only once per employee and evaluation run.

Supplying a Schema with Data

Tables TZP and TIP are the internal tables of time evaluation in which are stored basic data and the time pairs that have to be formed if time events have been recorded by an external subsystem. The infotypes are also used for time data—in particular, absences (2001), attendance (2002), and overtime (2005)—because these contain data entered manually.

Data transfer entails two operations:

- Table TZP is loaded with planned working time data from the employee's personal daily work schedule, including any substitution records that replace the schedule.
- Table TIP is loaded with time data for the day to be evaluated.

Time substitutions don't replace the employee's daily work schedule. Instead, they direct the schema to read planned working time data for the day from substitutions infotype 2003.

The time evaluation process includes the following key tasks:

- Check whether the employee has observed the begin and end times or the minimum daily working time.
- Evaluate absence times.
- Evaluate the duration of breaks.

These objectives are achieved by first generating an entry in table TZP for each time point and assigning an identifier to it that explains its significance. A time point might be the beginning of planned working time, for instance, or the beginning of a break. Table TZP contains the following fields:

- Time
- Time identifier code
- Time identifier explanatory text
- Duration of paid break
- Duration of unpaid break

The following time identifiers are standard:

01	Overtime or time outside employee's daily work schedule
02	Fill time

03	Core time
04	Break in core time
05	Break in fill time

The time events recognized by a time-recording system are downloaded to it each time-recording period, along with the planned time data, in the HR mini-master.

When the time event data is stored in table TZP, the next step is to transfer planned working time data for the day to be evaluated to table TIP. If the system is working by recognizing only exceptions to the work schedule, an extra time pair is transferred to represent the planned or scheduled working time for the day.

Time data for the day that's entered manually is transferred from infotype records to table TIP via the following functions:

P2001	Transfers absences to TIP
P2002	Transfers attendance to TIP
P2004	Transfers availability to TIP
P2005	Transfers overtime to TIP
A2003	Processes work center substitutions

If a substitution institutes a different working time, it doesn't need to be imported; the altered daily work schedule will have taken account of the changes before it was imported for the day. On the other hand, a substitution can include authority for a different rate of payment, in which case table TIP includes an ALP entry (the so-called *split indicator*), which identifies the alternative type of payment—an employee assigned to a different position in the work center, for example. The working time remains the same but the pay may change. In this case, the alternative rate is taken into account by the payroll functions and doesn't affect time evaluation.

Applying Error Checks in the Time Evaluation Schema

Checks are applied when the necessary data is assembled. You can arrange for the operation COLER to generate an error or warning message from within a personnel calculation rule.

Personnel calculation rule TE20 can be used as a daily error check. An error is reported if the employee is absent without authorization. The following factors are checked by TE20:

- The daily work schedule
- Was the employee at work?
- Has an absence been recorded for the employee?
- Has a full-day absence been recorded?
- Which day type is assigned to the day being evaluated?

Allowing Adjustments of Absences

If a time-recording system is in operation, the system can be allowed to make automatic adjustments to time pairs recording absences. Rule TE10 determines whether absence times and attendance times correspond. For example, an employee may enter an absence for an afternoon shift, having signed off from a morning shift. The system detects that there's a gap between signing off in the morning and the beginning of the afternoon absence—the absence time doesn't coincide with the attendance time. An error message can be issued.

By contrast, if the employee had entered an absence that began before the most recent clock-out time, the system would detect the overlap. It could then be configured to adjust the absence time pair so that it began at the moment when the employee actually signed off, rather than at the time entered for the start of the absence. This operation doesn't alter absences infotype 2001, so there's no change in payment as a result.

Handling Pair Formation Errors

A pair formation error can be detected if, for example, an employee forgets to enter a time posting. If the employee is still at work when time events are uploaded, there will also be a missing clock-out time. That will signal an error.

Personnel calculation rule TE30 checks the pair formation status of each time pair and issues messages if necessary:

- Pair status BLANK signifies that the pair is correctly formed.
- Pair status 2 indicates that there has been no clock-in entry.
- Pair status 3 indicates that there's no clock-out entry. If the employee isn't still at work, an error is reported. If the employee is still at work, the end of planned working time could be used as the clock-out entry for the time event. If this isn't the correct clock-out time, it becomes apparent on the next time evaluation run when the missing clock-out time is one of the entries. In this case, retroactive accounting is performed in the next payroll run.
- Pair status 7 indicates that there's no clock-in entry for offsite work. The normal begin time is copied from the daily work schedule, but there is no automatic retroactive accounting if this time proves to be wrong.
- Pair status 8 indicates that there's no clock-out entry for offsite work. The system raises a query to find out if the employee expected to return. If the employee is expected, the end time specified in the daily work schedule is used to delimit the time pair, and subsequent time entries can be used through retroactive accounting. If the employee isn't expected, the end time of the daily work schedule is used to complete the time pair, but no retroactive accounting can be performed.

Allowing Tolerances for the Daily Work Schedule

View V_T550A of the daily work schedule allows authorized users to define tolerances for working time begin and end. If any time posting falls within the tolerances so defined, the time-evaluation system function DPTOL substitutes the planned working begin and end times. If a posting falls outside the tolerance assigned, personnel calculation rule TL10 can be applied to make whatever adjustment you've specified. For example, you can deduct a set number of minutes for late arrival by adjusting the first or last time period of the day.

Classifying Times by Time Type and Processing Type

Classifying entails assigning a processing type and a time type to each time pair. The processing type identifies the rules to be used for time wage type selection. The time type indicates the meaning of the TIP entry and defines the time balances in which the entry is to be cumulated.

For example, time type 0050 is named Productive Hours because it's calculated by summing the time pairs stored as the following time types:

- Time type 0010—Attendances (pair type 1)
- Time type 0030—Attendances entered in infotype 2002
- Time type 0040—Overtime

You can have time types generated from time data in clock times or from the number of hours worked entered at a terminal. A different procedure is followed in each case to work out how the time evaluation should decide whether an employee is working less or more than the hours planned:

- If times are recorded as clock times, the planned working times are taken from the daily work schedule.
- If time are entered as hours, the time evaluation driver must consult the processing type or the time type class assigned to each attendance type and each absence type.

Table TIP contains the actual times as pairs. Table TZP contains the planned working times as pairs. Function TIMTP looks at the actual times and the planned times so that it can generate a new time pair in TIP for any discrepancy. These new time pairs are given a time identifier to indicate whether they are core time, fill time, or time outside the daily work schedule. You can add other time identifiers during customizing. The time type determination view V_T555Z lets you associate a processing type and a time type with each time pair identification code. Function TIMTP uses these entries to control the calculations.

When a time-recording system isn't being used, employees can enter their hours worked at a terminal. A dialog box controls this interaction, and the result is stored in attendances infotype 2002 or absences infotype 2001. For this information to be processed by time evaluation, attendance and absence data must be associated with suitable processing rules.

A typical first stage is to group all absences related to vacations in one class and illness absences in another. In customizing, the attendance/absence class view V_T555Y sets up the time type and processing type for each kind of TIP entry.

Customizing Time Data Evaluation

The main method of controlling how time evaluation is carried out is to customize personnel rule processing by saving a copy of a standard time evaluation schema under a new name and then editing it. A schema is a sequence of processing steps—called *functions*—used by the time evaluation driver RPTIME00. The details of the steps themselves are stored in control tables as personnel calculation rules.

You can customize the sequence of steps by editing the function calls at the schema level. You can customize individual personnel calculation rules by copying and editing a standard rule.

As a time evaluation calculation proceeds, various internal work tables are generated. Table TIP contains the input for one day in the form of time pairs. Each line entry is passed to a personnel calculation rule. When the rule performs its operations, some fields of the line entry may be changed. The processed line entries from TIP are passed to table TOP. This working table will be empty when a calculation rule processes every entry in TIP because the processed lines are now in table TOP.

Before the next personnel calculation rule is invoked, the contents of table TOP are put back into table TIP for another working cycle.

When all the rules have operated for the entire day for the single employee, the TIP table entries generate time balances in table TES. The time types used to indicate which entries are to be cumulated for each balance are determined from data in TIP and from status indicators held elsewhere, such as whether an employee is at work or on vacation.

The range of time-evaluation functions offered as standard is illustrated in the following set of examples:

- OPPT sets a switch for the entire schema that will determine whether the administrator responsible is mailed with messages generated by the schema.
- P2001 enters absences for the day being evaluated into table TIP.
- ACTIO calls a personnel calculation rule that performs some processing without referring to entries in table TIP.
- PTIP calls a personnel calculation rule that edits table TIP line by line.
- PBRKS reads the break specifications in the daily work schedule.

Processing Breaks in Time Evaluation

Time evaluation must take account of the official breaks and apply a percentage of this time when computing the daily hours worked.

Breaks can be stored in the following formats:

- Breaks with fixed times—for example, 9 a.m. to 9:15 a.m.
- Breaks within a specific time period—for example, a one-hour break between noon and 2 p.m.
- Dynamic breaks—for example, a break that begins x hours after the beginning of planned working time.

A work break schedule defines the following:

- When an employee may take breaks
- Whether a break is paid or unpaid
- What percentage of a paid break is to be paid

The time framework for breaks can be imported by the time evaluation driver under control of a personnel calculation rule. Function PBRKS can evaluate different breaks individually under control of the parameters set in customizing. A wider range of possibilities is open when clock times are recorded than when times are entered as hours. For example, unpaid break time can be deducted and paid breaks can be added to the employee's attendance time.

Calculating Overtime in Time Evaluation

After breaks are evaluated, the actual employee attendance times are available. They can be compared with the planned working times so that overtime can be discerned.

The next step is to assign processing type M to the overtime to identify overtime wage types to be used in payroll. Times recognized as planned working times are assigned processing type S, which signifies that the wage types for hourly pay are applied for hourly paid workers. Salaried employees aren't normally assigned any particular wage type for the planned hours they work.

Checking Overtime Approval

If overtime approval is required, the system determines whether a given employee has been given approval and, if so, for how many hours.

Standard overtime approval defines that employees don't have to get special approval for overtime work. Personnel calculation rule TO16 gives general overtime approval for all employees. Another method is to grant automatic overtime approval in the daily work schedule. If you want to grant standard overtime approval for individual employees, you can enter a value in the Standard Overtime field in infotype 0050. This is processed with personnel calculation rule TO10.

Individual overtime approval for specific employees can be allocated in attendance quotas infotype 2007. This method is used if overtime is used with the technique of allocating excess hours worked to the following month.

Using Time Balances

At the end of day, processing time evaluation forms balances. A *balance* is the sum of one time type for the day. For example, the balance of the productive hours time type is the sum of time type values for the following records:

- Attendances (pair type 1)
- Attendances entered in infotype 2002
- Overtime

These balances are used as follows:

- To compute an employee's flextime balance
- To update time accounts that employees can inspect at time recording terminals
- To create evaluations such as time leveling
- To calculate productivity for incentive wages

Forming Period Balances

A *period balance* is formed at the end of processing, not by using personnel calculation rules. Table T555A contains the time types that are defined for your system in customizing. Table T555A can be customized to determine whether each time type is to be added to the daily balance or to the balance for the time evaluation period. A time type for each balance must be in this table.

A *time balance revision* is an alteration made to the time balance for an individual employee. You can transfer hours from one time type to another; you also can transfer hours to a wage type or to an absence quota. If you want to assign a fixed value for a time type, a time balance revision can be applied.

Values for time balance revisions are entered manually in balance revisions infotype 2012. Function P2012 will import the time balance revisions if it's called in a schema.

Updating Results

The time balances stored in table TES during day processing are transferred to table ZES as the individual daily balances. Table ZL acquires the updated time wage types ready for transfer via an interface to payroll accounting.

Using Quota Maintenance in Time Evaluation

One automatic time evaluation operation is to update an employee's records in the following infotypes:

- Absence quotas (2007)
- Attendance quotas (2006)
- Leave entitlement (2005)

If these infotypes weren't previously created, time evaluation won't create them, so no updating occurs. However, you can use time evaluation to check, accumulate, and reduce attendance and absence quotas. Attendance quotas are automatically transferred to table ANWKONTI, absence quotas to table ABWKONTI.

The idea of attendance and absence quotas is to allow time evaluation to check whether an employee has attended sufficiently in a specific attendance period, and whether absences are within an appropriate amount for the period. The following operations can be initiated in a time evaluation schema by inserting the name of the operation in a personnel calculation rule's Variable Key field:

- OUTAQ acquires absence quota information.
- OUTPQ acquires attendance quota information.

The following processes can cause attendance and absence quotas to be accumulated and reduced:

- Automatic update of leave entitlement based on attendance times
- Accumulation of entitlement to a non-working shift for overtime compensation
- Deduction of approved overtime

Distributing Work Attendance Times to Controlling Objects

The attendance times, however entered, can be subsequently distributed to controlling objects such as cost centers, orders, or projects. Facilities are provided for you to make manual adjustments to the data before or after distribution to cost objects. If the data is already posted, only the differences are transferred.

There is full integration with CO-CCA Cost Accounting and PA-PAY Payroll. You must link an employee's time records with an object in the CO-Controlling application. There are three methods:

- Assign the employee to a controlling object by identifying a master cost center in the employee's organizational assignment infotype 0001.
- Create a record in cost distribution infotype 0027 for an employee who works in more than one department or division by entering the company code, business area, cost center, and percentage costs to be allocated.
- Enter controlling information when maintaining the employee's time records.

An employee's time infotype records can be linked to alternative CO-Controlling objects that aren't the main or own department cost object as specified in organizational assignment infotype 0001. The method is to assign the employee's individual working hours/days (or specific amounts) to alternative objects by using the Cost Assignment Specifications function. This assigns the primary personnel costs according to the specification.

The following procedure uses a cost assignment specification to assign personnel costs computed from an employee's time data to a Controlling object:

1. Select Human Resources>Time Management>Time Data>Maintain.
2. Enter the employee's personnel number.
3. Select the time infotype for which you want to maintain time data.
4. Enter the subtype and selection period (if applicable) and choose the Create function.
5. Select Goto>Acc/Log Specifics>Cost Assignment.

At this stage, the Cost Assignment Specification pop-up window offers entry fields for business area, WBS element, sales order, network, and company code, together with possible cost objects taken from the CO-Controlling application. The options are established in customizing. Saving the entries assigns the employee's time infotype records to the object identified.

Another way of associating time records with more than one cost object is to use the internal activity allocation procedure. This assigns particular activity types to one or more alternative cost centers so as to allocate the secondary costs incurred through work performed by an employee to Controlling objects other than the master object identified as the employee's own department in organizational assignment infotype 0001. The following procedure assigns the costs computed from an employee's time data to a Controlling object by using internal activity specifications:

1. Select Human Resources>Time Management>Time Data>Maintain.

2. Enter the employee's personnel number.

3. Select the time infotype for which you want to maintain data.

4. Enter the subtype and selection period (if applicable) and select Edit>Create.

5. Select Goto>Acc/Log Specifics>Activity Allocation.

6. The Activity allocation specification pop-up window offers CO-related entry fields as well as those for business area and company code. Enter the sender and receiver Controlling information pertinent to the time record and choose Transfer.

7. The receiver information is maintained in the Acct.assignm. section of the pop-up window. The sending cost center is generally the employee's master cost center, but can be overwritten. Save your entries to assign the employee's time infotype records to the Controlling object by using the activity type defined in the sender object.

The following time-management infotypes can be maintained with internal activity specifications:

- Absences 2001
- Attendances 2002
- Substitutions 2003
- Availability 2004
- Overtime 2005
- Employee remuneration information 2010

The employee's master cost center is normally credited as the sender, and the receiver cost center is debited for costs incurred in working elsewhere. For example, you may have a training cost center or one for consulting, which can be debited when the employee is engaged in these activities. These alternative cost centers must be assigned to the employee in cost distribution infotype 0027.

Several time-management records for one employee can be assigned to Controlling objects by using the weekly calendar screen. If you want to assign records for several employees, the Fast Entry of Time Data for Several Employees function is appropriate. The fast entry procedure can maintain the infotypes for the following purposes:

- Attendances 2002 and employee remuneration info 2010 for activity allocation
- Employee remuneration info 2010, recurring payments and deductions 0014, and additional payments 0015, for cost assignment

Entering Activity Allocation Specifications for an Employee's Personnel Costs

An employee may be allocated to work in another department at a task that's properly assigned to a third department. For example, an employee may be engaged for an activity type Repair Hours. The following procedure correctly updates the necessary attendance records by an activity allocation specification:

1. Select Human Resources>Time Management>Time Data>Maintain.
2. Enter the employee's personnel number.
3. Select the attendances time infotype.
4. Enter the subtype for productive hours and a date or range for the selection period and select Edit>Create.
5. Select Goto>Acc/Log Specifics>Activity Allocation.
6. Maintain the receiver information in the Acct.assignm. section of the pop-up window.
7. Enter the receiving cost center (6000) and the activity type in the Acct.assignm. section; enter the sending cost center (1000) in the Sender section.
8. Choose Transfer.
9. Save your entries.

Inspecting the Results of Time Evaluation

The *time statement* is a form that shows the balances and wage types calculated by the time evaluation driver RPTIME00. The evaluation results for specific organizational units can be collated by using the Cumulated Time Evaluation Results - Time Balances and Time Wage Types report.

The error processing function can list the messages generated in time evaluation. These messages can be error notifications, notes, and information messages. You can also correct any errors that have occurred by using the error processing function located in the Time Management function pool.

The following time evaluation services are provided in the form of standard reports that can be called:

- Result Lists in Time Evaluation
- Exploding Schemas and Personnel Calculation Rules
- Attendance and Absence Lists
- Work Schedule Reports
- Time Data Lists
- Error Lists in Time Evaluation
- Interface Reports

The time statement can be used for the following purposes:

- To compile a selective overview of the data stored in cluster B2
- To check the results of time evaluation
- To perform an online check of the flextime balances
- To send time statements to employees

If you specify a form ID as you start the time evaluation driver, the time statement is printed with the time evaluation log.

You can also have the time statement printed by a separate form run that's initiated by calling RPTEDT00, which is the Time Statement Form report. Either of the following procedures is suitable:

- Select Human Resources>Time Management>Time Evaluation>Time Statement.
- Select RPTEDT00 from the Time Management function pool.

If you want to create a customized time statement form, the following standard functions are available as reference models for editing:

- TF00—Day-by-day list of principal time balances
- TF01—Day-by-day list of principal time balances, header with address, and additional information
- TF02—Day-by-day list of principal time balances, header with address, and additional information in a detailed data display
- TFL1—Overview list of cumulated time balances
- TFL2—Overview list of cumulated time balances, printed out only if certain conditions are fulfilled

N O T E The conditions controlling TFL2 can be specified when the system is customized—for example, print only balances of employees with more than 15 hours of excess flextime. ■

Checking the Results of Time Evaluation

If time evaluation encounters an error, it can be configured to terminate or issue a message for each error for storage in the database. The time administrator for the employee can have the appropriate messages delivered, or they can be inspected in the time management work list.

Table T555E, Time Evaluation Errors, contains predefined error messages for certain errors, such as those that can arise in pair formation. These errors are classified as error type 3. The standard time-evaluation schemas also contain a complete array of error checks and messages. You can add customized error checks and define particular messages for specific errors.

Function COLER can be called in a personnel calculation rule. It can be customized to detect certain situations and store a message that subsequently can be read as an item in the report RPTERR00 (Time Management: Error Processing). This report also transfers these messages to the Time Management work list. The following functions are controlled by the parameter in variable 2 of function COLER:

- Terminate time evaluation for the employee
- Continue time evaluation and set the retroactive accounting indicator
- Generate specific information
- Generate a note

View V_T555E displays the time evaluation errors and allows you to select suitable error numbers or enter your own with the necessary message text. Variable 1 of function COLER can be primed with the numbers of the errors to be monitored.

Controlling the Printout of the Time Statement

The following parameters can be selected to control the time statement printout:

- Printout with recalculation, which also prints out the periods affected by recalculation up to the defined earliest recalculation date
- Include employees with errors
- Compress time wage types so that each time wage type appears only once daily on the statement
- Branch to time data information, which allows you to display the time data infotype records selectively

Analyzing Time Evaluation Results by Organizational Units

RPTBAL00 is the Cumulated Time Evaluation Results - Time Balances and Time Wage Types report. It can analyze and compare the results of time evaluation according to various aspects of organizational assignment. Examples follow:

- By business area
- By personnel subarea
- By foreman's area

This report also compares individual daily balances, period balances, or time wage types if they're specified as selection criteria.

Formatting the List Printout of RPTBAL00

Use the following menu path to call RPTBAL00: Human Resources>Time Management>Info System>Report Selection>Time Balance. When you're looking at the list screen for this report, you can delete fields that aren't required and insert fields by calling the Display Variant function.

If you require a subtotal for a numeric field in the list, place your cursor in the field name and choose Subtotal. This calls a function of the same name, which generates the subtotal.

If you mark a line and select the Choose Details function, all information on the line is displayed, including organizational information, responsible administrator, personnel number, and time type.

Administering Benefits

Introducing the PA-Ben Benefits Administration Component

The PA-Personnel Administration and Payroll Accounting component can be installed in various configurations and may be presented as a self-contained system. An alternative presentation identifies the various components as part of an integrated human resources system. Thus, R/3 HR Benefits Administration can refer to the same software as PA-Personnel Administration and Payroll Accounting, Benefits Administration.

Benefits Administration is managed as a hierarchical structure of benefit programs, each comprising one or more benefit categories. This structure allows the component to manage benefits programs for a wide range of employee populations and to accept new benefits programs at any time. There are no limits to the number of benefit types and individual benefit plans that can be supported and directed at particular subpopulations of employees.

Integrating Benefits Administration

SAP PA-Ben, Benefits Administration, is a component that can be integrated with PA-Pay, Payroll Administration, during customizing. Wage types have to be defined in the Payroll component that links to the benefit infotype records in order to support specific benefit plans. Standard payroll won't process benefits information.

PA-Ben can also be installed and configured to manage benefit plans without being integrated with Payroll.

Referencing National Supplements from the Benefits Administration Module

The variations in the tax and benefit systems of different nations are accommodated in the SAP R/3 HR-Human Resources system by appending the appropriate national supplements during customizing. Each special national supplement effectively adds to the suite of HR infotypes, which can be referenced when configuring the PA-Ben Benefits Administration module. Table 4.1 illustrates the special national supplements being complemented by new supplements under development.

Table 4.1 Adding HR Infotypes for Various Countries

Austria

Tax—For example, previous year, current year, subsequent year

Commuter lump sums

Social insurance

Family allowance

Sick certificates—For example, main person insured, insured spouse, insured child

Previous employer

Belgium

Social Insurance—For example, category, registration of substitute employee, pension number, Social Insurance number

Tax—For example, spouse, children, other persons in the same household, tax rule indicator

Personal data—For example, personal registration number, Royal Service number, Pension Insurance number, work permit number, Social Security number

Work schedule—For example, RSZ category, RSZ code, RSZ number, work regimen, work rhythm, work regulation, employee type (part time/full time), country indicator, work interruption, pay period

Contract elements—For example, Paritair Kommitee, Compensation Fund number, meal coupons, CAO/pension data

Canada

Residence status—For example, citizen/alien, passport data, work permit

Additional personal data—For example, ethnic origin, military status

Benefits—For example, employee welfare plans, medical, dental, vision, legal

Insurance—For example, life, AD&D, dependent

Deferred compensation and savings plans—For example, ESOP, RRSP, RRP, pension

Tax—For example, federal, provincial

Bond purchases—For example, denomination, recipient

Injury and illness—For example, extended accident or illness tracking, accident data

Workers' compensation—For example, entitlement, contribution, record-keeping, reporting

Union—For example, job title, seniority

Grievance tracking—For example, status, disciplinary action

Denmark

Tax

Private pension

Vacation or statutory holidays—for example, previous year, current year, subsequent year

ATP pension

France

Social Insurance—For example, Social Insurance number, fund model

Capital formation—For example, profit-sharing

Leave processing

Maternity protection

continues

Table 4.1   Continued

Germany

Tax—For example, previous year, current year, subsequent year

Social Insurance—For example, obligatory, voluntary, Retirees' Health Insurance

SI Supplementary Insurance

Capital formation—For example, saving through B&L association, saving by installments, life insurance

DÜVO—For example, registration, interruption

RWH/BWP

BAT benefits

Company pension plans

Wage maintenance

Direct insurance

Previous employer—For example, tax, Social Insurance

The Netherlands

The following functions are handled by the standard HR functions:

- Maternity protection cutoff dates
- Options for capital formation
- Travel expenses for trips between home and business

The special national features extension offers the following extensions to the general functions included in the international HR-Human Resources system:

- Employee taxes—For example, tax class, Sofi number, tax code indicator, deduction items, OT, annual salary
- Social Insurance—For example, person-related data such as the WW, ZW, WAO, ABP, VUT, and BPF codes
- Health Insurance funds—For example, private HI funds, compulsory HI funds
- Social funds—For example, application types, decisions, appeals, payment options
- Additional absence data—For example, data for tracking illnesses, dates for multiple treatment appointments, dates for work restrictions
- Accident data—For example, accident status, accident class, type of injury

Spain

Tax—For example, recipient key, annual gross

Social Insurance—For example, Social Insurance number, multiple work percentage

Various payees—For example, payee key, gross amount

Spain

Union—For example, union function, contribution

Seniority

Switzerland

Tax—For example, canton, municipality, tax liability

Social Insurance—For example, AHV number, FAK, ALV

Pension fund—For example, fund, insurance type, premium

Residence status—For example, status, expiry date

Family—For example, Child Allowance

The United Kingdom

Income tax

National Insurance; employee and employer contributions, arrears

Court orders, payments, protected earnings, administration fees

Pensions

Statutory sick pay

Statutory maternity pay

The United States

Residence status—For example, citizen/alien, passport data, work permit

Additional personal data—For example, ethnic origin, military status

Benefits—For example, medical, dental, vision, legal

Insurance—For example, life insurance, AD&D, dependent insurance

Savings plans and deferred compensation—For example, pension, 401(k), ESOP

Tax—For example, federal, state, local

Bond purchases—For example, denomination, recipient

Injury and illness—For example, illness tracking, accident data, OSHA, workers' compensation data

Workers' compensation—For example, entitlement, contribution

Union—For example, job title, seniority

Grievances—For example, status, disciplinary action, grievance tracking

US I-9 compliance

Introducing Benefit Plans

Employee benefit plan details are stored in a set of infotype records, categorized as follows:

- Health plans
- Insurance plans
- Savings plans
- Spending accounts
- Credit plans

These benefit plan categories can be divided into benefit plan types. For example, health benefits might be divided into dental, medical, and vision care plan types. Each plan has a plan identifier composed of a four-character code and a short plan description.

An individual benefit plan has the following parameters:

- The benefit provider, such as an insurance company
- Validity period of the plan record
- Cost/credit criteria, which are stored as separate criteria with a criterion ID that helps identify who is eligible for the plan
- Cost/credit groups defined by personal features such as the geographical location of the workplace or residence
- Plan status as active, locked, closed
- Eligibility rule that specifies who can enroll in the plan

Benefit plans are set up during customizing under control of the IMG-Implementation Guide.

Exploring the Structure of Benefits Plans

The benefit plan data structure is as follows:

- Plan category, from SAP classification as Health, Insurance, Saving, Spending, Credit
- Plan type within the plan category, such as Retirement Saving Plan
- Specific benefit plan, with its plan identifier, provider, and detailed records

The SAP plan category controls the sequence of screens used to administer each type of plan. Employee choice is exercised at the plan level.

Testing Eligibility

At the higher level (program eligibility), an employee can choose from a list of benefits. There can be more than one list, not all of them available to each employee.

At the lower or detail level, an employee's eligibility is tested by the criteria set by the benefit provider in the form of constraints on enrollment.

The Benefits application has features that automatically allocate each employee to a benefit group and a benefit status. A *feature* is a device for accessing a particular piece of information. For example, a benefit group could be defined in customizing to refer to the employees working at a specific location. Benefit status could be aligned with person subgroups, such as full time, part time, or temporary. By intersecting these two dimensions, you could identify a set of benefits programs:

- Full time at location A
- Part time at location A
- Temporary at location A
- Full time at location B
- Part time at location B
- Temporary at location B

Each program uses eligibility criteria to control enrollment based on benefit status and benefit group. However, the benefits providers taking part in any of these programs will have their own enrollment filters. Thus, each plan has detailed lower-level criteria. For example, you could define an eligibility group for a maternity plan as female hourly paid employees who have completed a three-month waiting period if they are newly hired and one month if they have transferred.

Calculating Costs and Credits

Each benefit plan may use different logical and numerical parameters. Logical or binary data could be smoker or sex. Numerical data could be age, length of service, or salary.

To simplify the data, groups are formed as follows:

- Salary groups define the salary ranges.
- Age groups define the age ranges.
- Length of service groups provide length of service.
- Cost groups enable you to set up user-defined cost rules such as geographical region.

The cost formula of a plan processes the cost information based on the cost calculation rules applied to the groups as specified in the formula.

Enrolling an Employee in a Health Plan

The Benefits component can assist in the employee hiring event by suggesting health plans for which the employee is eligible. The following steps enroll an employee in a health plan:

1. Choose Human Resources>Benefits> Administration>Enrollment.
2. Enter the employee personnel number and plan year.
3. Select the health plan category.

4. Choose the Enroll function and follow the instructions to create a General Benefits Data record (infotype 0171) for the employee, if one doesn't exist already.

5. If required, delimit non-selected plans to terminate them.

6. Make appropriate selections in the dialog box—background, foreground processing, or batch input session.

7. View the list of health plans for which the employee is eligible and the options for each. The system allows you to enroll the employee in only one plan per plan type. You can choose only one option within that plan.

8. Select the appropriate options for each plan in which you want to enroll the employee. If you want to enroll the employee in default plans, choose the Default Values function.

9. If required, choose the Cost Summary function.

10. Choose the Execute function.

11. If necessary, the system asks you to select the dependents to be included under the coverage. Follow the system through the Dependents screen for each plan, and select Continue to move from one screen to the next.

After you select the dependents, the system informs you of any delimited plans. It then informs you of the health plan records (infotype 0167) it will create when you choose Execute.

If you've selected foreground processing, the system requires you to press Enter to continue after inspecting each record being created.

N O T E The procedures for administering other plans follow the health plan model by offering a series of enrollment screens. ■

Printing Benefit Plan Enrollment Forms

The details of how an employee wants to be covered by a benefit plan are collected via a printed form. The system prints this form to ask about only the particular plans for which the employee is eligible. The following steps print an enrollment form:

1. Choose Human Resources>Benefits> Administration>Enrollment.

2. Enter the employee personnel number and plan year.

3. Enter the required period modifier. The system defaults to how often the employee is paid. You can override this field if you want to simulate different costs, depending on the period modifier.

4. Select the plan categories for which you want the employee to make selections.

5. Choose the Print Forms function.

6. Enter the relevant time period and personnel number selection.

7. Choose Enrollment Forms.

8. Press Enter.

9. Choose Print.

The following sequence prints a letter of confirmation:

1. Choose Human Resources>Benefits> Administration>Enrollment.
2. Enter the employee personnel number and plan year.
3. Select the All Categories check box.
4. Choose the Print Forms function.
5. Enter the relevant time period and personnel number selection.
6. Choose the Enrollment Forms function.
7. Press Enter.
8. Sehe Print function.

Understanding Benefits Infotypes

Many essential data records are created and maintained automatically as the personnel events are run in order to conduct such processes as hiring and organizational reassignment. However, some infotypes are specific to the Benefits component.

Using Infotype 0171, General Benefits Data

This infotype must have a record for the employee before enrollment in a benefits plan can take place. The main elements of infotype 0171 are as follows:

- Employee assignments
- Physician
- Non-discrimination testing, which stores an employee's status and may be used to control the permitted employee contribution amounts in the 401(k) plans
- Additional data, such as employee demographic data with respect to smoking

Using Infotype 0021, Family/Related Person

Infotype 0021 provides standard subtypes to represent the following family members and related persons:

Subtype 1	Spouse
Subtype 2	Child
Subtype 3	Legal guardian
Subtype 4	Testator
Subtype 5	Guardian
Subtype 6	Stepchild
Subtype 7	Emergency contact
Subtype 8	Related person
Subtype 10	Divorced spouse

Using Infotype 0219, External Organization

Records in infotype 0219 contain details of beneficiaries who aren't family or related persons. Each record has a validity period and identifies the external organization type, which provides an organization description. Additional data fields are provided to specify precisely the external organization.

Interpreting Infotype 0167, Health Plans

A record in infotype 0167 is created for every health plan in which the employee is enrolled.

- ■ *Plan data* is a section that records the name of the health plan and option chosen by the employee. Exactly who is covered by the health plan is identified in this section of the record.

- ■ *Employee data* includes the Area/Grp/Status and Cost Group fields that contain information from the General Benefits Data (infotype 0171). The employee eligibility is denoted by the eligibility group, which matches that of the plan.

- ■ *Coordination of benefits* is a section containing provider and policy number information about any other benefit coverage that would have to be coordinated for processing claims.

- ■ *Plan dates* include the eligibility date, which depends on the plan conditions. An eligibility override date is allowed. A participation date to record when the employee first participated in the plan is also stored here.

- ■ *Plan attributes* include the plan type, eligibility group, and eligibility rule that apply to the plan.

- ■ *Cost* includes the As Of date field, from which the cost of the plan is calculated. The cost and period are determined by the option in the Plan data box.

A similar record must be created in infotype 0168 for each insurance plan in which the employee is enrolled.

Interpreting Infotype 0169, Savings Plans

A record in infotype 0169 is required for each savings plan in which the employee is enrolled. The Plan data, Employee data, Plan dates, and Plan attributes fields are similar to those in infotypes 1067 and 0168.

- ■ *Contribution data* specifies whether any post-tax contributions should start immediately in tandem with pre-tax contributions or not until the plan-defined pre-tax limit is reached. The account number to which the contributions are to be paid also can be stored here.

- ■ *Plan parameters* include the employer contribution rule, the vesting rule, and the investment group assigned to the savings plan.

Interpreting Infotype 0170, Spending Accounts

A spending account allows employees to specify the amount of pre-tax income to be contributed over a benefit plan year in anticipation of expenses, such as health care, dependent care, or legal benefits. A record in infotype 0170 has to be created for every separate spending account. The Plan data, Employee data, Plan dates, and Plan attributes fields are similar to those in infotypes 1067 and 0168.

■ *Account status* includes the total of the account and the date when this was calculated.

Interpreting Credit Plans (Infotype 0236)

A *credit plan* allocates an amount to the employee, additional to earnings, used to offset the costs of other benefit plans. The employee pays or receives the difference each pay period. Infotype 0236 stores the details of credits allocated to an employee. A separate credit plan record is created for each benefit plan in which the employee has chosen to enroll.

The Plan data, Employee data, Plan dates, and Plan attributes fields are similar to those in infotypes 1067 and 0168.

■ *Employee groups* includes the fields Area/Grp/Status and Credit Group from the General Benefits Data infotype 0171. The credit group denotes employees who share the same credit calculation rule.

■ *Credit amount override* is associated with the frequency at which it's paid to the employee.

■ *Credit per pay period* specifies the calculation used to pay employees each time they're paid. The start date is also stored here.

Monitoring of Dates (Infotype 0019)

Infotype 0019 holds the significant dates and deadlines for an employee. Standard SAP recognizes the following date/deadline types as valid entries to the field Date/Deadline, when accompanied by a date:

Subtype 01	Expiry of probation
Subtype 02	Temporary work relationship
Subtype 03	Pay scale jump
Subtype 04	Work permit
Subtype 05	Challenge
Subtype 06	Training period
Subtype 07	Dismissal protection
Subtype 08	Expiry of inactive contract
Subtype 09	Expiry of temporary contract
Subtype 10	Staff meeting
Subtype 11	Vaccination date
Subtype 20	End of maternity protection

Subtype 21	End of maternity leave
Subtype 30	Follow-up medical
Subtype 35	Submit PI number
Subtype 36	Submit AHV-ID
Subtype 40	Prior attachment
Subtype 70	Next appraisal
Subtype 71	Work permit expires

A deadline date must be entered for each date/deadline type. In the field processing indicator, you can enter whether the deadline is being processed (has not yet arrived) or is completed.

Reminder is a section of infotype 0019 that stores a reminder date and the lead/follow-up time. You can enter the reminder date directly, allow the system to propose a reminder date depending on the date/deadline type, or enter a lead time as a number with a unit and the operation indicator.

The following rules are applied automatically because each date/deadline type will have been assigned the correct operation indicator in customizing:

- If the operation indicator for the relevant date/deadline type has the value blank or – (minus symbol), the reminder date must be before the actual date/deadline.

- If the operation indicator has the value + (plus symbol), the reminder date must be after the date/deadline.

If you enter a number and unit for the lead or follow-up time, the system won't use the reminder date if one has beentered.

Interpreting Date Specifications (Infotype 0041)

If you select Date Type when your cursor marks a date entry on a display, a window will appear containing the information held in the relevant record of the infotype date specifications (0041). The same source of information can be used with a printed document from payroll or the leave program.

The user can define concrete date types named in records of infotype 0041. These dates can then be used to refer to dates or deadlines that can't be derived from the organizational assignment history. For example, a hiring personnel event will record the date, and that event will appear in the employee's organizational assignment history. By contrast, a benefit plan might be assigned a start date on which no event occurred and therefore wouldn't be recorded automatically in the employee's organizational assignment history.

Reporting in the Benefits Component

A *benefits report* is a program that collects information from benefit enrollment records. The scope of a report is normally restricted by specifying a time period, a personnel number range, and an organizational data element such as a department. Each report displays a screen of employees and their relevant data according to your search specification.

Displaying Change of General Benefits Data

Report RPLBEN13, Change of General Benefits Data, lists any deviations from the default values in an employee's General Benefits Data (infotype 0171). A deviation indicates that the system-allocated default value has been overwritten by a manual entry. The default value is displayed next to the actual value.

The following steps display changes in employee General Benefits Data:

1. Choose Human Resources>Benefits>Infosystem>Reporting Tree.
2. Select Change of General Benefits Data (RPLBEN13).
3. Enter the relevant time period and personnel number selection.
4. Define the benefit area(s) that you want to examine.
5. Enter the benefit group(s) and employee status(es) for the employees you want to select.
6. Choose the Execute function.

Displaying Benefit Plan Participation

The following steps use report RPLBEN02 to display the participation dates of each employee enrolled in a particular benefits plan:

1. Choose Human Resources>Benefits>Infosystem>Reporting Tree.
2. Select Participation (RPLBEN02).
3. Enter the relevant time period and personnel number selection.
4. Define the benefit area(s) that you want to examine.
5. Enter the benefit group(s) and employee status(es) for the employees you want to select.
6. Enter the benefit plan(s) that you want to examine for participation.
7. Choose Execute.

Finding Eligible Employees

The following steps use report RPLBEN01 to generate a list of all employees who are eligible for a particular benefits plan:

1. Choose Human Resources>Benefits>Infosystem>Reporting Tree.
2. Select Eligible Employees (RPLBEN01).
3. Enter the relevant key date and personnel number selection.
4. Enter the benefit area, benefit group, and employee status for the employees you want to select.
5. Enter the benefit plan(s) for which you want to select eligible employees.
6. Choose Execute.

Displaying Change of Eligibility

The system assumes that the benefit area, benefit group, and employee status values stored in the records of General Benefits Data (infotype 0171) are correct for the employee. However, a plan they're participating in may not be in their allocated program. They may not be eligible according to the eligibility rule for that plan as it's specified in their correct program. Other inconsistencies in the data of infotype 0171 may be held on their behalf.

The following steps use report RPLBEN09 to detect and list employees who are no longer eligible for a benefit plan and give the reason in each case:

1. Choose Human Resources>Benefits>Infosystem>Reporting Tree.
2. Select Eligibility Change (RPLBEN09).
3. Enter the relevant time period and personnel number selection.
4. Define the benefit area(s), benefit group(s), employee status(es), and benefit plan(s) that you want the report to examine for changes.
5. Select the Execute function.

Displaying Employee Demographics

Age and sex information, along with other information, is sometimes collated for health insurance purposes. The following steps use report RPLBEN11 to form employee demographics and sort the list according to whether the employees smoke:

1. Choose Human Resources>Benefits>Infosystem>Reporting Tree.
2. Select Employee Demographics (RPLBEN11).
3. Enter the relevant time period and personnel number selection.
4. Enter the basis date. The default value here is the current date at system runtime.
5. Enter the age groups you want to examine.
6. Enter the benefit area(s), benefit group(s), and employee status(es) you want the system to examine.
7. Choose Execute.

Displaying Cost Overviews

The costs of health plans and insurance plans can be analyzed to reveal the effects of different factors such as salary and length of service. The following steps use the report RPLBEN14 to display a cost overview:

1. Choose Human Resources>Benefits>Infosystem>Reporting Tree.
2. Select Cost Overview (RPLBEN14).
3. Define the benefit area that you want to examine.

4. Enter the plan type(s) and benefit plan(s) whose costs you want to display.

5. Enter the plan validity dates in the selection period.

6. Select the Health Plans or Insurance Plans radio button.

7. Choose Execute.

Displaying Benefit Plan Summary

The following sequence uses report RPLBEN12 to display a benefit plan summary in the form of a tree:

1. Choose Human Resources>Benefits>Infosystem>Reporting Tree.

2. Select Plan Summary (RPLBEN12).

3. Define the benefit area(s) that you want to examine.

4. Enter the plan category(ies), plan type(s), and plan status(es) of the plans you want to display.

5. Enter the plan validity dates in the selection period.

6. Choose Execute.

Plans are ordered according to plan category and plan type. Each plan is broken down to display options, costs/credits, benefit program, plan eligibility, and termination.

Health and insurance plans have costs; credit plans have credits. All other categories have neither.

You can jump to the features relevant to each plan set up.

Displaying Spending Account Premiums

The following steps use report RPLBEN08 to display the spending premiums that employees contribute to spending accounts:

1. Choose Human Resources>Benefits>Infosystem>Reporting Tree.

2. Select Spending Premiums (RPLBEN08).

3. Enter the relevant key date and personnel number selection.

4. Define the benefit area(s) that you want to examine.

5. Enter the benefit group(s) and employee status(es) for the employees you want to select.

6. Enter the benefit plan(s) that you want to examine for spending account premiums.

7. Choose Execute.

The list of names is sorted according to pay frequency. Grand totals of employees, employee cost, and employer cost are cumulated from the subtotals for each benefit plan on the lines above.

Displaying Health Premiums

The cost of health plans is shared between employer and employees. The following steps use report RPLBEN03 to display the health premiums:

1. Choose Human Resources>Benefits>Infosystem>Reporting Tree.
2. Select Health Premiums (RPLBEN03).
3. Enter the relevant key date and personnel number selection.
4. Define the benefit area(s) that you want to examine.
5. Enter the benefit group(s) and employee status(es) for the employees you want to select.
6. Enter the benefit plan(s) that you want to examine for health plan premiums.
7. Choose Execute.

The list of names is sorted according to pay frequency. Grand totals of employees, employee cost, employer cost, and provider cost are cumulated from the subtotals for each benefit plan on the lines above. (In this report, *employer cost* refers to the difference between total cost of a plan and the cost to the employee.)

Displaying Insurance Premiums and Savings Premiums

Report RPLBEN04 displays insurance premiums by carrying out a similar procedure to report RPLBEN03, as previously described. Report RPLBEN05 displays savings premiums in a similar fashion.

Displaying Vesting Percentages

The following steps use report RPLBEN06 to display vesting percentages for the employer contribution to employees' savings plans on a specified date:

1. Choose Human Resources>Benefits>Infosystem>Reporting Tree.
2. Select Vesting Percentage (RPLBEN06).
3. Enter the relevant time period and personnel number selection.
4. Specify the basis date. The default for this field is the current date at system runtime.
5. Enter the benefit area, benefit group, employee status(es), and benefit plan(s) for which you want to examine vesting percentages.
6. Choose Execute.

Displaying Change of Benefit Election

An employee can change the benefit election in a benefit plan. For instance, an employee could change the coverage of a health plan from spouse only to family. The following steps use report RPLBEN07 to display any changes of benefit election:

1. Choose Human Resources>Benefits>Infosystem>Reporting Tree.
2. Select Benefit change (RPLBEN07).

3. Enter the relevant time period and personnel number selection.

4. Enter the election period. This is the period you want the report to examine for changes to enrollment (infotype) records.

5. Enter the benefit provider and the benefit plan you want to examine.

6. Choose Execute.

Records whose validity starts after the election period but have been changed within it won't be listed; records whose validity ends on the last day of the election period will be listed. For each case, the report will indicate whether a new record exists that renews the employee's enrollment.

Using HR Reports During Benefits Administration

The menu sequence Choose Information Systems>General Report Selection accesses the following HR reports:

- Date monitoring (RPPTRM00)
- Employee directory (RPLMIT00)
- Employee entries/withdrawa(RPLNHTU0)
- Logged changes in infotype data (RPUAUD00)

Administering COBRA

The Consolidated Omnibus Budget Reconciliation A(COBRA) of 1985 requires employers to offer continued health plan coverage to employees and their dependents if certain qualifying events occur that would otherwise curtail the group health plan coverage. Examples of qualifying events are termination, reduction of hours, an employee's death, or divorce.

The administration of COBRA is a legal requirement only in the United States. The functionality is designed specifically for this country. The COBRA Administration component identifies qualified beneficiaries from master data records and prints letters of notification, including personalized COBRA election and enrollment forms.

Using the COBRA Qualified Beneficiary (Infotype 0211)

Infotype 0211, COBRA qualified beneficiary, is used to create a record for each person who is a qualified beneficiary of an employee's health plan. A person is a qualified beneficiary if he or she has experienced a COBRA qualifying event. Records in infotype 0211 are created automatically by the Benefits COBRA procedures.

- *Event data* stores the data concerning the qualifying event experienced by the individual—namely, the COBRA event type, the date it occurred, if it was a second event, and the date it was detected by the Event Collection function. The event data section also holds the benefit area, the group and status of the covered employee, through whom the qualified beneficiary is covered, and the state details.

■ *COBRA data* stores the COBRA status that reports the stage reached in the administration for that qualified beneficiary. If the COBRA coverage was terminated early, the termination reason explains. The notification date, reply sent date, and payment due dates are alstored here.

Collecting Qualified Beneficiaries

COBRA processing begins by identifying qualified beneficiaries. These are individuals who have experienced certain qualifying events. They may be employees or an employee's dependents, such as a divorced spouse or a child who has lost dependent status. The system detects qualified individuals by referring to a list of collected qualifying events. The events are separated according to event type and event status. You can interact with the fields in a list in order to refine the selection of employees.

The following steps collect qualified beneficiaries:

1. Choose Human Resources>Benefits>Administration>COBRA.

2. Enter the benefit area of the covered employees you want to collect. You can also enter the benefit group and benefit status, if required.

3. Select the qualifying event(s) for which you want the system to collect covered employees. By default, the system searches for all types of qualifying events except employer bankruptcy.

4. Choose Collect and view the Collection of COBRA Qualifying Events report screen.

5. Enter the relevant time period and personnel number selection.

6. Select whether you want all or just new COBRA events.

7. If necessary, change the default age limit for dependent status. (This parameter isn't relevant to disabled dependents.)

8. If necessary, change the default If Student status.

9. Enter the key date for bankruptcy if this is the qualifying event for which you're searching; this is when the regular benefit coverage will end.

10. Choosrocess.

Identifying Employee Criteria for a Qualifying Event

The COBRA Administration component searches for a different pattern of employee and dependant criteria for each qualifying event it's looking for.

Checking for Termination of Employment

This qualifying event is detected in the personnel events infotype 0000, using the condition that the reason for termination isn't equal to death.

Checking for Death of Employee

This qualifying event is detected in the personnel events infotype 0000, using the condition that the reason for termination equals death.

Checking for Reduction in Work Hours

This qualifying event is detected by comparing the planned working time infotype 0007 at the Reduction in Hours field and the eligibility rule for the existing health plan to see if the number of work hours required is greater than the employee's work hours.

Checking for Entitlement to Medicare

This qualifying event is detected by a change from blank to selected in the Medicare check box in the additional personal data infotype 0077.

Checking for Divorce

This qualifying event is detected as the family/related person infotype 0021, new subtype 10, divorced spouse, subtype 1 delimited.

Checking for Legal Separation

This qualifying event is detected by looking at infotype 0021 and then infotype 0106, legal separation.

Checking for Loss of Dependent Status

This qualifying event is detected through infotype 0021/106, birthday of dependent.

Checking for Bankruptcy of Employer

This qualifying event is detected from the personnel event infotype 0000, status 2 = retired.

When a list of qualified beneficiaries is detected, the system can be tasked to print letters of notification and forms for COBRA benefit election and enrollment, personalized for each qualified beneficiary. When letters of notification are issued, the system creates the COBRA qualified beneficiary (infotype 0211) records and delimits existing employee health plan records in infotype 0167.

The delimiting of a health plan is total if the employee is the sole qualified beneficiary. The termination rule for that plan is followed. However, the procedure is more complex if the employee's spouse or a dependent child is a qualified beneficiary. The employee's health plan record is terminated according to the termination rule of that plan, but the system generates a new record for the employee, excluding the qualified beneficiaries. They are now administered by the COBRA system because infotype 0211 will have records of them as COBRA-qualified beneficiaries.

Administering Payroll

In this chapter

Identifying the Basic Tasks in Payroll Accounting

Four essential tasks take up most of the effort in personnel administration because they have such obvious effects on payroll:

- Hiring an employee
- Moving an employee within the organization, or *reassignment*
- Arranging for an employee to leave the company
- Maintaining an accurate database of employee information

There's also a strong case for arguing that a fifth task is to be able to locate personnel information when it's needed. However, this task is assumed to be highly automated by the standard SAP R/3 functions in the Human Resources application. In particular, the technique of storing master data in defined formats referred to as *infotypes* is essential to the R/3 system organization. As a pertinent example, infotype 0002, Personal Data, is held in the HR database. Personal Data includes the following fields:

- Name
- Date of birth
- Marital status

Where certain data, such as the employee's name, is absolutely essential, the infotype will appear on a data-entry screen with a question mark in each field for which a valid entry must be made before the screen can be posted for storage in the database. When an implementation of R/3 is customized, non-mandatory fields can be specified, provided that this won't disrupt the system.

The individual records stored in the format of an infotype can be edited or "maintained" on a data-entry screen for a single employee. Also, a fast entry function allows the infotypes of several employees to be maintained together by displaying only those fields needed for the purpose.

Finding Employee Records

Efficient search and retrieval techniques are essential when the personnel database comprises a very large number of separate records—infotypes—for each employee.

The first step is to enter the personnel number of the employee or select a number from the list that will appear if you select the Possible Entries drop-down arrow icon at the side of the Personnel Number field. When the system has been given a valid personnel number, it will allow a choice of the infotypes to be displayed.

After you identify the employee of interest, the following methods are available for accessing the infotype records that belong to this employee:

- Select a known infotype by entering its title or its number in the Infotype field.
- Select a static menu.

A *static menu* identifies a number of fixed collections of related infotypes chosen for their relevance to a particular task, such as the following:

- Basic personal data
- Contract data
- Planning data
- Time management data

The system will generate a dynamic menu if a keyword is entered in the Infotype field. This will retrieve all the infotypes that include the keyword in their title and offer the list as a menu from which you can select the ones you need.

A *personnel file* is a particular type of dynamic menu made by retrieving all the infotype records stored in the system for a specific employee.

Using Incomplete Matchcodes

Matchcode fields (marked with a small triangle) will accept a partial entry. The result will be all records that satisfy this search specification for this employee. The possibilities will be offered as a list from which a further selection can be made. The matchcode can be a complete word or numeric value, or it can include signs that mask any characters that you're not certain of. An incomplete matchcode search uses as much of the beginning of the target field as you can remember or as much of the beginning as is necessary to uniquely identify the infotype record you need.

Using Complete Matchcode Searches

If you have some accurate information about an employee, you can use a complete matchcode search to access the relevant infotype records:

1. Click the Possible Entries drop-down arrow icon next to the Personnel Number field.
2. Select a matchcode for which you have information, such as Last name - First name.
3. The Restrict Value Ranges pop-up window allows you to enter the employee's last name and any other information you have.

The result will be a unique personnel number or a list of those numbers that meet your range restrictions. If you enter a + sign for characters that you don't know, the system will operate the masked matchcode search procedure and attempt to find a list of matching records.

Selecting a Known Infotype Record

The following steps retrieve an infotype based on the name or number:

1. Select Human Resources>Personnel Admin.>HR Master Data>Maintain Master Data.
2. Enter the infotype name or number in the Infotype field.
3. If the infotype has a subtype that you require, enter the subtype number. Press F4 if you need to see a list of possible subtypes.

The current infotype record will appear. You can search for non-current infotype records by specifying the time period in which the data should be valid.

Creating Dynamic Menus

Follow these steps to have the system compile a menu for a particular purpose:

1. Select Human Resources>Personnel Admin.
2. Choose either Maintain or Display Master Data.
3. Enter a word or text string in the Infotype field.
4. Press Enter.

You are offered a menu comprising all infotype titles that begin with the word or text string you've just entered. For example, if you enter the characters Att, the system will present all the Attendances infotypes for the current employee.

Using the Personnel File

A *personnel file* is a browsing list for one employee of all the infotypes, displayed in ascending numerical order and then sorted by their validity. All the infotype subtypes will appear following their parent infotypes. The following steps are appropriate:

1. Select Human Resources>Personnel Admin.>HR Master Data>Personnel File.
2. Enter the employee's personnel number.
3. Select the Display function. The first record will be the current record in Events infotype 0000.
4. Choose the Next Record function to continue forward and the Previous Record function to move back.

If you want to see all the records and subtype records for one infotype, call the Overview function and mark the record of interest, and then choose Select.

Using the PD Search Feature

The normal way to locate a data object is to provide its object ID. The PD-Personnel Development application, however, has a database with an advanced search feature that accepts the following forms of search specification:

- Asterisks as wildcards to represent any sequence of characters anywhere in the text
- Plus sign to represent a single missing character
- Restricted search with logical conditions

A logical condition can be used to limit the search for an infotype. The following are standard examples:

- A specific infotype must or must not exist.
- A given relationship must or must not exist.

■ A particular object status is required.

■ The defined validity period is required.

■ The evaluation path must be checked.

You can add customized search restrictions to this list.

Working with Personnel Events

The Personnel Event function groups together all infotypes needed to input the data that arises when a personnel procedure is performed. Standard SAP R/3 provides the following procedures as personnel events for updating the HR master database:

■ Hiring an employee

■ Organizational reassignment, which is used for recording promotion, demotion, and lateral transfer

■ Early retirement or normal retirement

■ Leaving the company

■ Re-entry into company (rehire)

A personnel event isn't complete until all necessary infotypes are created and updated to give the system a full set of data about the employee concerned.

The personnel event controls the sequence and access to the necessary infotypes to ensure that none are forgotten and the procedure runs as smoothly as possible. The details of a personnel event can be customized.

A personnel event will be preconfigured to present a sequence of particular infotypes defined as an infotype group for the purpose. The function Change Infogroup can be used to change the details of the infotype group used by the event.

A change in one field of an infotype might require that certain other infotypes be updated at the same time. The details can be specified as a dynamic event. For example, when an employee leaves the company, various actions should be carried out immediately. The employee might have had objects on loan. A company ID might have to be canceled. If there's an organizational reassignment, permission to use a particular system might have to be withdrawn.

During customizing, a dynamic event can be set up to automatically call SAPoffice to mail each responsible administrator when an employee leaves or is reassigned. These reactions can be triggered by a change in the Events infotype.

Interpreting the Events Infotype

Events combine related infotypes into infotype groups, or *infogroups*, and control the updating of the information stored in them. In particular, most events create a record in Events infotype 0000.

An employee's status is recorded in the Events infotype, and any change of status automatically generates a new record. The following status indicators are standard:

- Customer-specific (Status 1) is available for any purpose defined in customizing.
- Employment (Status 2) is used by PA to select records for reporting and purging archives of unwanted records.
- Special payment (Status 3) controls the employee's entitlement to special payment for automatic special payments within payroll accounting.

Using Time Constraint Validation

The Events infotype has time constraint 1, which specifies that an infotype record for each employee must be retained in the system from the date of hiring.

Data records with time constraint 1 can be purged from the database at the end of a processing run if they meet the condition that Status 2 equals 0, which occurs when an employee leaves the company. However, the infotypes Events (0000), Organizational Assignment (0001), and Personal Data (0002) are always retained to provide a basic record of each previous employee.

Using the Events Infotype for a Personnel History

You can list Events infotype 0000 to selectively display the significant fields needed to assemble a history of the employment events and, thus, the career development in the company of one or more employees or ex-employees.

Running Personnel Events with Fast Entry

In the standard SAP system, you can use the Fast Entry of Personnel Events function with the Hiring and Organizational Reassignment events. The Fast Entry function presents all infotypes belonging to an event in an ordered sequence. Some fields in the infotypes will be filled with default values suggested by the system. For example, if you record the "Position" assigned to an employee, the system will automatically suggest an appropriate entry in the "Payroll accounting area" field. However, during fast entry, the screen won't display any fields filled with default values.

The fast entry screen includes all the required entry fields of every infotype specified in the event's infogroup. Running an event entails processing a sequence of infotypes by completing or editing at least all the required entry fields.

You might not have all the necessary data to run an event to completion. In this case, you can interrupt the event and resume it later. You can also skip particular infotypes if you know that you won't have all the necessary information.

Running a Personnel Event

To run an event, follow these steps:

1. Select Human Resources>Personnel Admin.>HR Master Data>Personnel Events.
2. Enter the employee's personnel number and the date from which the event is valid, as well as the employee's personnel area, employee group, and employee subgroup.

3. Select the event you want to run.

4. Select the Choose function. You will be in events infotype 0000.

5. Enter data into the required fields, overwriting any default values if necessary.

6. Save each infotype. The next one is displayed until the Personnel Events screen reappears to signal that the event is successfully completed.

The employee's personnel number and the date from which it is valid are automatically transferred to all infotype records in the event. Organizational Assignment infotype 0001 is used to generate a record holding the employee's personnel area, employee group, and employee subgroup. This record includes a link to the PD-Personnel Planning and Development component if one is installed on your system.

Skipping an Infotype During an Event

Sometimes you need to leave out an infotype because the necessary data isn't available:

1. From the infotype in an event sequence that you want to skip, select the Next Record function.

2. Confirm the dialog box by choosing Yes to signify that you want to leave the current screen without saving data.

3. Continue working on the next infotype in the event sequence.

Restarting an Event

When an event is saved before the full set of infotypes is completed, you can resume the interrupted event by following these steps:

1. Select Human Resources>Personnel Admin.>HR Master Data>Personnel Events.

2. Enter the employee's personnel number and the date from which the event is valid.

3. Choose the event that you previously interrupted and select the Choose function.

4. Select the Execute Info Group function in Events infotype 0000.

5. Step through the infotypes of the event by selecting the Next Record function, making any alterations necessary and saving each infotype in turn.

The system changes to Create mode when you reach the first infotype that hasn't been previously saved.

Changing an Infotype Group Temporarily

The Change Infogroup function enables you to include one or more additional infotypes to be maintained as temporary members of the infotype group, but this applies only to the currently running event. The following steps use the Change Infogroup function:

1. Select Human Resources>Personnel Admin.>Personnel Events.

2. Assign a personnel number, choose an event, and then press Enter.

3. Make entries as required in Events infotype 0000.

4. Choose the Change Infogroup function.

5. Change the infotype group by editing the displayed list of infotypes in sequence.

6. Save the changes and continue running the event.

Using Fast Entry of Personnel Events for an Employee

The Fast Entry function allows you to display and change only selected fields from an event's infotypes. After the Fast Entry event is saved, the system displays any infotype containing an error.

The following steps use the Fast Entry procedure on events:

1. Select Human Resources>Personnel Admin.>HR Master Data>Fast Entry: Events.

2. Enter the Validity begin date for the event.

3. Activate the indicator for the desired personnel event.

4. You also can enter the employee's personnel area, employee group, and employee subgroup.

5. If the Personnel Planning and Development component is integrated, maintain the Position field on the fast entry screen with the information on the employee's personnel area, employee group, and employee subgroup.

6. Select the Choose function and maintain the data for the required entry fields of the infotypes.

7. If you want to add additional data to an infotype, select the Further Infotype Data check box for the corresponding infotype.

8. After you save your entry, you are branched to the corresponding Further Information screen if you've marked an infotype.

Understanding Payroll

The task of payroll is to calculate the gross remuneration for each employee based on individual payments. From the gross remuneration, the system deducts various insurance contributions and taxes.

Each type of individual payment can be managed in the format of a dedicated data structure assigned for storing information about the payment. This data structure is referred to as a *wage type*. For example, there will be one wage type for overtime payments and another for payments associated with leave periods. Wage types can be grouped with other data elements as infotypes focused on a particular business purpose.

Referring to Basic Pay

Basic pay is an amount calculated from fixed data elements stored within payroll accounting in infotype 0008. It's often used as the basis for computing other wage types.

Basic Pay infotype 0008 for an employee can be updated during the running of any of these personnel events:

- Hiring
- Change of job
- Change in pay
- Leaving

N O T E   An employee's basic pay records are retained after the Leaving event so that retroactive accounting runs can be performed.

The data for an employee's basic pay can comprise up to 20 wage types per accounting period. The employee's subgroup and personnel subarea control which wage types are permitted. Each wage type can be specified with a pay rate that can be overwritten.

If you copy an infotype record for another pay period or for another employee, the pay scale type, pay scale area, capacity utilization level, and working hours per period are redetermined unless their values vary from the standard default values for that period, in which case the special values are copied.

The following steps maintain basic pay data using a personnel event:

1. Choose the appropriate personnel event for the employee and the key dates in question.
2. Maintain all the infotypes suggested as a default by the personnel event until you reach infotype 0008 Basic Pay.
3. Check the collective agreement data and change the assignment to a pay scale structure, if necessary.
4. Check the suggested wage types from the wage type model.
5. Enter an amount for directly valuated wage types.
6. If necessary, enter a number and unit for indirectly valuated wage types (such as for wage types in which the amount is calculated as a percentage based on the total of other wage types).
7. Enter more wage types if necessary and if the customizing settings allow this.
8. If necessary, delete non-required default wage types.
9. Check the wage type total.
10. Save your entries.
11. Continue processing all the subsequent infotypes as suggested by the personnel event you selected.

Performing a Pay Scale Reclassification

Pay scale reclassification is needed when an employee is moved to a different pay scale group, pay scale level, or both. These events can be predefined in customizing, but a different date entered in Basic Pay infotype 0008 will take precedence.

Pay scale reclassification must take place within the payroll period before the payroll run. The following steps perform a pay scale reclassification:

1. Select System>Services>Reporting.
2. Enter report RPITUM00 and then choose the Execute function.
3. Select employees individually or according to payroll administrator or organizational unit.
4. Set the parameters by initiating a Create Batch Input session. A simulation will take place if you don't activate the Create Batch Input parameter. The reports RPLTRF00, RPLTRF10, and RPSTRF00 can be run to create lists of employees on the specified key date with their pay scale structure and further information on their current classification.
5. Check the results log.
6. Process the batch input session to reclassify the Basic Pay infotypes of the selected employees.

Performing a Pay Scale Increase

The system normally is customized to carry out automatic pay scale increases for those employees whose basic pay is calculated indirectly, rather than taken as a fixed amount.

An indirectly calculated amount can be adjusted by a particular amount or percentage. Alternatively, an extended pay scale increase can be arranged by using variants of the increase formula.

The following steps perform a simple pay scale increase:

1. Select System>Services>Reporting.
2. Enter report RPU51000 and then choose the Execute function.
3. Use the fields Pay Scale Structure and Wage Type to specify the employees for whom the pay scale increase should be performed using the customizing system.
4. Enter the amount or percentage of the increase.
5. Enter rounding data.
6. Enter the date as of which the customizing settings must be changed.
7. Enter your system name in the field Password.
8. Execute the report.

Arranging Recurring Payments and Deductions

Recurring payments and deductions are additional wage elements that aren't necessarily used in every payroll period. They follow a timetable determined by the frequency specified in infotype 0014, Recurring Payments and Deductions. Basic pay is assigned to the master cost center for an employee, but other accounts can be assigned for recurring payments and deductions.

Recurring payments can include transportation allowances, rent allowances, holiday pay, and Christmas bonuses. Recurring deductions can include tax paid on inputed income for benefits provided by the employer, such as a company car.

The following steps define a recurring payment or deduction for an employee:

1. Select Human Resources>Personnel Admin.>HR Master Data>Maintain.
2. Enter the personnel number of the employee.
3. Enter 14 in the Infotype field.
4. Choose the Create function.
5. Specify a validity period for the recurring payment/deduction in the fields Valid From - To.
6. Specify the wage type that the employee will receive as a recurring payment/deduction in the Wage Type field.

N O T E To display a list of allowed wage types, press F4.

7. If necessary, specify the wage type amount, number, and unit in the Amount and Number/unit fields.
8. If necessary, specify the first and then all subsequent periods in which recurring payments/deductions should occur in the First Payment Period and Interval in Periods fields. If you want to display allowed entries and examples, press F1.
9. If necessary, use the First Payment Date and Interval/unit fields to specify the date on which the first payment must be effected and the interval in which all further payments must occur. If you want to display allowed entries and examples, press F1.
10. Save your entries.

The following steps change the account assignment:

1. Select Goto>Cost Assignment.
2. Specify your assignment data in the Cost Assignment dialog box.
3. Choose the Execute function to override the account assignment defined in Organizational Assignment infotype 0001.

Arranging Additional Payments

If a payment such as a bonus is to be made once only on a fixed date, it's classified as an additional payment. Infotype 0015, Additional Payments, is maintained with the details, including a different account assignment if necessary.

The following steps define an additional payment for an employee:

1. Select Human Resources>Personnel Administration>HR Master Data>Maintain.
2. Enter the personnel number of the employee.

3. Enter **15** in the Infotype field.

4. Choose the Create function.

5. Specify the wage type that the employee will receive as an additional payment in the Wage Type field. If you want to display a list of allowed wage types, press F4.

6. If necessary, specify the wage type amount, number, and unit in the Amount and Number/unit fields.

7. Enter the date on which the additional payment must be accounted for in the Date of Creation field, or accept the default, which is the last day of the current payroll period.

8. If necessary, use the Default Date fields to specify a period and year other than those in the payroll control record. This causes the last day of this payroll period to be set as a new value in the Date of Creation field.

9. Save your entries.

Administering Salary

Salary administration enables you to automate compensation management. Selected individuals or groups of employees are remunerated according to the performance and *compa ratio* (compensation ratio of basic pay divided by mean salary) of each employee within the limits of a specified budget.

There are three stages to salary administration:

- Plotting a matrix of proposed percentage pay increases based on employee performance using the compa ratio, basic pay/mean salary. The system reads the basic pay from the Annual Salary field of Basic Pay infotype 0008, and the mean salary value is taken from pay scales for annual salaries.

- Preparing a proposal report that shows current salaries and those proposed by the matrix using the compa ratios for high, medium, and low performance, which are taken from Appraisals infotype 0025.

- Confirming or overriding the proposals to generate a release report that actually updates employee records for use by payroll.

Generating Proposals

The following steps generate employee pay raise proposals:

1. Select Human Resources>Personnel Admin.>HR Master Data> Maintain>Environment>Salary Administration>Proposals.

2. Enter the relevant time period and personnel number selection.

3. Enter the effective date.

4. Enter the compensation modifier and the compensation matrix ID.

5. Enter the reason for the salary change.

6. Select the Process function to display the report list screen with totals.

Modifying Proposals

From the Proposal Report List screen, the following steps allow modifications of individual proposal lines:

1. Select the individual employee names whose proposed salary increases you want to modify.

2. In the Detail screen of the report list output, make alterations to the Change Amount or the Change Percentage field.

3. Press Enter.

4. Return to the Report List screen and select the Refresh function to inspect any adjustments you've made.

The Proposals screen offers the following functions:

- ■ Current salary, to inspect the currently valid Basic Pay infotype 0008

- ■ Appraisals, to inspect the employee's Appraisals infotype 0025 records

- ■ Matrix, to inspect or change the sources of the salary proposals

Basic Pay infotype 0008 uses subtype 0 for the current basic pay and subtype 1 for the proposed basic pay in the form of temporary records. The Release report uses these when updating the employee basic pay records individually online or in batch mode.

The following steps update Basic Pay infotype 0008 records:

1. Select Human Resources>Personnel Admin.>HR Master Data>Maintain>Environment>Salary Administration>Release.

2. Enter the relevant time period and personnel number selection to list employees who have both Basic Pay (infotype 0008 subtype 0 and 1) records within the periods you specified in the report initial screen.

3. Select the Perform Update function.

4. Select batch or online processing.

5. Save each screen as the system leads you through the infotype creation.

Calling Related Reports

The following reports make no changes to the data:

- ■ Compa ratio analysis RPLCMPPU1

- ■ Salary structure RPLCMPPU 2

The following steps display a compa ratio analysis:

1. Select Information Systems>General Report Selection>Goto>General Reporting.

2. Enter `RPLCMPU1` in the Program field.

3. Select the Process function to begin the compa ratio analysis report.

4. Enter the relevant time period and personnel number selection.

5. Enter the pay scale group and pay scale level, if you require.

6. Select the Process function.

The compa ratio analysis shows the employee's job and the average annual salary and then the employee's details with his actual annual salary. The final column gives the compa ratio for each employee. You can select a line in the list screen to jump to the employee's Basic Pay (infotype 0008) records.

Displaying Salary Structure

You can inspect pay scales by following these steps:

1. Select Information Systems>General Report Selection>Goto>General Reporting.

2. Enter RPLCMPU2 in the Program field.

3. Select the Process function.

4. Enter the parameters that you require to refine the selection in the Salary Structure - List Report initial screen.

5. Select the Process function.

For each pay scale and pay scale level, the salary structure analysis shows a minimum, average, and maximum salary.

Displaying HR Infotypes

All HR data is stored in infotype records that are accessed in response to the entry of a valid personnel number followed by the selection of one or more infotypes offered. The following processing functions are available for working with HR infotypes:

- Maintain
- Display
- Fast Entry
- Reporting

The Display function displays an infotype record onscreen, but no updating is possible in Display mode. The List function displays an overview of all records stored for a selected infotype.

Data security is maximized by adopting the "Two-Person Control Tactic" in conjunction with the general SAP authorization check.

The authorization check depends on *authorization objects*, which are data structures containing up to 10 authorization fields. Employees are authorized to access a system or data element if their authorization profiles are adequate, which depends on their profiles meeting all the conditions specified in the authorization object associated with the system or data element. Thus, each field of an infotype could require a particular authorization.

Appreciating Time Constraints on HR Master Data

As an infotype is updated, the previous data is archived. Each infotype record also has a defined period of validity. Therefore, an employee could have several infotype records that vary only in their validity period. The system manages this automatically by using time constraints. Three primary time constraints are numbered and various additional constraints of a secondary nature are lettered:

- *Time constraint 1* allows only one record to be valid for an employee's infotype, with no gaps or overlap. This constraint is used on infotypes that must be accessible at any time. This time constraint is indicated by a screen message.

- *Time constraint 2* allows an infotype record for an employee if required, but only one record can be valid. Previous records are delimited if a new record is created, and a screen message appears.

- *Time constraint 3* allows an infotype to have any number of coexistent records for an employee because the individual records don't affect each other.

- *Time constraint A* allows only a single infotype record to exist. This record has an automatic validity period of 01/01/1800 to 12/31/9999. An infotype record with time constraint A can't be deleted.

- *Time constraint B* is similar to time constraint A, except that infotype records can be deleted if they're assigned it.

- *Time constraint T* signifies that the infotype records are constrained according to the subtype.

Displaying a Current Infotype Record

Current data on an employee can be inspected from the relevant infotype record as follows:

1. Select Human Resources>Personnel Admin.>HR Master Data>Display.
2. Enter the employee's personnel number.
3. Select the infotype from the default selection menu.
4. Choose the Display function.

Displaying a Previous Infotype Record

A previous infotype record will have a validity period that doesn't include the current date. The following steps identify it for display:

1. Select Human Resources>Personnel Admin.>HR Master Data>Display.
2. Enter the employee's personnel number.
3. Select the infotype for which you want to display a previous record.
4. Choose the List function. A list of all records for the infotype appears.
5. Select the record you want to display from the list.
6. Choose the Display function.

Displaying the List of Infotype Records

The following steps display a list of all the records for an employee in the chosen infotype:

1. Select Human Resources>Personnel Admin.>HR Master Data>Display.
2. Enter the employee's personnel number.
3. Select the infotype for which you want to display all records.
4. Choose the List function.

Displaying Individual Records from a List

When a list of an employee's infotype records is onscreen, you can select any record of interest and choose the Display function to see the details. If you mark some or all listed records by using the Select function, you will see the current record if you choose the Display function. By repeatedly choosing the Next function, you can step through the records until the message No subsequent record exists for current selection appears.

Maintaining and Changing HR Infotype Records

If you call the Maintain function, you can amend records as well as add new ones for an employee. When an infotype record is maintained, a copy of the previous record is retained for the archives so that it can be recalled to contribute to a history of the changes to the employee's data throughout her career.

If you call the Change function and alter data on an infotype record, no copy of the record is archived. Thus, the Change function is used mainly to correct existing data rather than to document important changes to the personnel information.

Deleting an Existing Infotype Record

If you use the Delete function on an infotype record with time constraint 1, the previous record will have its validity automatically extended to make it current. In other cases, the Delete function will remove records from the database without any historical record. You normally aren't allowed to delete an infotype record unless it had time constraint 1, except during the testing phase of implementing an R/3 system.

Deleting a Current Infotype Record

The following steps delete a current infotype record:

1. Select Human Resources>Personnel Admin.>HR Master Data>Maintain Master Data.
2. Enter the employee's personnel number.
3. Select the infotype record you want to delete.
4. Choose the Delete function. The current infotype record will appear in Delete mode, as stated on the menu title bar.
5. Choose the Delete function again to confirm the deletion.

If you activate general reporting during customization, a historical record is retained in the system for future evaluations of historical data and a document is created that documents the deletion of the infotype record. These records can be inspected by using the Log Records function.

Using Data Object Identification

A data object has an identification code that can be used to split infotype subtypes into individual objects. This facility allows you to generate an independent history for each object. For example, Family infotype 0021 subdivides into the following subtypes for Family types:

- Spouse→type 1
- Child→type 2
- Guardian→type 3, and so on

Time constraint 2 is associated with the individual subtypes so that a history can be generated for each subtype. To enter details for more than one child, you need to attach time constraint 3; otherwise, the records will overlap. Introducing an object ID allows you to generate one history per child. This infotype codes the object ID by child number.

Entering Payroll Data in the Payroll Past

Changes made to an employee's infotype records can affect the employee's pay. You can change infotype records relevant to payroll for a period for which an employee has already been included in a payroll accounting run. If you do this, the system marks the relevant records and prepares to run retroactive accounting for this employee. A message warns you if you make such changes.

Changing the Retroactive Accounting Date

Various factors affect the date from which retroactive accounting should take place:

- If you add a new infotype record by using the Create or Copy function, the begin date of the added infotype record will be used as the retroactive accounting date.
- If you delete an existing record by using the Delete function, the begin date of the deleted record will be used as the retroactive accounting date.

If you maintain an existing record by using the Change function, three conditions control the retroactive accounting date:

- If you change the data division of an infotype record relevant to retroactive accounting, a retroactive accounting run is triggered by using the validity begin date of the current infotype record.
- If you change the validity begin date, the new begin date is used as the retroactive accounting date if the new begin date is earlier than the original begin date.
- If the new begin date is later than the original begin date, the original begin date will be used as the retroactive accounting date.

- If you change the validity end date, the begin date of the changed record will be used as the retroactive accounting date if the new end date is later than the original end date.
- If the new end date is earlier than the original end date, the new end date will be used as the retroactive accounting date.

Controlling Payroll After Leaving

If you want to continue paying an employee after he leaves the company, it's not sufficient to enter a suitable date in the Accounted To field of Payroll Status infotype 0003, because this field won't be consulted by payroll after the leaving date is posted by the Leaving event.

In such circumstances, the correct method is to enter the intended payments in Recurring Payments and Deductions infotype 0014. The entry should be in Additional Payments infotype 0015 for a non-recurring payment. The Accounted To field in these payment infotypes is consulted by payroll until the date specified in the Do Not Process After field.

Locking a Personnel Number for Payroll

If an employee is rejected by a payroll run due to an error in her master or time data, the `Personnel number locked` indicator should be used to prevent the payroll driver from selecting this personnel number until the problem is sorted out.

A payroll error will select the `Payroll correction` indicator, which will cause the system to write the personnel number to matchcode W. This dynamic matchcode is used to process payroll errors.

If you've corrected the source of the problem, you can deactivate the `Payroll correction` indicator. This will delete the employee's personnel number from the matchcode W list.

Interpreting Payroll Control Records

Payroll normally begins by addressing a payroll accounting area one period at a time. All the employees in this area are processed as a batch. The status of this payroll accounting area will be set to `Exit payroll` when the area is finished processing.

All the employees in the payroll accounting area are assigned the date of processing in the Accounted To field of their Payroll Status infotype 0003 records if their payroll processing is successful. This date can't then be changed.

N O T E Although a productive system obeys strict accounting rules, a test system can be manipulated for simulation purposes in various ways that don't affect company accounts.

Using Master Data Fast Entry

If you need to create or maintain the same infotype or subtype record for several employees, the function to use is Fast Entry. This function assembles the infotype "required entry" fields for a selection of employees so that their data can be processed efficiently.

The following methods can be used to build a list of employee personnel numbers for use in Fast Entry:

- Compile the personnel numbers manually before entering the Fast Entry screen.
- Enter the personnel numbers directly into the Fast Entry screen.
- Generate the personnel numbers by using a report based on specific search criteria.

The following Fast Entry functions are available to update employee data in a specified infotype:

- *Create* allows you to create infotype data for many employees at once for a specified infotype.
- *Create using default* allows you to create infotype data for numerous employees by using default values that can be modified as necessary after they're transferred to the entry screen.
- *Maintain* allows you to change infotype data that already exists in the system.
- *Delete* allows you to delete existing infotype data for numerous employees.
- *Lock/Unlock* allows you to change the status of records from unlocked to locked by activating the Lock indicator for each record.

If you try to process more than 20 personnel numbers at one time, the system will arrange them in groups. You can access the next group with the Further Pers. Numbers function after saving the records of the previous group.

Creating Master Data Records with Fast Entry

The following steps create master data infotype records for numerous employees using Fast Entry:

1. Select Human Resources>Personnel Admin.>HR Master Data>Fast Data Entry.
2. Activate the indicator for Entry in the Fast Entry screen under the heading Personnel Number Entry.
3. Select the desired infotype by choosing it from the menu provided or by entering the infotype number in the Infotype field. Standard SAP, before customizing, allows the following infotypes to be selected:
   - Recurring Payments/Deductions infotype 0014
   - Additional Payments infotype 0015
   - Fiscal Data (D) infotype 0012

4. Choose the Create function to access all the fields of the chosen infotype.

5. Enter the personnel numbers, directly or by matchcodes, of the employees for whom you want to create new infotype records.

6. Maintain the required information for each employee record.

7. Save your entries.

Creating Master Data Records by Using Fast Entry Defaults

The following steps create master data infotype records for numerous employees by using fast entry default values:

1. Select Human Resources>Personnel Admin.>HR Master Data>Fast Data Entry.

2. Select a personnel number entry method.

3. Select or enter the desired infotype number.

4. Choose the Create Using Default function.

5. Enter default data in the applicable fields provided.

6. Select Next Screen. The system generates 20 entries by using the default data.

7. Enter the personnel numbers, directly or by matchcodes, of the employees for whom you want to maintain records.

8. Make any modifications necessary and save your entries.

Deleting Master Data by Using Fast Entry

The following steps delete infotype records for numerous employees by using Fast Entry:

1. Select Human Resources>Personnel Admin.>HR Master Data>Fast Data Entry.

2. Activate the indicator for Entry in the Fast Entry screen under the heading Personnel Number Entry.

3. Select or enter the desired infotype number.

4. Enter the applicable subtype in the Subtype field.

5. Maintain the relevant validity period.

6. Choose Edit>Delete.

7. Enter the personnel numbers, directly or by matchcodes, of the employees for whom you want to maintain records.

8. Select Enter.

9. Enter d in the Operation Indicator field (labeled O) of each record you want to delete, or use the Select function to highlight all displayed records.

10. Use the Delete function.

Locking/Unlocking Master Data by Using Fast Entry

The following steps lock/unlock infotype records for numerous employees through Fast Entry:

1. Select Human Resources>Personnel Admin.>HR Master Data>Fast Data Entry.

2. Activate the indicator `Preselect Manually` under the heading Enter Personnel Numbers.

3. Select or enter the desired infotype number.

4. Enter the From and To dates for the relevant validity period.

5. Select Enter to display an empty data table.

6. Enter the personnel numbers, directly or by matchcodes, of the employees whose fast entry infotype records you want to lock/unlock.

7. Use the menu path Edit>Lock/Unlock.

8. Activate the `Lock` indicator for each fast entry infotype record you want to lock, or deactivate the `Lock` indicator for each record you want to unlock.

9. Save your entries.

Creating a Batch Input Session when Processing Fast Entry Data

The following sequence will process multiple fast entry data records by using a batch input session:

1. Select Human Resources>Personnel Admin.>HR Master Data>Fast Entry Data.

2. Activate the indicator for Create Batch Input Session found under the heading Save Option.

3. Continue with the sequence for the intended Fast Entry function.

When you save your fast entry data, a system message gives you the name of the newly created batch input file.

Administering the Pay Scale Structure

The pay scales are associated with a structure that defines a job, a position, and a department or other organizational unit that comprises a defined group of employees. If your system isn't integrated with HR's PD-Planning and Development component, the pay scale structure must be set up in PA control tables during customizing. If the PD component is integrated, the tables are set up and maintained in PD. In this integration, the system automatically initiates a transaction in the PD component when you assign an employee to a job, position, and organizational unit during personnel administration.

The following advantages accrue if the PD component is integrated:

- The Position data is linked to the employee group, employee subgroup, personnel area, personnel subarea, company code, business area, cost center, job, and organizational unit data.

- Personnel events address the extra infotypes offered by the PD component and validate any entries that vary from the default values suggested.

- Organizational Assignment infotype 0001 accepts an employment percentage for the position and uses it in the position-staffing schedule, as well as prompts the user to allocate the employee to other positions for the unassigned staffing percentage.

PA allows only one position if it's not integrated with PD.

Defining the Pay Scale Structure

A pay scale structure is assembled from the following data elements:

- Pay scale type
- Pay scale area
- Employee subgroup grouping for the collective agreement provision
- Pay scale group
- Pay scale level

Any of the following infotypes assign an employee to a pay scale structure when they're created:

- Basic Pay infotype 0008
- Recurring Payments and Deductions infotype 0014
- Additional Payments infotype 0015
- Wage Maintenance infotype 0052

Pay scale types are maintained in customizing to represent the scope of a pay scale or collective agreement. The scope can be defined, for example, by a single company, a trade union, or a whole industry. The system stores each defined pay scale type as a two-digit code within a "personnel country" grouping.

A pay scale area corresponds to the geographical area in which a pay scale or a collective agreement is valid. Within a pay scale area, pay scale groups and levels can be defined per pay scale type and indicator.

Default values for pay scale types and groups defined for each personnel subarea are suggested when a Basic Pay infotype 0008 record is created.

The "employee subgroup grouping for the collective agreement" provision is used to assign an employee to a pay scale group, of which the following are examples:

- Industrial workers/hourly wage
- Industrial workers/monthly wage

- Salaried employees
- Non-pay scale employees

Within such a grouping system, pay scale groups and levels can be defined per pay scale type and pay scale area. If employees are being paid using indirect valuation on an hourly or monthly basis, the calculations can be managed by setting up an "employee subgroup grouping for personnel calculation rules and collective agreement" provision.

Remuneration is computed by using a pay scale level within a pay scale group. These values are applied to the amounts of time or product defined as particular wage types.

Understanding Wage Types

A wage type defines how an employee will be rewarded in pay or holidays. Wage types are divided into two main groups:

- *Primary wage types*, also referred to as *dialog wage types* because users can enter them into infotypes. The primary wage type group also includes wage and salary types generated automatically from certain time pairs, for example.
- *Secondary wage types* are derived by the system during processing.

A wage type can represent a payment or a deduction. A time constraint can be applied to a wage type, such as a bonus, to control how often it can be used in an accounting period.

The entry combination for a wage type determines whether it's entered with or without amounts, with volume specifications or a unit of time or measurement.

Indirect wage type valuation can be arranged by indicating a module name or variant as well as the corresponding rounding off preference. The amount is then calculated by using tables and not entered or stored in Basic Pay infotype 0008.

Using Wage Types

Wage types have the job of labeling items created during payroll runs.

From an accounting viewpoint, a wage type classifies an expense as, for example, wages, salaries, taxes, or insurance. Cumulative wage types can also be used to compile totals of other wage types. The results of payroll accounting are also expressed in terms of particular wage types defined for the purpose. These wage types are then used to trace the flow of payments and their dates.

For example, a record identified as a wage type MA10 will be recognized as a container for a standard salary element that should be accounted as an operating expense. By contrast, wage type /559 will be identified as a bank transfer that contains a payable amount and therefore should be posted to a clearing account.

The standard R/3 system includes a catalog of wage types to which further wage types can be added during customizing by copying and editing model wage types.

A wage type consists of three fields: Amount (AMT), Rate (RTE), and Number (NUM). You can use these fields in various ways. For example, a wage type might be a fixed amount in the accounting currency. Another wage type might have the amount calculated by multiplying the number of hours worked by the rate of remuneration per hour. Time wage types can be written with a number of hours that are valuated by using a rate determined by conditions specified in customizing.

Wage type characteristics define how a wage type can be used to receive information, the type of entries that can be made, and how the wage type is subsequently processed.

Direct valuation of a wage type takes place when an infotype is used to supply a specific amount. For example, infotype 0015, Additional Payments, can be used to enter a special payment wage type in the amount of $500. By contrast, indirect valuation computes the amount of the wage type by referring to data held elsewhere in the system.

Transferring Payroll Results

The HR-Human Resource management system is recommended for use in the same SAP client as FI-Financial Accounting and CO-Cost Accounting. However, payroll results can also be transferred if the HR module is used on a different client or system. The release status of the HR module doesn't have to correspond to the release of the other modules. HR can also accept transfers to and from SAP R/2 and third-party financial accounting and cost accounting systems.

Payroll results are transferred to financial accounting and cost accounting for each payroll period. There are two steps "subsequent to payroll": Prepare reporting and Transfer to FI/CO. There might also occur what are known as "further subsequent steps," such as making payments to bank clearing accounts.

Use the following menu sequences to initiate the two subsequent steps from the initial Payroll screen:

- Subs. Activities>Per Payroll Period>Reporting>Prepare Reporting
- Subs. Activities>Per Payroll Period>Reporting>Transfer to FI/CO

After the payroll results are transferred from payroll accounting, any "further subsequent activities" must take place in the relevant departments, such as human resources, financial accounting, and cost accounting.

The destinations of payroll results are controlled by the wage types relevant to posting, such as basic pay, overtime, net pay, tax deductions, and health insurance deductions. Associated with these wage types during customizing will be pertinent information such as master cost center and company code assignment.

Payroll accounting can be configured to create additional wage types to assist in directing the results to the proper receiver destinations. For example, you might find it useful to maintain a controlling account to cumulate the remuneration in pay or leave arising from work on public holidays. A wage type can be defined in customizing for this purpose.

The next step after a payroll period run is to prepare reporting, during which each wage type intended for posting is given a symbolic account assignment to generate a line item. A wage type to be assigned to an additional account is also recorded as a line item. Line items from the payroll run are then stored in a work file.

The transfer to FI/CO step is accomplished by a separate transfer program that interprets the symbolic account assignment of each line item in the work file and makes a final account assignment using the automatic account determination procedure in FI.

As the final account determinations are made, a list is compiled that will become the basis for the posting document. This list is usually printed and stored for documentary purposes. It's referred to as the *paper document.*

As well as preparing the paper document, the second step of payroll results transfer prepares batch input sessions that will be controlled by Post Document transaction FB01. Additional batch input sessions can also be prepared for KB11, Enter Transfer of Primary Costs.

When transaction FB01 actually posts the transfer to FI, any data intended for CO is transferred indirectly by using accounts marked as "profit/loss carry forward accounts." Similarly, if a posting is required to one or more clearing cost centers, a summarized posting is assigned for transfer by FB01. If retroactive accounting runs in the payroll past have taken place that affect previous fiscal years, the amounts can be posted to special periods for the fiscal years concerned.

Wage types relevant to cost accounting can be posted to fixed cost centers, to fixed orders, or to standard orders, rather than to the employee's master cost center or to an otherwise determined cost assignment.

Processing "further subsequent activities" entails dealing with personnel expenses identified in the transferred payroll results.

Simulating a Payroll Run

The main function of a payroll simulation is to test that the master data has been correctly maintained for the employee personnel numbers in the run. The payroll control record for a period being simulated is inactive, so the payroll results aren't saved. During a simulation, the master data records aren't locked, so they can be altered if errors are detected. The payroll log of a simulation can be displayed and printed.

The following steps simulate a payroll run:

1. Select Human Resources>Payroll.
2. Specify the personnel country grouping and payroll accounting area, unless these parameters are preset.
3. Select Payroll>Simulation.
4. Specify the payroll accounting area and period in the block Payroll Period.
5. Overwrite the default Payroll area field, if necessary.

6. In the block Deleting the last payroll result, make an entry in the Personnel Number or Payroll Area field by specifying an individual value or a range of values.

7. In the Payroll Schema field, specify the name of the schema with which the payroll run will be performed or accept the default country-specific payroll schema.

8. In the field "Forced retroactive accounting as of," enter a date for the retroactive accounting run that you want to trigger and which the system doesn't recognize automatically.

9. Set a flag for the indicator Test run (no update), if this isn't already set, so that the run will be a simulation.

10. Set any available flags that control how the simulation results will be presented and how the simulation can be interrupted if necessary.

11. Select Program>Execute or Program>Execute+Print.

Any employees rejected by a payroll run are identified in matchcode W, which can be used to initiate a second simulation for those employees alone.

Performing the Payroll Run

The generic steps for running payroll are as follows:

1. Release the payroll.
2. Start the payroll.
3. Check the payroll results.
4. Correct the payroll.
5. Exit the payroll.

Releasing the Payroll

The first step in running payroll is to select the personnel records by nominating one or more payroll accounting areas. These records must then be released for payroll. This action ensures that master data changes will be allowed only if they affect the future. Records released for payroll are locked against any present or past changes that might affect payroll accounting.

The following steps release the payroll for one payroll accounting area:

1. Select Human Resources>Payroll.
2. Specify the personnel country grouping and payroll accounting area, unless these parameters are preset.
3. Select Payroll>Release Payroll.

The following steps release more payroll accounting areas:

1. Select Tools>Set Modifiers>Payroll Area.
2. Specify the next payroll accounting area.
3. Select Payroll>Release Payroll.

Starting the Payroll

The payroll is executed by a country-specific payroll driver. This driver uses country-specific personnel calculation schema, but only on personnel numbers assigned to a payroll accounting area that has been released.

The following steps start the payroll:

1. Select Payroll>Start Payroll.
2. Specify or accept the default payroll accounting area and the period in the block Payroll Period.
3. In the Selection block, specify an individual value or range of values in the Personnel Number or Payroll Area field.
4. In the field Payroll schema, specify or accept the default name of the schema with which the payroll run will be performed.
5. In the field "Forced retroactive accounting as of," enter a date for the retroactive accounting run that you want to trigger that isn't recognized automatically by the system.
6. Ensure that a flag hasn't been set for the indicator Test run (no update).
7. If necessary, set a flag for the Store generated schema? indicator.
8. If necessary, set a flag for the indicator Close payroll gaps. If the indicator is set for an employee and payroll accounting hasn't been performed for one of her past payroll periods, the payroll is also run for the period in question.
9. If necessary, set flags for the indicators Display log, Sorted output of tables, and Log times.
10. Set a flag for the indicator Unconditional interrupt or User-specific interrupt or Switch off interrupt.
11. If necessary, set a flag for the indicator Display print selection screen. If a flag is set for the indicator, a print selection screen is displayed in which you can set print parameters before the payroll log is printed.
12. Select Program>Execute or alternatively Program>Execute+Print. A log is displayed when the payroll run is complete.
13. Scroll down to the end of the log and check whether personnel numbers were rejected or not selected. If personnel numbers are rejected or not selected, don't exit the payroll program. Instead, check the payroll results and correct master data and time data. Rejected employee numbers will have been stored in matchcode W.

Don't exit the payroll program if you intend to perform a split run in order to perform payroll accounting at a later date for specific wage elements pertaining to the payroll period. A split run is managed like a correction run.

CAUTION

Exit the payroll program only if you don't intend to perform a split run and all personnel numbers are successfully processed.

Checking the Payroll Results

If you freeze the current payroll status before checking the payroll results, the relevant master data will be locked and no new payroll run can take place. The following steps set the status `Check payroll results:`

1. Select the initial screen Payroll Accounting for *country*.

2. Select Payroll>Check Result.

3. Select Tools>Payroll Result.

4. Enter an individual personnel number or a range of personnel numbers in the Personnel Number field.

5. Enter the period for which payroll results must be selected in the Period for For-Periods field. Use the Status Indicator field to specify whether current or past payroll results are to be checked.

6. Flag the List of Payroll Records check box, from which individual payroll results can be displayed.

7. Flag the Choose Individual Tables check box to inspect the individual results tables.

8. Choose Program>Execute or Program>Execute+Print.

9. Select the payroll record you want to check.

10. Use the Choose function.

11. Select the table that contains the contents you want to check.

12. Use the Choose function.

13. The function key List Payroll Results enables you to return to the list of payroll records.

Correcting the Payroll

If you need to correct infotype data because personnel numbers have been rejected or not selected by a payroll run, the records in the payroll accounting area must first be unlocked by releasing them for corrections.

Payroll Status infotype 0003 includes a flag in the Payroll Correction field for all rejected personnel numbers. These numbers will then appear under matchcode W. When the corrections are all made, this matchcode can be used to select these records for a payroll correction run.

The following steps set the status `Correct payroll:`

1. Return to the initial Payroll Accounting for *country* screen.

2. Select Payroll>Corrections.

The following steps correct master data for employees who were rejected or not selected:

1. Select Environment>Master Data>Maintain.
2. Correct data in the appropriate infotypes.
3. Release the payroll again.
4. Start the payroll again by using matchcode W.
5. Check the payroll log again for rejected personnel numbers.

Continue to correct master data until matchcode W is empty because payroll accounting has been performed for all personnel numbers. You can't exit the payroll program until matchcode W is empty.

The significance of exiting the payroll program is that this event causes the payroll period for the respective payroll accounting area and the current year to be incremented in the payroll control record. This records that payroll accounting is complete for that payroll accounting area of personnel numbers for that period.

Displaying Matchcode W

Matchcode W collects personnel numbers that were rejected because of incorrect data. Personnel numbers can also be rejected because payroll accounting has already been performed for them in the selected period. Note that rejections of this sort aren't stored in matchcode W.

To display matchcode W, follow these steps:

1. On the menu screen Payroll Accounting for *country*, select Tools>Control Record.
2. Specify a payroll accounting area.
3. Choose the Display function.
4. Select Edit>Incorrect Personnel Numbers.

The following steps run the program using matchcode W:

1. Select the function key Matchcodes.
2. Select matchcode W (payroll correction run).
3. Select Program>Execute, or Program>Execute+Print or Execute in Background.

Exiting Payroll

When you exit payroll, the payroll period is incremented in the payroll control record and the payroll accounting area is released for further processing.

The following steps exit the payroll program, provided matchcode W is empty:

1. Select the initial screen Payroll Accounting for *country*.
2. Select Payroll>Exit Payroll.

You won't be allowed to exit if any parts of a split payroll run remain incomplete.

Deleting the Last Payroll Result

You can maintain Payroll Status infotype 0003 before running the payroll to exclude from the payroll run employees that belong to a particular payroll accounting area. However, if you discover that a payroll run includes an employee in error, this particular result can be deleted unless data medium exchange has already occurred for the employee or a productive system control record is already complete.

Locking with the Payroll Status Infotype

Payroll Status infotype 0003 serves the following locking functions:

- *Run Payroll Up To* is a date field that identifies the last date on which payroll will be run for the employee, which might be after the leaving date.
- *Do Not Process After* field can contain a date up to which the payroll can be run for the employee, if necessary.
- *Pers. No. Locked* is used to prevent payroll being run for this employee.

Locking a personnel number for payroll can't take place in the following circumstances:

- A payroll result already exists for the period in which the payroll should be run, and you're trying to lock the personnel number when correcting the payroll results.
- Remuneration has already been effected for the employee in the current payroll period.

To stop payroll from being run for an employee, delete his last (most recent) payroll result. If you delete the last payroll result, the previous result takes its place as the last result. You can't delete an employee's payroll result until you finish processing his master data.

The following steps delete an employee's current payroll result and record the action in the application log:

1. Select Human Resources>Payroll *country payroll_accounting_area.*
2. Choose Tools>Payroll Result>Delete *personnel_number.*

   The system will display a list of all payroll results created during the last payroll run—one result for each period plus any results for retroactive accounting.

3. Choose Program>Delete, and confirm the deletion as requested by the dialog box.

The application log records whether payroll results are deleted, which payroll results have been deleted, and who deleted them. This log is accessed by command SLG1, Evaluate Application Log, and applied to object HRPU, which is the deletion log for the last payroll result. You can limit the list of entries by dates and times.

Using Off-Cycle Payroll

Normal payroll works on a schedule to create payroll results for employees. *Off-cycle payroll* allows the following processes to be performed at any time:

- Displaying payroll history
- Adjusting payroll results
- Generating on-demand checks
- Replacing checks
- Reversing payroll results
- Generating manual checks

Displaying Payroll History

An inspection of an employee's payroll history is a useful starting point for calling other functions in off-cycle payroll. The history comprises a list of all the payroll results stored in the system for the employee in reverse chronological order.

The following steps display an employee's payroll history:

1. Select Human Resources>Payroll>Off-Cycle>Payroll History.
2. Enter the employee's personnel number or choose the Matchcode function to search for the desired personnel number. If you've been working with a particular employee, the employee's personnel number will appear onscreen.
3. Choose the Continue function.

Reversed payroll results appear highlighted. Replacement checks appear with an asterisk in front of the check number. If you haven't printed the check, the check number is blank. If you haven't transferred the direct deposit, the direct deposit number is blank.

Select any payroll result, except a reversed result, and choose the Display function to see the details.

Adjusting Payroll Results

The occasions for adjusting a payroll result include the following:

- You've produced a check incorrectly and the check is no longer available, perhaps because it has been cashed.
- You've already transferred an incorrect direct deposit record.

Performing an adjustment requires that data be created or changed within the payroll period. A retroactive calculation is triggered by the adjustment so that the next payroll result will be updated with the corrected information.

The following steps adjust a payroll result:

1. Select Human Resources>Payroll>Off-Cycle>Adjustment Check.
2. Enter the employee's personnel number or choose the Matchcode function to search for the desired personnel number.
3. Choose the Adjust Data function.

4. Select the Personnel Administration or the Time Management Information function to correct the necessary data and then choose the Continue function.

5. Choose the Change or Create function to change or create data in PA or choose Time Management so that the system will process a retroactive calculation.

6. After adjusting the data, return to the Adjustment Check screen and choose the Start Payroll function. You can choose the Display Result function to display payroll history for the employee.

7. Enter the desired adjustment date and choose the Start Payroll function. The system defaults the current date.

8. After reviewing and verifying the successfully calculated payroll results, choose the Continue function.

9. Choose the Save function to save the payroll results, the Cancel function to reject the results, or the Results function to review the calculated results.

10. After choosing the Save function, choose the Print Check function to print, if necessary.

11. For employees who use direct deposit, choose the Issue Check function to pay the current calculated result with a check or the Direct Deposit function to pay the result with a direct deposit.

12. Enter the same adjustment date as shown in step 7.

13. Choose the Print Check function to print the check.

Generating On-Demand Checks for Regular Pay

A newly hired employee, a dismissed employee, or an employee who will be taking vacation during the regular payroll run might have to be given a check without the payroll being run. To generate a check, you must create a payroll result associated with a specific open pay period.

The following steps generate an on-demand check for regular pay:

1. Select Human Resources>Payroll>Off-Cycle>On Demand Check>Regular Pay.

2. Enter the employee's personnel number or choose the Matchcode function to search for the desired personnel number. If you've been working with a particular employee, the employee's personnel number will appear onscreen.

3. Choose the Start Payroll function.

4. Enter the check date and choose the Start Payroll function.

5. Determine whether the calculated payroll result is correct on the Successful Regular Payroll Run screen, and then return to the previous screen.

6. After reviewing and verifying the successfully calculated payroll results, choose the Save function to save the calculated payroll results, or choose Cancel or Result to view the results again.

7. After choosing the Save function, choose the Print Check function to print. For employees with direct deposit, choose the Issue Check function to pay the current calculated result with a check or the Direct Deposit function to pay the result with a direct deposit.

8. Enter the pay period run and choose the Print function to print the check.

Issuing an On-Demand Check for a New Hire

A newly hired employee might not be paid because the paperwork didn't arrive before the payroll run. In this case, the hiring event has to be performed for this employee to establish the personnel data and an on-demand check has to be issued. The following steps issue an on-demand check for a new hire:

1. Select Human Resources>Payroll>Off-Cycle>On Demand Check>Regular Pay.
2. Enter or select the employee's personnel number.
3. Select Environment>Personnel Admin. to perform a new hire event for the employee, using the appropriate hire date.
4. Return to the On Demand Check for Regular Payment screen and choose the Start Payroll function.
5. Enter the check date and choose the Start Payroll function.
6. Choose the Save function to save the calculated payroll results.
7. After choosing the Save function, choose the Print Check function to print.
8. Enter the pay period run and choose the Print function to print the check.

Replacing Checks

The following sequence will issue a new check with a new number as a replacement for a check that was lost, stolen, or damaged before it was cashed:

1. Select Human Resources>Payroll>Off-Cycle>Replacement.
2. Enter or select the employee's personnel number.
3. Choose the Continue function.
4. Mark the check to be replaced and choose the Replace function.
5. Enter the reason for replacement and choose the Replace function.
6. Choose the Print function to print the replacement check.

Now when you display payroll history, the replacement check will appear with an asterisk in front of its check number.

A damaged payroll check that hasn't been cashed can be replaced by entering `unusable` as the reason for replacement.

Reversing Payroll Results

Reversing a check is possible if it's uncashed. Reversing a direct deposit is possible if it hasn't been credited to the employee's account. If you've issued more than one check or direct deposit in a payroll period, you have to reverse each one to enable the system to revise the taxes. Use the Reverse function when you have marked the payroll result to be reversed.

The following steps reverse a payroll result:

1. Select Human Resources>Payroll>Off-Cycle>Reversal.
2. Enter or select the employee's personnel number.
3. Choose the Continue function to proceed.
4. Select a payroll result to reverse and choose the Reverse function. You can select the Result Info function to display detailed pay stub information for the selected payroll result only while it hasn't been reversed.
5. Verify the payroll result to reverse and choose the Reverse function.
6. Choose the Reverse function again to confirm the reversal process.
7. Enter the reason for the reversal in the Reverse Reason dialog box and choose the Reverse function.

When performing a reversal, the system voids the corresponding payroll information in FI and then reverses the payroll result in HR.

If a payroll run has created incorrect results, they can be discarded immediately without consequences for the accounting system. However, if a check has been created with an assigned check number but not yet cashed, or if a direct deposit has been created but not yet transferred to the employee's bank account, the reversal procedure must be carried out to nullify the incorrect payment.

Communicating Payroll Information to Employees

A payroll account is a customized printout of payroll data for a payroll period, or more often for a whole year. The following steps create a payroll account for your employees:

1. Select Lists/Statistics>Payroll Account.
2. In the Period block, specify a data and person selection period or use the Payroll Period function.
3. In the Selection block, make an entry in the Personnel Number or Payroll Area field by specifying an individual value or a range of values.
4. Enter the name of the form you set up in the customizing system in the Form for Payroll Account field.
5. If necessary, set a flag for the indicator Display last result only? to ensure that retroactive accounting differences are displayed as well as the currently valid payroll results.
6. If necessary, overwrite the default value in the Number of Columns Per Page field.
7. If necessary, set a flag for the indicator Separate form for legal person?. This ensures that a separate form is created if the output function encounters a change of legal person during printing.
8. Select Program>Execute, Program>Execute+Print, or Program>Execute in Background.

The report that creates the payroll account allows you to double-click from displaying the payroll account to the remuneration statement for any marked payroll result.

A payroll journal comprises tables of payroll data for several employees for one payroll period. The format and content are established in customizing.

Creating a Remuneration Statement

A list of all payments and deductions made for an employee during a payroll run is created before payment is effected. The presentation format of a remuneration statement is determined in customizing, in addition to personal and general notifications that can be nominated for inclusion in the statement when appropriate.

Notifications infotype 0128 stores additional information in the form of texts assigned to Subtype 1 if they are general and to Subtype 2 if they are personal and maintained individually for a particular employee.

Infotype 0128 allows the following parameters to be entered:

- Text name, for Personal Notifications Subtype 2
- Language, for Subtype 2
- Short title for standard fixed text notifications
- Sequence number used to order printing when more than one notification is issued
- Source system for administrative information concerning the origin or reason for the notification
- Payroll type to control the type of payroll accounting run for which the notification is used

The following steps create a remuneration statement:

1. Select Payroll>Remuneration Statement.
2. Specify the payroll accounting area and period in the block Payroll Period.
3. Accept or overwrite the default payroll area.
4. Use the Selection block to specify personnel numbers or payroll areas by specifying individual values or a range.
5. Enter the name of the form set up in the customizing system in the Form Name field.
6. If necessary, overwrite the default values in the fields Output Language, Print Current Period, Print Retroactive Runs, Layout of Retroactive Runs, and Sort Retroactive Runs.
7. If necessary, enter a number between 1 and 9 in the Number of Test Forms field. The corresponding number of test forms are printed out.
8. If necessary, set a flag for the indicator Print superlines, which contains values for more than one wage type.
9. Select Program>Execute, Program>Execute+Print, or Program>Execute in Background.

Arranging Unqualified Advance Payments

An unqualified advance payment can be calculated from employee master data. It normally represents an estimate of the remuneration earned to date. This type of advance payment is known as an advance payment based on master data. The payment is assigned to a wage type, but the accounting isn't completed until a normal payroll run, possibly at the end of the following period. The payment is termed *unqualified* because it isn't considered to be attached to any one accounting period. The following employee infotypes are consulted to find out if any unqualified advance payments are due:

- External Bank Transfers (infotype 0011)
- Recurring Payments/Deductions (infotype 0014)
- Additional Payments (infotype 0015)

If you arrange a split payroll run, you can have some payroll elements accounted and perhaps a qualified advance payment made to cover the elements not accounted in the first part of the split payroll run. The payroll program is set to Correction mode when you want to include these remaining payroll elements. A split payroll run constitutes an interruption of the normal sequence of payroll activities because more than one payroll or payment is run for an employee in a single accounting period.

Maintaining Employee Tax Information

Each sovereign country retains the right to exact taxes according to laws established for the purpose. Payroll processing acknowledges these differences by consulting employee tax information records and then using a country-specific personnel calculation schema to perform the necessary calculations. For example, an employee might be liable to pay federal, state, and local taxes, as well as unemployment insurance.

The following nations have payroll procedures that have been assembled in the form of software components that can be installed and integrated as required:

Australia	The Netherlands
Belgium	South Africa
Denmark	Spain
France	United States
Great Britain	Other countries
Japan	

Any of these components can be updated and adjusted during customizing.

The data needed to calculate an employee's withholdings in most national taxation schemes must include the following records or their equivalent:

- *Address*, for which there can be separate records for the permanent address used as their tax residence and their home address, if different

- *Residence Tax Area* (infotype 0207), a group of local, state, and federal authorities to which the employee pays tax
- *Work Tax Area* (infotype 0208), which calculates the amount of taxes paid to each authority for an employee who works across several tax areas, according to the percentage of time worked in each
- *Unemployment State* (infotype 0209), which identifies the authority for unemployment insurance and can include data required by an authority for statistical reporting by work site
- *Withholding Information* (infotype 0210), which includes details from an employee's Federal Employee Withholding Allowance Certificate, State Employee Withholding Allowance Certificate, and the equivalent certificate for local tax authorities
- *Additional Withholding Information* (infotype 0234), for example, for special payments to a tax authority
- *Other Taxes* (infotype 0235), which might specify alternative methods of calculating taxes for this employee
- *IRS Limits* (infotype 0161), which records whether an employee has limits or exemption amounts set by the Internal Revenue Service (IRS) or equivalent state and local authorities

Generating Other Tax Types

In certain exceptional circumstances, you might need to create other taxes to be applied to an employee for a particular authority. You can alter the calculation of the tax by changing the formula used or exempt an employee entirely from a tax. The new arrangements are recorded as infotype 0235, Other Taxes. These special procedures or exemptions will override the standard calculation of the tax types for that authority.

Using the Tax Reporter

Tax authorities define the wage types used when payroll calculations are reported. Each company might have to report to several tax authorities, each with its own reporting requirements. For example, U.S. law can require the following reports:

- Form 941, Employer's Quarterly Federal Tax Return
- Form 941C, Monthly Reporting for Delinquent Employers
- Form W2, Information Reporting for Employees

Preparing the Tax Reporter

The tax reports required by law are determined by the way the system is integrated with the various components for computing taxes for the national authorities. The Tax Reporter component offers reports according to this customizing.

The following steps use the subsequent activities functions to prepare the Tax Reporter:

1. Select Human Resources>Payroll>Subs. Activities>Period - Unrelated> Payroll Supplement>Tax Reporter>Preparation.

2. Enter the desired payroll area, tax company, tax authority, and tax form group in the appropriate fields.

3. Select the Preparation type from On-demand, Monthly base, Quarterly base, and Annual base.

4. Enter the preparation date, or click the Correct button on the toolbar to set the preparation date to today's date.

5. Choose Edit>Fill Interface or Edit>Fill in Batch.

After preparing the Tax Reporter, the report is generated by following these steps:

1. Select Human Resources>Payroll>Subs. Activities>Period - Unrelated> Payroll Supplement>Tax Reporter.

2. Select Generation, Simulation, or Preview.

3. Enter the desired payroll area, tax company, and tax authority in the appropriate fields.

4. Select the Preparation type from On-demand, Monthly base, Quarterly base, and Annual base.

5. Enter the preparation date.

6. Choose the menu path Tax Reporter>Create or Tax Reporter>Create in batch.

Interpreting Employee Deductions

The term *employee deductions* includes union dues, insurance contributions, charitable donations, and so on, but not tax and garnishment deductions. Employee deductions can be processed by payroll, as can priorities and arrears. Limits on deductions can also be processed at the same time.

The data for employee deductions is held in the employee's Recurring Payments and Deductions infotype 0014 records. Each deduction is represented as a wage type. Individual wage types hold data as values in "characteristics" that can include the amount to be deducted, when and how often the deduction should be taken, arrears processing, and limits on deductions. The particulars of each characteristic of a wage type are determined in customizing. Wage types can be assigned a payment model as a default that will display the deduction frequencies and other details of the model when the wage type is identified. The payment model suggestions can be accepted or modified as the wage type is used. Deductions can be scheduled in various ways to coincide with or overlap accounting periods by creating records in the employee's Recurring Payments and Deductions infotype 0014.

Limits on deductions can be recorded in infotype 0014 to ensure that, for example, no more than 5 percent or $200 be deducted from the total gross amount an employee receives per month. However, if you want to allow certain employees to have different limits, you can create records for them in their Limits on Deductions infotype 0165. These limits will then apply to wage type classes and be expressed as amounts per time interval, such as per month or per quarter. You can also set up limiting rules that can be referenced when applying limits to employee deductions. A limit defined in infotype 0165 for an individual employee will take precedence over the standard limit set in customizing.

Processing Priorities and Arrears

If a deduction exceeds a set limit, the payroll automatically allocates the amount not taken to the following payroll period. If more than one employee deduction is active, there must be a system of priorities.

Each wage type class can be assigned a priority, and each wage type in that class can also be assigned a priority. By this means, employees whose limits aren't high enough to meet all their scheduled deductions will find that their payroll processing has taken the highest priority deductions first and processed them first in arrears.

Managing Employee Garnishments

A *garnishment* in the United States is a legal procedure authorizing a deduction from an employee's earnings to satisfy a debt. Some authorities refer to it as a *court payment order*.

Garnishments operate within limits imposed by federal and state laws or their equivalents. These limits restrict the amount of an employee's earnings that can be taken by a creditor before the employee is paid.

For example, the Consumer Credit Protection Act (CCPA) protects consumers in the United States from unfair or harsh collection practices. Title III of the CCPA, also known as the Federal Wage Garnishment Law, specifically protects employees by restricting the amount that can be garnished from their wages for the payments of a creditor debt, alimony, and child support. It also regulates state garnishment laws and protects employees from losing their jobs as a direct result of any one debt.

Obeying State Laws

If the law in effect in the state the garnishment originated in is silent with respect to creditor garnishments or is less favorable to the employee than the federal law, the employer must abide by the provisions of the Federal Wage Garnishment Law. If state law requires that a greater portion of an employee's wages be exempt from creditor garnishment, the employer must abide by the provisions of the law in effect in the state of origin.

The following types of garnishment are differentiated:

- Child and spousal support
- Federal and state tax levies
- Creditor
- Voluntary wage assignment

Maintaining the Garnishment Infotypes

The complexity of garnishment arrangements requires a considerable volume and variety of information to be stored in the system. This data is held in three infotypes:

- The Garnishment Document (infotype 0194)
- The Garnishment Order (infotype 0195)
- The Garnishment Adjustment (infotype 0216)

Beginning with the Garnishment Document (infotype 0194), internal numbers and sequence numbers are used to connect data for the same garnishment between the infotypes.

To create a Garnishment Document, proceed as follows:

1. Select Human Resources>Personnel Admin.
2. Choose the Maintain function from the toolbar.
3. Enter the employee's personnel number.
4. Enter infotype 0194 (Garnishment Document) in the infotype field.
5. Choose the Create function from the toolbar.
6. Enter information in the fields of the Garnishment Document infotype 0194. Entries for case number, priority, internal number, status, and category are mandatory.
7. If the status of the garnishment is pending, choose Calculate End Date to have the end of the obligation calculated when the report is run.
8. Save your entries.

After the Garnishment Document is saved, the Garnishment Order (infotype 0195) fast entry screen is automatically displayed.

Exploring the Garnishment Document

Garnishment Document infotype 0194 includes the following information:

- General garnishment information such as status, important dates, priority, and category
- Vendor information
- Originator information
- Garnishment processing information, such as applicable service charges and remittance information

The Case No. field contains the unique number of the document that identifies the legal instrument. The InternalNo field contains the unique garnishment number assigned by the system that's used for working with the records.

A garnishment's status can be Pending, Active, or Released. The status Rejected isn't normally encountered because it refers to documentation entered for an employee who has subsequently left.

The Rcvd Date is the date the Garnishment Document was received, which is set automatically as the date the record was created by default.

The Rlsd Date is the date when the employee is released from the Garnishment Document obligation and will be set automatically when you enter the Status as Released and save.

The Priority field value controls the order in which the garnishment will be deducted in respect to other garnishments. Highest priority will be deducted first, and the lower the value, the higher the priority. If more than one support garnishment with the same priority exists, there will be a proration (sharing in proportion) of the nonexempt amount independent of the received date. Support garnishments usually have priority over any other garnishment type.

If a conflict occurs because two non-support garnishments have the same priority, the garnishment received first will be deducted first.

The Origin field records the region in which the garnishment is originated and is used when deciding how the nonexempt amount will be calculated.

The Category field classifies the garnishment document in a category system determined in customizing.

The Vendor Data is the information about the party that receives the money, such as the vendor of goods being paid for by a garnishment order or the recipient of a support order. When entering vendor data, the user merely chooses the correct vendor and the relevant vendor information is displayed. This vendor information can be maintained only from the Controlling module.

The Originator code identifies the type of source that originated the document. The originator might or might not be the vendor or payee. Directly under the Originator field you enter the originator's information. This information is used for the delivery of periodic answer letters.

The Single Check Indicator field is marked to override the default procedure of paying all garnishments to one vendor by a single check.

The originator of a Garnishment Document can be sent answer letters under control of the fields Answer Ind., Elapsed Days, and Startdate Ans.

The Plaintiff field contains the name of the person on whose behalf the Garnishment Document was issued.

The Remit Rule field contains a specification in the form of a rule. The rule can be manually entered as a special rule. The default rule is the company remittance rule or, failing that, the government remittance rule.

The ServCharge field can be blank or can contain a value determined by a special service charge rule, the company service charge rule, or the government service charge rule.

When an edited Garnishment Document is saved, the Garnishment Order (infotype 0195) fast entry screen is displayed on which Garnishment Order information can be entered for several different types of orders. The suggested values can be overwritten as required.

N O T E   If adjustments to a garnishment are needed, such as a refund, a stopped payment, or an additional deduction, they're entered in the Garnishment Adjustment infotype 0216. ■

Garnishment Order infotype 0195 stores the processing data for a garnishment request:

- Initial balance of the claim
- Periodic deduction information
- Information on nonexempt and exempt limits

Accessing the Garnishment Document List

The following steps list all the garnishment cases for an employee:

1. Select Human Resources>Personnel Admin.
2. Choose the Maintain function from the toolbar.
3. Enter the employee's personnel number.
4. Enter the number **0194** (Garnishment Document) in the Infotype field.
5. Choose the List function from the toolbar.
6. Select Edit>Sorted By, and use the menu if you don't want the garnishments to be sorted by the delimiting dates.
7. Use the History function to view the garnishment history for the particular employee.

Changing a Garnishment Order

If you want to change a garnishment order, you can access the infotype and maintain the fields. The preferred sequence is to access the Garnishment Document that lists all garnishment cases for the employee. From the Garnishment Document of the selected case, use the Change function to display the Garnishment Order, which you can edit as long as it hasn't yet been processed in a payroll run. After a Garnishment Order begins, you must copy it and make the necessary changes to the copy. You then adjust the begin date and save the copy, which replaces the previous order.

Running Garnishment Reports

The garnishment history report for a specified employee displays the corrections and deductions for the employee's history, as well as remaining balances and the total to date. Any service charges rendered by the company, as well as remittance information, are included.

The garnishment review report displays all customizing parameters used in processing garnishments and the tables that the information is stored in.

The garnishment statistics report displays by personnel area, personnel subarea, employee group, and employee subgroup the total number of employees with garnishments and without garnishments.

Changing Garnishment Status After a Payroll Run

A garnishment batch input report should be run after every payroll run to change garnishment status. These reports do one of the following:

- Change all expired garnishments from the status of Active to Inactive
- Change all relevant garnishments from Pending to Active
- Delimit all chosen garnishments

The infotype information is then updated automatically by a batch input.

Using the Garnishment History Report to Change the Garnishment Due Date

A garnishment's due date might remain in the system after the garnishment expires and the debt is paid. This date can be corrected by running the garnishment history report:

1. Select Human Resources>Personnel Admin.
2. Choose the Maintain function from the toolbar.
3. Enter the employee's personnel number.
4. Enter the number 0194 (Garnishment Document) in the Infotype field.
5. Choose the List function from the toolbar or select Edit>List.
6. Select the desired garnishment case from the list.
7. Select the Change function or the Display function from the toolbar.
8. Select Environment>Garnishment History or select the History function from the toolbar.
9. Choose the Remittance function from the toolbar.
10. Place the cursor on the due date you want to change. If there are payments from different payroll runs, you can select from a list which payments you want to change the due date for.
11. Enter the new due date.
12. Save the entry.

Generating Garnishment Letters Automatically

You can automatically create answer letters and notice letters for individual employees or employee groups by flagging the garnishment infotype of the employees concerned if either letter is to be generated when the report is printed. Letters can be displayed and edited before printing.

Notice letters are sent in cases of bankruptcy, termination, notification, release, and leave of absence. These letters are controlled by the status of the garnishment as shown in the Garnishment Document infotype 0194.

Answer letters use information from previous payroll runs to create an answer letter to the vendor. This letter might or might not be requested by the vendor.

Applying Tax and PAYE Calculation Rules

PAYE, Pay As You Earn, is a method of extracting taxes from payroll under Great Britain's legal system.

The PAYE information is stored in the records of Tax infotype 0065. New employees have PAYE contributions deducted at a rate that assumes they are entitled to no tax-free allowances. The correct deductions are applied when their tax coding is known and the balance is collected or refunded as appropriate. However, no recalculation of tax takes place when a change of tax code is applied because the deductions are based on cumulative tables that specify the total tax due to date for each tax period and the tax actually paid to date.

New tax records have to be created every time an employee's tax liability changes, and also at the beginning of each tax year, whether or not the employee's situation has altered.

Tax refunds are withheld from striking employees. When employees resume work or leave the company, the refund can be paid. A flag is activated for the period of industrial action. A new tax record is created for the period of the strike.

If an employee's tax liability changes, a new tax record has to be created.

Form P45 is a record of the taxable pay and tax paid by an employee who has left a previous employment. A form P6 from the tax office is provided for those who weren't previously employed. These documents provide the information entered for a newly hired employee to control the tax calculations for the first year of their new employment.

Leaving details are entered when a P45 is issued and the payroll can apply basic rate of tax to any late payments made to the employee. A new tax record can be created automatically, containing employees' leaving details when their P45 is issued using the Sample P45 Slip report (RPCP45G0).

The following steps create a Tax infotype 0065 record for a new employee:

1. Select Human Resources>Personnel Admin.>Maintain Master Data.
2. Enter the employee's personnel number. Use the Matchcode function to find a number you don't know.
3. Select the Tax record (infotype 0065) by entering the name or infotype number in the Infotype field.
4. Choose the Create function.
5. If you're entering tax details after the employee's data is included in a payroll run, enter the date on which you received the information. A message will warn you that this is after the employee's start date. Otherwise, leave the date as it appears by default.
6. Enter the employee's tax code, tax code source, and correct tax basis.
7. Enter the employee's previous employment details from his P45.
8. Save your entries.

Changing an Employee's PAYE details

The Inland Revenue might change an employee's tax code, or you might receive new taxable pay and tax paid figures. This information can come at any point during a person's employment. Each time this happens, you must generate a new tax record. The previous tax record will be automatically delimited to avoid overlapping with the new record.

Changing PAYE Details for an Employee Who Leaves

An employee who leaves has to be given a form P45, and this action is recorded in Tax infotype 0065. The following steps update the PAYE details for a leaver:

1. Select Human Resources>Personnel Admin.>Maintain Master Data.
2. Enter or select the employee's personnel number.
3. Select the Tax Record infotype 0065 by entering the infotype name or number in the Infotype field.
4. Choose the Copy function and view the Copy Tax screen.
5. Change the From Date to the date on which the P45 was issued.
6. Change the employee's tax code and tax basis, if necessary.
7. Activate the P45 issued indicator and enter the appropriate date.
8. Save your entries.

If the employee was on strike at the time of leaving, any tax refund being withheld will be paid with his final pay.

Another technique for entering leaving details is to run the report RPCP45GO, Sample P45 Slip, which suggests default entries that users can accept or edit before saving the data.

Processing National Insurance Contributions

National Insurance is part of Great Britain's taxation system. Each employer and employee makes a compulsory National Insurance Contribution (NIC) to Inland Revenue. In return, the employee is credited with National Insurance contributions that are used to enhance his sickness and retirement pension entitlements. In certain circumstances, a National Insurance holiday can be entered for a new employee in which neither employee or employer is liable for National Insurance contributions.

National Insurance infotype 0069 acquires the employee's National Insurance number automatically from the employee's Personal Data (infotype 0002) record. Default values are adopted for the NIC until the actual information is entered. If you create a National Insurance record after a payroll runs, a retro-calculation is triggered.

The records of National Insurance infotype 0002 provide fields to record such information as the following:

- *National Insurance Category* controls the amounts of the employee and employer NICs.
- *Exception flags* signify that the employee pays an annual NIC as a company director, has form RD950 to confirm that NICs are paid in another employment, or pays NICs daily as a sessional worker.

Any employees belonging to an approved pension scheme pay NICs at a "contracted out" rate.

Any changes in an employee's National Insurance status must be marked by creating a new National Insurance record valid from the exact date of the change so that the payroll might apply the new contributions. Arrears can be recovered in accordance with legal rules, and overpayment is refunded after end-of-year reporting.

Processing Court Orders

A court order is a legal requirement on an employer to deduct a specified amount from an employee's earnings and remit it as directed by the order.

Court Orders infotype 0070 is used to create a record of each court order and specify its relative priority. The payroll automatically ensures that arrears, protected earnings, and arrears of protected earnings are processed correctly. For example, if there are two court orders against an employee, each with the same priority, the first order to be processed will be the one with the earlier "Begin validity" date.

An Object ID is assigned automatically to each order and is used in the payroll results to differentiate the payments under the different orders.

The Identification References and the Monetary Values are on the order document that you receive from the court or local authority.

Payroll automatically keeps a total of arrears and arrears of protected earnings so that no retro-calculation is required for court order processing. If a grand total is specified, payroll will stop making deductions when the total is reached.

The Administration Fee field suggests the current default processing fee for the particular court order. This default can be edited.

The following steps create a court order record for an employee:

1. Select Human Resources>Personnel Admin.>Maintain Master Data.
2. Enter or select the employee's personnel number.
3. Select the Court Orders record (infotype 0070) by entering the infotype name or number in the Infotype field.
4. Choose the Create function and view the Create Court Orders screen.
5. Set the date from which the order is effective in the From field.
6. Enter the Identification and Monetary values from the form that you received from the court or local authority.
7. Enter the administration fee according to your company policy.
8. Save your entries.

N O T E A court order might attempt to deduct earnings that would violate an employee's protected earnings. The payroll will automatically deduct no more than the difference between the employee's attachable arrestable earnings and his protected earnings. The unclaimed balance is identified as "arrears of order" and is deducted next month in addition to the specified court order deduction. ■

Understanding the Payroll Driver

Payroll accounting is executed by running the international version RPCALCx0 in the SAP Human Resources Management System. This version contains no data specific to any country. It therefore performs only the gross calculation of pay for payroll accounting.

The net pay calculation for payroll accounting must be performed by programs that have been developed explicitly for the countries in which they're running. These explicit, country-specific versions can be created from the basic international report program RPCALCx0. The method entails editing the standard tables for flow control and payroll customizing. This customizing can be carried out safely under control of the IMG (Implementation Management Guide).

In addition to the payroll driver developed from report RPCALCx0, a country-specific payroll accounting system requires a specific accounting schema. This schema defines the steps to be performed by the payroll driver. In particular, the schema ensures that all information required by the payroll driver is available for calculating an employee's pay in a specific payroll period.

Table 5.1 lists the payroll driver reports for payroll accounting and their standard accounting schemas.

Table 5.1   Country-Specific Payroll Driver Reports and Schemas

Country	Report	Schema
USA	RPCALCU0	U000
Belgium	RPCALCB0	B000
Denmark	RPCALCM0	M000
Germany	RPCALCD0	D000
German civil service	RPCALCD0	D1KA
France	RPCALCF0	F000
Great Britain	RPCALCG0	G000
The Netherlands	RPCALCN0	N000
Austria	RPCALCA0	A000
Switzerland	RPCALCC0	CH00
Spain	RPCALCE0	E000
All other countries	RPCALCx0	X000

The country identifier appears in the schema and toward the end of the report program name. The payroll driver and the accounting schema carry out a gross and a net calculation of pay.

The schema goes through an initialization procedure before beginning the actual gross calculation of pay of each employee's data in turn. When the net calculation is completed, the schema might encounter an end-of-selection statement, which holds the results so that further processing of data can take place after payroll accounting.

The gross calculation of pay section of the accounting schema entails six steps linked per employee:

1. Read basic data.
2. Read payroll account of the period last accounted.
3. Read time data.
4. Calculate the individual gross values.
5. Carry out factoring.
6. Cumulate gross amounts.

The net pay calculation of the accounting schema can be divided into a country-specific part and a general part:

- Country-specific calculation of insurance contributions
- Country-specific calculation of tax
- Transfers
- Cumulation of net amounts

An accounting schema carries out its task by calling a sequence of functions. Each function can access information, process it, or both. A function can call on a personnel calculation rule to manipulate a logically related selection from the information already assembled. Each rule can comprise several subordinate rules that, in turn, carry out a sequence of operations.

Consulting Payroll Files

The files P*nnnn* contain the personnel master records for each personnel number that has been entered online through infotypes. The *nnnn* placeholder stands for the infotype number in the HR database of master and time data.

The file PCL1, HR cluster 1, contains primary data originating from master and time data entries such as production time tickets or time events. The file PCL2, HR cluster 2, contains derived secondary data such as payroll results or time pairs, along with any generated schemas.

PCL1 and PCL2 are organized to form clusters in which related information can be stored in one record. This structure accelerates database access and reduces the storage requirements.

When the payroll driver is running, the P*nnnn*, PCL1, and PCL2 files can exchange information under control of the accounting schema.

The payroll driver uses internal tables to store data between processing steps:

- The temporary input table IT contains wage types that can be processed by functions or operations.

- The temporary output table OT contains wage types that have been processed until the end of a processing step, when they're stored in table IT.

- The permanent results table RT in cluster RX of PCL2 at first contains the results of the previous accounted period loaded to the old results table ORT.

The results of a processing step are stored in the output table OT or the results table RT. At the end of a processing step, the data from the OT is loaded back into the IT, where it's available for further processing steps.

Using Valuation Bases on Wage Types

If a wage type is created by an entry to an employee's master data, the wage types will have values in the fields—the wage type will be valuated. For example, the AMT (amount) field will contain a monetary value, or the NUM (number) and RTE (rate) fields will contain values that can be multiplied to calculate the monetary value of the wage type.

By contrast, a time wage type will be written to the payroll driver with only the Number field, usually containing a number of hours. This number must be multiplied by a rate when the payroll is run. The value of this rate is determined in customizing for each wage type, such as basic pay, overtime, and holiday working.

The system of rates consulted during payroll accounting is called the *valuation basis*. The valuation basis can be related to the wage types alone or to the collective agreement. The valuation basis can also be related to the remuneration of the particular employee as indicated by his pay scale level.

Infotype 2010, Employee Remuneration Information, is provided so that unforeseen wage types can be entered in the system for premiums and bonuses for hazardous or unpleasant work, for example. If the employee has an entry in this infotype, it will be considered by the payroll in preference to the normal valuation bases.

A system of modifiers is available that can be used to control when a particular wage type is consulted. The personnel calculation rule also can include a control structure to implement the company policy on wage types.

More than one valuation basis can be consulted in situations such as Sunday working, which attracts a premium in addition to the premium for working on a public holiday.

Valuating Absences

There can be several ways of interpreting an absence recorded for an employee:

- An employee is on leave and is entitled to a leave allowance.
- An employee is ill for a long period of time. Certain country-specific criteria might affect the way in which the absence is valuated.
- An employee has taken unpaid leave. His pay must be reduced accordingly.

Absence valuation rules are defined in customizing by grouping absence types and subtypes from Absences infotype 2001. The following standard procedures can be used (in combination if necessary):

- An absence is valuated as if the employee had worked.
- Absences involve a reduction in pay calculated by factoring.
- An absence is valuated according to the average number of hours or days worked, or as a constant using a fixed amount.
- Special processing is triggered for certain absences.

Absence processing entails the following general steps:

1. Set payroll modifiers.
2. Import absences by using country-specific features.
3. Valuate the absences by using country-specific features.

Setting Payroll Modifiers

Function MOD in schema *XT00* provides an international calculation procedure for valuating absences that's used if no country-specific or country-grouping procedures are available.

N O T E   The *X* character is replaced by the country ID letter in the name of a specific schema, function, or personnel calculation rule. Table 5.1 illustrates this country letter nomenclature. ■

MOD calls personnel calculation rule XMOD, which uses operation MODIF A to define an employee grouping for absence valuation. This grouping is used to select an absence valuation rule from Valuate Absences table T554C.

The meaning and, hence, the labeling of the employee grouping is taken from personnel calculation rule XMOD, which can be customized. For example, you can use different employee groupings for absence valuation for hourly paid and salaried employees.

Importing Absences

When a personnel number is associated with an employee grouping for absence valuation, function RAB reads the absences recorded for the employee during the relevant period from records in Absences infotype 2001. Function RAB makes corresponding entries in Absences table AB. Each absence is assigned a work center split indicator, which might be needed if the employee changed work centers during the payroll period.

Recognizing Country-Specific Features when Importing Absences

A sickness absence, for example, can attract different payment rates according to its length. To account for this feature, an absence record can be split into smaller sections according to the legal specifications for the country. These absence splits are held in internal table AB.

Function XNAB can apply a different absence valuation rule to each section of the absence split. Function PAB subsequently uses the appropriate procedure to trigger valuation.

Although preliminary valuation has taken place, the actual amounts aren't finalized at this stage in the payroll accounting process because it might be necessary to apply monthly factoring.

The absence valuation rule initiates the following actions:

- Wage types are entered in OT.
- Time wage types are selected via the Time Wage Type Selection table (T510S) and entered in the internal time wage types table (ZL).
- Special processing is carried out, if specified.

A *bucket* is an information collector that's structured into number fields such as calendar days, absence days, and absence hours. These numbers are determined by reference to the employee's personal work schedule. The following buckets are associated with the listed counting classes:

NAU	Unpaid absences
NAP	Paid absences
NAX	Public holidays

Record layout fields are also copied to buckets from the line entries in Absences table AB. The following are examples of named record layout fields:

ABWAF	Public holidays in payroll period, days with day type > 0
ABWSF	Public holiday hours in payroll period, days with day type > 0

Valuating Absences by Averaging

If an employee takes paid leave, the rate per day for additions above basic pay can be calculated by averaging the overtime and bonus payments from the previous month.

Wage type data used to build average bases is accumulated in a "bonuses" bucket for each employee in each payroll period. For example, you can arrange to collect the number of working hours, the amount, or the rate associated with each wage type. The following wage types must be collected with the number of hours and amounts when forming average bases:

- Bonus for nightwork
- Bonus for holiday work
- Bonus for Sunday work

When absence valuation takes place, the number of payroll periods to be considered and which periods they should be must be specified in the formula used to calculate a rate for the collected bonuses wage types. The total amount of all wage types collected in the bonuses buckets for the designated periods is divided by the total number of working hours in the collected periods to arrive at a working hour rate. Alternatively, you could compute daily rates.

An employee's absence can now be assigned an allowance, in proportion to the length of the absence, based on an average bonus taken from this employee's records.

Absence valuation rules can be chosen to build average bases according to employee groupings such as all salaried employees, or according to groups of absence types such as paid leave. However, the allowance paid to the employee in accordance with the principle of averages will use the average bases for each individual employee and is employee specific.

Using Frozen Averages

Valuating absences by using frozen averages is an alternative to the normal method using the principle of averages. The allowance rate calculated by the principle of averages is stored and applied without recalculation for subsequent periods.

The duration of an employee absence determines when frozen averages are to be used.

Applying Factoring

Factoring entails calculating remuneration for an exact period using the pro rata principle. The remuneration will comprise primary wage types assigned to an employee as basic pay, recurring payments, or additional payments.

The principle uses of factoring are as follows:

- To reduce payments made to an employee because she joins, leaves, or is absent from the company during a period
- To calculate remuneration for an exact period because of substitutions, changes in basic pay, organizational reassignments, or changes in the personal work schedule
- To calculate cost accounting wage types for an exact period, such as the productive and unproductive constituents of payments for paid attendances and absences

Factoring is performed at the end of the gross part of payroll accounting and will follow country-specific personnel calculation rules for factoring. Normally, each situation requires a different factor. Standard factor calculations are provided from which customized variants can be created.

A factor is usually a value between 0 and 1. A factor of 1 signifies a whole period, and fractional values represent the portion of the period for which an employee is to receive a pro rata payment. The primary wage types for the employee are multiplied by the factor for the exact period.

The calculation of a factor for a specific period is controlled by a personnel calculation schema that can be programmed to take account of data in any of the following infotypes:

- Events 0000
- Organizational Assignment 0001
- Planned Working Time 0007
- Basic Pay 0008
- Recurring Payments/Deductions 0014
- Additional Payments 0015
- Absences 2001
- Substitutions 2003

The factoring schema calls a country-specific sub-schema to handle any non-standard calculation requirements.

Issuing Form P45 to an Employee Who's Leaving

After her final pay is calculated by the payroll, an employee about to leave must be given a form P45 that she will need when she applies for work again. RPCP45G0, Sample P45 Slip, is a report that can be run to prepare the P45 data for employees who are leaving. When this report runs, it will use batch input to update all Tax infotype 0065 records of the leavers.

The following steps issue a P45:

1. Select Human Resources>Payroll>Period-Unrelated>Payroll Extras>P45 Processing.
2. View the Report Selection screen for the Sample P45 Slip report (RPCP45G0).
3. Select the payroll period during which the employee's final pay was processed by payroll.
4. Enter or select the employee's personnel number.
5. Enter the details needed by the form.
6. Choose Execute.

The leaver's tax and pay information for the current tax year is printed in P45 format. New records in Tax infotype 0065 are created for them. These records contain an active P45 issued indicator and the date on which the P45 was issued.

The following steps print a dummy P45 without updating the employee's records:

1. Select Human Resources>Payroll>Period-Unrelated>Payroll Extras>P45 Processing.
2. View the report selection screen for the Sample P45 Slip report (RPCP45G0).
3. Select time period Other Period.
4. Enter the system's highest date (31.12.9999) in the To Date field.

5. Enter or select the employee's personnel number.

6. Enter the details needed by the form.

7. Choose Execute.

Administering Pensions

An employee might elect to join a pension scheme and have her contributions administered in payroll.

An employee's own pension scheme information is recorded in Pensions Administration infotype 0071. A fresh record has to be created if any changes occur. For example, an employee might change schemes or elect to make additional voluntary contributions (AVCs).

The different varieties of pension schemes are managed by establishing infotype subtypes. The following are examples of pension scheme subtypes:

- Percentage
- Mixed value
- Flat rate
- A pension scheme using bespoke calculations
- A specific company pension scheme

The system automatically generates an object ID for each scheme if an employee pays into more than one scheme. Onscreen, the Reference field contains the standard figures agreed for the scheme. The Actual column is used to record any values that the employee has arranged that vary from the Reference values. If an employee elects to make a different contribution, a new record must be created to alert payroll. If the payroll has already run for the period of the first altered contribution, the new record will trigger a retro-calculation.

Arranging a Mixed Value Pension Scheme

The mixed value scheme allows an employee's contribution to be adjusted according to his pay level:

- *Low*, in which the low range contribution is deducted if the employee earns less than the low amount
- *Medium*, in which the medium range contribution is deducted if the employee earns between the low and the high amounts
- *High*, in which the high range contribution is deducted if the employee earns more than the high amount

The following steps add an employee to a mixed value pension scheme:

1. Select Human Resources>Personnel Admin.>Maintain mAster Data.

2. Enter the employee's personnel number. Use the Matchcode function to find a number you don't know.

3. Select the Pensions Administration record (infotype 0071) by entering the infotype name or number in the Infotype field.

4. Select the Mixed Value subtype.

5. Choose the Create function and view the Create Pensions screen.

6. Enter the date from which the employee wants to join the scheme.

7. Overwrite the standard employer or employee contributions in the Actual field(s), if necessary.

8. Enter any regular AVCs the employee wants to make in the Supplements field.

9. Save your entries.

Arranging AVCs to a Pension

An employee might elect to make additional voluntary contributions to one or more pension schemes. The AVCs can be regular or ad hoc in their timing, and flat rate, percentage, or mixed in their value.

The details of regular AVCs can be entered in the Supplement field of the pension scheme to which they contribute. However, if the AVCs are likely to be irregular, it's probably best to create a so-called "dummy" scheme—one for each irregular contribution limited to the particular payroll period in which it's made.

The duration of a dummy scheme comprises the start and end dates of the relevant period. An actual amount should be entered. Any defaults suggested by the system must be deleted.

Processing Statutory Sickness Pay and Statutory Maternity Pay

SSP and SMP processing depends on identifying absences due to sickness or maternity and then evaluating them by reference to the rules for statutory sickness payments and statutory maternity payments. These calculations take place before the payroll run each period. They're controlled by the SSP and SMP Processing function, which is available in the Payroll Accounting menu for Great Britain.

SSP and SMP processing evaluates absences by using an employee's Qualifying Day Patterns (QDPs). A *qualifying day* is a day on which the employee should have worked. A QDP doesn't necessarily have to coincide with the employee's work schedule.

QDPs are defined and generated by using the Time Management Implementation Guide. They can also be displayed and updated from the Payroll menu.

The evaluation data produced by the SSP and SMP processing is used to update the absence calendar. The following infotype records for each employee are updated:

- Payroll Status (infotype 0003)
- SSP PIW Record (infotype 0085)

■ SSP/SMP Exclusions (infotype 0086)

■ SMP Record (infotype 0088)

SSP and SMP processing lists all employees processed and a detail screen. This complete list groups personnel numbers by employee subgroup and shows the number of SSP- and SMP-relevant absences. If you mark an entry and choose Select, the detail screen for that employee is shown.

The importance of the detail screen for an employee is that it shows how the Qualifying Day Pattern logic would affect the employee's entitlements if it were applied. Thus, the display acts as a simulation of SSP and SMP processing.

If an employee has an SSP Control record in infotype 0084, it will be consulted. Otherwise, the default Qualifying Day Pattern will be applied. At this stage no absence calendars or infotype records have been updated.

The data for the absence calendar is shown in calendar format so that you can see which SSP-relevant absences are waiting days or SSP payable days. The maternity absences are displayed according to whether they are SMP non-qualifying or payable days at upper or lower rates.

The infotype records that will be changed are listed individually with the new data that will be entered. Having seen what the effects will be, you can edit the records, if necessary. Provided the Update indicator was active when the processing took place, you can now choose Perform Update to have the entries posted.

Payroll consults the infotypes that have been updated by SSP and SMP processing. This will involve only a small proportion of employees, so it might be advisable to select only those for whom qualifying absences have been recorded in the period.

The absence calendar for an employee contains any SSP and SMP relevant absences for a particular employee. The following calendar formats can be viewed for each selected employee in turn, for several years if required:

■ *Weekly overview*, showing absences week by week for the whole year with SSP- and SMP-relevant days marked

■ *Monthly overview*, showing absences month by month for the whole year with SSP- and SMP-relevant days marked

■ *Yearly overview*, showing dates of all SSP- and SMP-relevant absences, differentiated by type of absence and the amount of SSP or SMP paid per week

Managing Business Trips

In this chapter

Managing Integrated Travel Expenses

The PA-TRV Travel Expenses module provides a seamless software system for managing business-related trips from application through approval, to update and correction, by means of retroactive accounting. The scope of the component includes domestic and business trips, in the home country and abroad, for individuals and groups.

The approach is standard SAP: maximize the integration between modules and components of the SAP R/3 system and any non-SAP connections; minimize the redundant storing of data.

The component is intended to be integrated with the SAP R/3 system in an open system architecture—UNIX, for example. It can also be used as part of SAP R/2 systems on mainframe hosts. The PA-TRV Travel Expenses component can also be used as an output interface to external systems.

The following SAP R/3 modules and components are normally installed and configured before the PA-TRV Travel Expenses component is set to work:

- FI-Financial Accounting
- CO-Controlling
- CO-OM Overhead Cost Control
- HR-Human Resources

HR Travel Management is the title of a fully integrated system in which various modular components can be installed and configured as required. The intention is to offer a system for managing business trip expenses from initial travel request through to financial accounting, with provision for subsequent corrections and retroactive accounting as necessary.

The traveling person or another staff member can enter the data. The data can be recorded before or after the trip. When a travel request is entered, the system automatically creates a workflow structure that simplifies the subsequent administration of the trip details.

Each type of business will have its own type of business trip; each employee may have particular requirements; certainly, each country visited will have its particular regulations that must be observed. All these particulars can be entered at the time or predefined so that they can be suggested by the system as default values, to be edited if necessary.

Bearing in mind that the purpose of business data processing is to make businesses more profitable and that routine work can be tedious and prone to error, it is expected that a travel management program should offer at least the following facilities:

- Automatically calculate tax
- Automatically process credit card transactions for a particular trip
- Accept receipts in any currency
- Accept supplementary receipt information
- Provide long-term optical archiving of travel receipts

- Marshal travel costs according to such classifications as employee, trip destination, and receipt
- Allocate expenses to numerous account assignment objects, such as cost center, order, project, or cost object
- Reimburse costs incurred during a trip
- Select payment methods such as payroll accounting, accounts payable accounting, or data medium exchange

These facilities are the basic requirements for an integrated travel expenses management system.

Identifying the Components of PA-TRV Travel Expenses

The TRV module of PA comprises three groups of functions:

- *Basic version* provides the transactions, forms, and evaluation tables needed to carry out travel expense accounting in accord with the tax law of the country in which the R/3 system is installed.
- *Cost distribution* allows the component to redistribute travel costs from the employee level to such cost objects as trip, receipt or cost type, or stopover.
- *International supplements* allow variations of the basic evaluation procedure according to the requirements of other nations.

The supplements for tax calculations and country-specific payroll calculations are organized according to the divisions of the INT-International Development module:

- IN-APA Asian and Pacific Area
- IN-EUR Europe
- IN-NAM North America
- IN-AFM Africa/Middle East
- IN-SAM South America

Using Basic Version Functionality

The functions of the basic version component can be grouped as follows:

- Lump-sum accounting, where the amounts are taken from standard rates regardless of the expenditure actually incurred
- Representation of company regulations
- Procedures and administration

The following features support lump-sum accounting:

- Lump-sum accounting for accommodations, meals, and commuting costs
- Itemizing per invoice as accommodations, meals, commuting costs, business entertainment, or incidental costs
- Trip itemization and lump-sum accounting
- Reduction of lump sums and maximum amounts by predefined adjustments for active or passive business entertainment events

The PA-TRV Travel Expenses component affords flexible arrangements for recording and automatically applying the rules and customs of the individual company:

- Definition of permitted circumstances via table entries
- Reduction of the daily rate for meals if a trip lasts less than one day
- Statutory trip types, errands, or business trips
- Trips with stopovers
- Round trips
- Special business trips with day excursions to different customer sites
- Company-specific regulations that apply to trips representing the company and may apply different rates according to the employee's status and according to the nature of the trip or the territory in which it's made
- Company-internal event trips, such as attending a seminar, attending a course, or a customer advisory service trip
- Trip-specific account assignment to company code, plant, cost center, order, or project
- Employee-specific overall proportional cost distribution to company code, plant, or cost center

The essential functions for managing overseas trips are grouped as follows:

- Automatic currency conversion
- Border crossing
- Foreign trips worldwide

The component supports a number of essential administrative procedures and facilities, such as the following:

- Application and approval procedures, trip approval notification at the planning stage, approval notification immediately before departure, advance of travel expenses, and cancellation of a trip
- Internal or external number range assignment for trip number
- Model trip plans, which can be edited
- Table-controlled statement per employee
- Interfaces to other SAP applications

- Day-specific accounting
- Special function keys to control fast data entry
- Short form of travel expense accounting procedures for external services

Interfaces to other SAP applications are established if the following applications are installed and configured:

- FI-Financial Accounting
- CO-Controlling
- CO-OM Overhead Cost Control
- HR-Human Resources and PA-PAY Payroll

Day-specific accounting is achieved by storing tax-free and company-internal refund rates in tables, which are also accessed to provide determination of additional amounts or income-related expenses.

Applying Cost Distribution Functionality

The organizing focus of the costs to be distributed can be an individual employee or a trip. If several employees go together on a trip, the total costs associated with the trip can be distributed, in equal shares for each employee, to the company code, plant, or cost center with which that employee is associated.

Another cost distribution variant available in this component is to allocate to each cost center, project, or order the deviation account value representing the difference between planned and actual costs of the trip.

You can also enter a percentage distribution structure for each trip and have it applied to the following item types to distribute the amounts to the appropriate company code, plant, cost center, order, or project:

- Total cost of the trip
- Costs pertaining to individual stopovers
- Individual travel expense receipts

You can also assign an individual expense receipt to a specific cost object and so prevent it from being distributed with the other expenses of the trip.

Each employee master record will include an infotype for cost distribution and an infotype subtype for travel expenses. Therefore, you can call for a display of the proportional overall cost distribution of an individual employee over a range of trips. You can see whether he or she tends to spend more money on one thing than another and how these priorities change over a succession of trips.

It may make sense to allocate a percentage distribution for planning purposes to the overall costs of a trip, which can then be assigned to cost centers (as an example). You can also separate the expenses of the individual stopovers and distribute one or more of them according to a percentage scheme.

Individual receipts can be distributed in proportion or in absolute amounts to the cost objects specified in your distribution plan.

Using International Supplements

International travel expense accounting may require additional information to be recorded and extra calculations to be performed.

Mileage distribution can be recorded for specific dates and the number of passengers, and luggage can be recorded on the basis of distance. Company lump sums can also be attributed on the basis of distance. Vehicle characteristics such as horsepower, engine capacity, and price can be recorded and taken into the valuations.

Mileage rates by country of destination can be applied. Cumulative miles covered by each employee can be recorded on a flexible time basis. Users can define mileage ranges over which lump-sum payments per mile can be specified.

The INT-International Development module can provide for lump-sum accounting for additional expenditure on meals under the following circumstances:

- Border crossing for inward and outward legs of trips
- Trip duration, which can be calibrated in calendar days, 24-hour periods, or times of day
- Days on which an employee is traveling for less than 24 hours, which can be evaluated according to the number of hours in transit or the time of day
- Lump sums and maximum amounts, which can be reduced on account of lunch coupons given out monthly

Certain trip activities can each attract a fixed lump sum, and all employee-specific travel expense regulations controlling travel privileges can be altered for each trip. Cash advances are deducted from subsequent payments.

Consulting Personnel Master Data

The following employee personnel data is required by the PA-TRV Travel Expenses component:

- Name of employee
- Organizational assignment—For example, to plant, cost center, or person in charge
- Travel privileges—For example, authorization to run an expense account and the particular internal regulations under which it may be operated
- Banking connection for direct payment

Reviewing the Travel Expenses Procedures

Central data recording can be used, or the travel expense procedures can be managed on a decentralized basis. Travel expense data recording without the submission of a prior application occurs in the following order:

1. Employee submits a travel expense claim form.
2. Data on the trip is checked and recorded.
3. The trip claim is approved.
4. Travel expense accounting action takes place in the PA-TRV Travel Expenses component.
5. Data is transferred to the FI-Financial Accounting module and to the CO-Controlling, CCA-Cost Accounting component.
6. The marked claim document is returned to the employee.

Your company may require prior approval of a trip and use this occasion to provide help with booking travel tickets and accommodation. The benefits of advanced travel expense planning may include the following opportunities:

- Coordination of the means of transport for several employees making trips
- Overview of travel and hotel usage patterns
- Discount negotiations on means of travel and hotel bookings
- Advance payments through the FI-Financial Accounting component to be credited to the employee's bank account or paid directly in cash or foreign currency

If the employee must obtain prior approval, the following steps are enacted:

1. Employee submits a travel expense claim form with a request for an advance.
2. Data on the trip is checked and recorded.
3. Trip advance payment is approved.
4. Travel expense planning action takes place in the PA-TRV Travel Expenses component.
5. Data is transferred to the FI-Financial Accounting module and to the CO-Controlling, CO-OM Overhead Cost Control component.
6. Trip advance is paid to the employee.
7. After the trip, the employee submits a record of the trip and the expenses incurred.
8. Data on the trip is checked and the records supplemented and updated.
9. Trip claim is approved.
10. Travel expense accounting action takes place in the PA-TRV Travel Expenses component.
11. Data is transferred to the FI-Financial Accounting module and the CO-Controlling, CO-OM Overhead Cost Control component.
12. Marked claim document is returned to employee.

A development of this travel expense procedure is to have the employee enter the data to which the central facility applies the checking and financial actions.

Processing Trip Data

A single trip—from a short-distance errand to a long-distance business trip to a complex trip abroad—can be processed for individual employees. The following choices are offered if you want to review the documents on previous trips:

- Trip period
- Trip destination
- Customer
- Processing status of the trip

You can use any of these search specifications to locate a previous trip to copy as the basis for a new trip.

Creating a Trip

The system will require your personnel number and a trip schema, unless you opt to copy a previous trip. A *trip schema* is an instrument for controlling the sequence of screens. You can create a new trip schema or edit the table that contains a standard trip schema.

Data entry is required under the following headings:

- Beginning/ending time and date of trip
- Trip destination
- Number of domestic and foreign miles driven
- Number of passengers for calculating the passenger lump sum
- Lump-sum accounting for meals
- Number of overnight stays with lump-sum accounting
- Cost center for travel expense account posting if this isn't to be the master cost center for the employee
- Trip activity types, such as seminar, customer visit, and so on
- Border crossing on return trip

Entering Individual Receipts

Trip receipts relevant to accounting are recorded. Each is assigned an expense type key that determines the FI-GL General Ledger account to which expense receipts are to be posted. The keys and their associated FI-GL General Ledger accounts can be established to suit your company. This normally takes place during customizing.

These keys can also be used for statistical summaries of standard and user-defined travel expense types.

Foreign currency can be entered on the trip receipt along with the exchange rate. The system can provide a default exchange rate and, if necessary, a default currency identifier based on the trip destination.

Recording Business Entertainment

If an employee is invited to a meal for business reasons, the lump-sum payable for meals on that day is reduced by an amount determined by a predefined table. The maximum travel expense amount is also reduced. The default entry for every day assumes that there is to be no deduction of travel expenses for business entertainment received.

Documenting Advances

Entries on a trip with the status of Travel Expense Application and that concern advances are evaluated by the PA-PAY Payroll program and the FI-Financial Accounting system. If the advance is approved, the employee will receive it in the next payment run.

If an advance is approved for payment in cash, that amount has to be posted to a specific vendor or customer account. Each employee to receive an advance must be represented as a vendor so that the financial accounting procedures will assign the advance to the correct accounts. The cash advance claim serves as documentation for this posting.

The exchange rate is entered automatically when the currency is identified. The rate may be changed manually at any time, which leaves a change record in the system.

Advances can be refunded in the same manner.

Noting Stopovers

In addition to the main destination, one or more stopovers may be entered, with their exact times of entry and departure.

Maximum amounts for travel expense claims and the lump sum or blanket allowances for meals and accommodation are determined from predefined tables for each country. The 24-hours rule is applied: Standard rates and individual receipts are assigned for each day of a trip according to the last country the person was in before midnight, local time.

Effecting Mileage Distribution

Passenger allowance to an employee is payable on the miles actually traveled by the passenger. The function allows this to be recorded in preparation for distribution to the cost objects. Mileage per employee is cumulated in this function.

Assigning Trip Texts

Text can be assembled from standard text elements or written freeform through the SAPscript word processing facility. It can be used for two-way communication between the travel expenses accounting office and the employee, and as additional documentation for trip activities. The format and printing destination depend on the purpose of the text.

Maintaining Trip Status

The Trip Status maintenance screen offers a choice of status indicators. Which of them are open to alteration depends on the user's authorizations and the stage reached in the trip travel expenses transaction sequence. The following possibilities are offered as standard:

- Approval status—Application, Application Approved, Trip Occurred, Trip Approved
- Accounting status—Open, For Accounting—To Be Settled, Canceled

Function keys control the recording of trip status data. If the accounting status is Open, there will be no accounting action, but changes to the document will be stored. If the status combination is Approved and For Accounting—To Be Settled, the trip is settled on the next billing run.

Using Fast Entry

Fast entry allows you to enter several domestic trips for one employee in the same transaction.

Each trip in a multitrip fast entry is assigned an internal trip schema that controls the trip number allocated and marks the trip as domestic. For a trip lasting more than one day, you must enter the starting and finishing dates and times. All other trip data is entered on the line for the beginning date. The following fields will be filled by the system with default values:

- Area—The area to which the employee is normally assigned
- Errand or Business Trip—The distance of the destination
- Status—Defaults on entry or when a detail is changed to Trip Approved—To Be Settled, on the assumption that the travel expense claim is being submitted after the trip takes place

To postpone a trip, you can change the date fields.

A Copy function is provided to accelerate entering several one-day trips for the same employee.

The system prints for each employee a list of the trips that have been validated and settled.

Trip Accounting

The accounting period for travel expenses can be user defined. The normal choices are weekly, every two weeks, or monthly.

If an error is detected during a travel expense accounting run, the cause of error is logged and corrections have to be made by the User Travel Accounting department.

Settlement is carried out only if the status of the trip document indicates that the travel expense application is approved and the trip is to be settled or, in the case of a planned trip, the trip is approved and is to be settled—for instance, by paying an advance to the employee. The settlement action normally includes the following processes:

- Conditions are accessed to determine the calculation procedures to be followed according to the country of destination, the area, the refund class or group, and any deductions to be incurred.
- Lump-sum charges and maximum charges are determined.
- The refund, tax-free, and additional amounts are calculated.
- Adjustments are made to take account of the duration of the first and last days of the trip.

Using Standard Forms

Two standard forms are provided as suggestions for printing the results of a trip settlement transaction for the employee's benefit:

- Detailed statement
- Condensed statement

Control of the printing of the standard forms is affected by reference to SAP R/3 tables, to which you have access in order to manipulate the form and content of the printed statements.

Each day for which meals were taken is evaluated separately. The lump-sum accounting for accommodations, meals, and commuting expenses for each main destination or stopover is displayed first. Then follows the accounting data for the individual receipts.

The condensed statement is particularly useful for external service employees who make the same trip every day; it allows you to present the accounting results of many standard trips in compact form.

Entering Data with the Trip Costs Personnel Event

A *personnel event* a presentation of selected infotypes that facilitates comprehensive and accurate data entry. In particular, the trip costs personnel event is designed to generate a mini-master record, which can be adjusted automatically to suit the requirements of the context in which the trip costs are being entered.

A personnel master record for the traveling employee normally exists in PA, although it's possible to create master records from the Trip Costs component.

Infotype 0017, travel privileges, specifies which kinds of travel document this employee is allowed to enter. It also stores the reimbursement amounts needed by the accounting program.

Every trip must be assigned to a master account. Therefore, an employee must be assigned to a cost center before entering trip data. The following alternative methods affect this assignment if it hasn't already been determined:

- Enter a cost center for the employee in the organizational assignment infotype 0001
- Enter a cost center for the employee in the travel privileges infotype 0017
- Enter a cost center for the employee in the costs assignment, infotype 0001, subtype 02

If the employee is to be paid throughbank via the data medium exchange, the particulars have to exist in the system as a record in the bank details infotype 0009.

The trip costs (mini-master record) personnel event presents the infotypes for data entry in the following order:

- Create event (infotype 0000)
- Personal data (infotype 0002)
- Create organizational assignment (infotype 0001)
- Travel privileges (infotype 0017)
- Create addresses (infotype 0006)
- Create bank details (infotype 0009)
- Communication credit card number (infotype 0105, subtype 0011)

If necessary, the following steps create a new employee by using personnel event trip costs (mini-master):

1. Choose Human Resources>Trip Costs.
2. Choose Environment>Personnel Events.
3. Assign a personnel number, if relevant, or accept the number if one is provided by the system.
4. Assign a beginning date.
5. Select the event type trip costs (mini-master).
6. Fill in the Personnel Area, Employee Subgroup, and Employee Group fields.
7. Choose the Choose function and view the Create Events screen (infotype 0000).
8. Verify any data found.
9. Change or supplement the data, if necessary.
10. Save your entries.
11. Enter the data needed step by step in the following screens.
12. Save.

Maintaining Master Data for PA Trip Costs

Trip cost management data is held in the following infotypes:

- Organizational assignment (infotype 0001)
- Personal data (infotype 0002)
- Addresses (infotype 0006)
- Bank details (infotype 0009)
- Travel privileges (infotype 0017)

The following steps present the chosen infotype and let you update the personnel master data records for an employee:

1. Choose Human Resources>Trip Costs.
2. Choose Environment>Maintain Master Data.
3. Enter the employee's personnel number.
4. Select the relevant infotype.
5. Choose Edit>Change or the Change function.
6. If no data is entered for this infotype, you must create a data record. To do so, choose Edit>Create or the Create function.
7. Change or supplement the data.
8. Save.

A similar sequence is used to reach the Display function if you don't intend to alter trip costs infotype data.

Automatic Setup of Vendor Master Records from PA Trip Costs

To account imbursements of trip costs, each employee must be entered as a vendor with a vendor master record. As of R/3 release 3.0D, a batch input session can be initiated to create person-specific vendor master records for each employee. This allows posting and payment of trip costs in financial accounting. With R/3 releases before 3.0D, vendor master records are created and maintained manually in FI-Financial Accounting, separate from HR master data.

The system consults a reference vendor master record and uses it as a model to generate a person-specific vendor record containing information taken from the following infotypes in HR:

- Infotype 0000 (events)
- Infotype 0001 (organizational assignment)
- Infotype 0002 (personal data)
- Infotype 0006, subtype 1 (permanent residence)
- Infotype 0009, subtype 0 or 2 (bank details)

Using Preliminary Entry of Trip (PET) Costs

If you have access to a PC, laptop, or notebook computer, you can use the PET program to carry out preliminary trip cost entries. The results are preliminary because they've yet to be posted to an R/3 system.

Effecting Payment for Travel Expenses

There are several methods of effecting payment for travel expenses. It may take place along the channels of the SAP R/3 integrated system or via a standard interface to a non-SAP system.

Paying via the FI-Financial Accounting System

Transfer of trip data to vendors or customer accounts for settlement of the travel expenses of an employee making a trip to their plant, or elsewhere on their behalf, can take place at varying time intervals.

If a trip that has been posted is subsequently changed, the differences are posted. If additional amounts occur, they have to be transferred to PA-PAY Payroll.

Paying via PA-Payroll

All travel expenses relating to trips that are fully entered and evaluated are paid out on the next payroll run.

Paying via External Non-SAP Financial Accounting or Payroll Accounting Systems

The programs to effect a transfer will have been configured to access the external systems, so you can directly access the travel expense accounting results database or a predefined sequential data set, depending on the system.

Paying via the DME-Data Medium Exchange

The DME provides a fully configured means of paying from the PA-TRV Travel Expenses component.

Evaluating Trip Data

Three points of view have to be taken into consideration when evaluating trip data:

- The maximum tax-free lump sum and maximum amounts legally refundable by the employer
- The travel expense regulations and practices established in your company
- The amounts to be billed

There are three significant amounts to be billed:

- The amount that can be refunded tax-exempt to the employee under the legal regulations in force at the time
- The amount actually refunded by the company to the employee
- The amount that can be debited to other accounts

An *additional amount* is defined as an amount paid to an employee over and above what's legally refundable free of tax. This additional amount is included in payroll accounting and may attract tax deductions in the normal way.

If the amount refunded is less than the amount that can be refunded tax-exempt, the difference can be taken into account when claiming income-related expenses in the annual wage tax adjustment.

The tables used to evaluate trip expenses contain the dates when regulations come into force. If such a change takes place during a trip, the differences can be computed automatically.

The PA-TRV Travel Expenses component offers the following evaluation variants:

- Lump-sum amounts valid on the first day of a trip are valid throughout the trip.
- The lump-sum amounts valid on the last day of a trip are applied throughout the trip.
- The evaluation refers to the lump-sum amounts valid for each day of the trip.

Representing Company-Specific Regulations

Trip travel expense data can be evaluated by a combination of two standard methods available in the PA-TRV Travel Expenses component:

- Employees are assigned to refund levels valid for all their trips.
- Each trip is assigned to an area, which is an accounting instrument defined to suit your company's requirements.

For example, employee-specific lump sums and maximum amounts are defined according to the refund level to which the employee is assigned. The refund class or refund group may define the level at which the accommodations and meals are refunded. Vehicle regulations specific to your company may be specified by the refund class or group.

The area method of representing company-specific regulations can be used to apply differential rates in the following example circumstances:

- Additional allowance for trips to capital cities
- Trips between different company sites
- Seminar attendance

If an employee works for several company codes or plants, there is an indicator in the specification of his or her travel privileges, so that the travel expenses can be distributed and posted appropriately.

Area and Vehicle Regulations

Tables are used to set up area and vehicle regulations that specify the amounts refundable for different vehicle classes and travel expense areas. The effect is to impose logical conditions, as in the following examples:

- If an employee is entitled to refunds under regulation A, the basic mileage rate is $x; under regulation B, it's $y.

- The regulation A exception mileage rate for trips to Area 1 is $x + 10%; for trips to Area 2, it's $x + 5%.

- The regulation B exception mileage rate for trips to Area 1 is $y + 8%; for trips to Area 2, it's $y + 4%.

Accommodations and Meals

Tables are also used to specify the allowances for accommodations and meals, in order to award different amounts according to the regulation associated with the employee's refund group. Again, there can be any number of exceptions to the basic rates that are to be applied if the trip destination is in an area that attracts different accommodations and meals refund lump sums.

Using a Cash Office to Pay Advances

The cash office can pay the approved amount as an advance of travel costs and make a manual entry to post the advance to financial accounting. After the trip, the advance paid is entered in the trip data to provide a history record by using the Maintain function. The cash office indicator should be set to identify the method of payment.

When this document is saved, certain fields are blocked for further entry to assist in auditing. The advance data can be subsequently changed only by adding further advances. However, this posting could trigger a second posting of the amount to financial accounting, were it not for the control feature TRVCT, which must be set to ensure that the trip advance amount is used purely for statistical purposes.

When the trip data is entered, approved, and accounted, the trip expenses are posted to financial accounting with the trip accounting results.

During the next payment run in financial accounting, the relevant accounts are balanced and the remaining trip costs are reimbursed to the employee by bank.

If the cash office making an advance creates a travel request by using the Advance Data Entry function, the system automatically assigns the cash office indicator, approves and accounts the travel request, and posts the document to financial accounting.

When the trip data is finalized after the trip, it's added to the travel request, which is then saved with the status of Trip Completed.

Paying Advances by Financial Accounting

Rather than make a payment from a cash office, you can record the advance on a receipt document when the travel request is created. Payment then takes place in the next payment run. Later, the trip data is added to the travel request and the trip expenses are balanced against the advance so that a settlement of the difference can be made.

Paying Advances with Data Medium Exchange

If an advance is entered manually without a cash office indicator, the amount will be paid by using the DME-Data Medium Exchange program.

It's also possible to pay an advance from a cash office and subsequently settle the balance of trip expenses by payment through the Data Medium Exchange program.

The various arrangements for managing trip expense advances are controlled by feature TRVPA, which is set up during customization. This feature also determines how the system controls the creation and processing of travel requests. For example, switch WRC in TRVPA decides whether a weekly report must be posted during a trip.

The details of your company's trip accounting policies can be read into the system by *user exits*, which are programmed functions designed to accommodate requirements that can't be achieved by normal customizing.

For each data table there is a routine that allows users to prepare the system for reading the data. There's also a corresponding routine that can be used to provide interpretations of the table's fields after the company-specific data is loaded. In particular, the interpretation routines normally determine which wage type for posting is to be assigned for each type of trip expense.

The following trip data tables are available with their corresponding routines:

T706A	Deductions
T706B	Trip expense types
T706D	Default values for dialog
T706F	Travel costs
T706H	Meals/Time
T706L	Country; country group assignment
T706M	Input tax for international per diems
T706P	Miles accumulation periods
T706S	Trip schema
T706U	Accommodations
T706V	Meals

Maintaining the Authorization Object for HR Trip Data

An *authorization object* lists a maximum of 10 authorization fields. The authorization objects are listed in table TOBJ.

All the authorization fields existing in any authorization object are defined with their attributes in table AUTHA in the repository.

An authorization object becomes an authorization when some or all fields are assigned values.

Several authorizations for an object can be collected in one global authorization. A *profile* is a list of authorization objects with the corresponding authorizations (or global authorizations).

A user's authorizations for the various authorization objects in the SAP system depend on the profiles assigned to the user in the user master record. The authorization object for HR Business Trip Management is called P_TRAVL and consists of the following authorization fields:

BUKRS	Company code
AUTHS HR-REISE	Status new when trip is saved
AUTHF HR-REISE	Operation and Status old
AUTHP HR-REISE	Personnel number check
KOSTL	Cost center
PERSG	Employee group
PERSK	Employee subgroup
VDSK1	Organizational key
WERKS	Personnel area
PTZUO	Employee grouping for business trip management

Administering the Personnel Planning and Development Modules

Planning Human Resource Requirements

In this chapter

Introducing the PD-Personnel Planning and Development Module

Personnel planning determines who is required to perform a job or task and when they are needed. *Personnel development* makes sure that the aspirations of the personnel planners can be realized by selecting suitable applicants who have the broad educational qualifications and specific training requirements that ensure sufficient suitable staff will be available to do the jobs when they're required.

The functionality of the PD-Personnel Planning and Development module is serviced by the following standard business program components:

- PD-OM Organization and Planning
- PD-WP Workforce Planning
- PD-PD Personnel Development
- PD-RPL Room Reservations Planning
- PD-SCM Seminar and Convention Management

The integrated system is also referred to as the HR Planning System. Some components can be used in the standalone mode.

N O T E As R/3 software has developed, the earlier SAP convention of using a letter code ID for the minor components has been abandoned in favor of naming a component in full to avoid misinterpretation. ▨

The SAP standard business software in the Human Resources domain is under continuous development as this aspect of business grows in complexity and becomes ever more critical as the productivity of individual workers is increased by technological improvements in production and communication methods.

The business activities addressed by the PD-Personnel Planning and Development Module include the following:

- Organization and Planning (the basic component)
- Workplace and Job Description
- Applicant Data Administration
- Applicant Screening
- Qualifications and Requirements
- Career and Succession Planning
- Workplace and Job Grading
- External Training Administration
- Education and Training Administration
- Education and Training Planning

- Manpower Planning I (Long-Term)
- Manpower Planning II (Short-Term)
- Cost Planning
- Personnel Assessment and Trend Procedures

Planning a Workforce with the PD-WP Component

The PD-WP component is available to manage the details in installations where a very large volume of processing is entailed in job and workplace specification. Where this component is installed and configured, your displays of job charts and staffing schedules indicate how you can evaluate the supplementary job information when you need it.

The component makes available a wide range of data and evaluative processing, which can be initiated in the context of the PD-Personnel Planning and Development module. This area of Human Resources management is under continuous research and development as the nature of work undergoes evolutionary and sometimes revolutionary changes. Job evaluation methods must be elaborate to track these developments.

The following sections illustrate some additional functions provided by the PD-WP Workforce Planning component.

Planning Compensation

Pay scale groupings or absolute amounts can be stored—precisely or in ranges of values—to be the planned compensation for any of the following job description elements:

- Workplace
- Job
- Position
- Task

Standard evaluations can be called to provide the following results:

- Planned monthly costs for each organizational unit
- Comparison of planned payments with actual costs

Using Job Description Supplements

Information can be stored on any job description elements regarding the following matters:

- Authorizations necessary to perform the task element or to change its specified task description
- Auxiliary elements of the job description not detailed in the main description of the job or task—for example, whether a specific qualification is required by law to do the job, or whether special equipment is used at a workplace

Maintaining Health Care Data

Medical histories can be entered against particular workplaces where, for instance, follow-up data has been collected on previous incumbents of jobs dealing with hazardous materials or processes. A workplace can be marked to indicate the requirement for preventive medical examinations at prescribed time intervals.

Applying Restrictions

Some jobs and workplaces require special protective clothing to be worn and therefore might not be suitable for persons who have difficulty wearing it. The workplace might be inaccessible or difficult to access by persons with certain disabilities. Some positions might be unsuitable for particular persons because of the hours worked or the types of activity performed. If a workplace has emergency exits that are difficult to access or hazardous emergency procedures, it might be unsuitable for certain persons. These matters have to be raised at some stage in the recruitment and appointment process.

Consulting Location Data

Although the location of a job in a workplace and the identification of the position or positions held there are matters documented in the central organization master data records, the supplementary records of the Workplace and Job Description component can be used to store additional information of importance:

- Building identification
- Room number
- Telephone number
- Fax number
- Network address
- Complete postal address

This location data is used to compile telephone and organization directories, for example.

Planning Working Hours

The planned working time, to any level of accuracy, can be stored as data attached to an individual workplace or position. If the position is filled, the PD-Personnel Planning and Development system can compare the planned working hours with the contractual working hours of the person appointed. When positions are summarized up to higher levels of the organizational structure, evaluations can be conducted not only on the basis of positions filled but also on the planned or actual working hours.

Assigning Persons to Groups

Certain personnel indicators can be used to establish person subgroup types into which individuals can be classified. Certain positions or workplaces can be reserved for persons in a specific person subgroup.

Some companies, for instance, reserve certain positions for hourly paid employees and others for those paid on a monthly basis. In some cases, certain positions are reserved for members of a particular trade union or for persons who are accredited members of a particular professional organization.

Assignment of a person to a person subgroup type can be determined by an SAP R/3 condition that specifies the logical relationships between two or more personal attributes, such as "Within a given age range" and "Charter member of the XYZ Institute."

Building Task Structures

The information stored about a task can be in the nature of a comment on the duties involved rather than a description of the steps or technical stages. For example, the task can be characterized in terms of the main function of the person holding the position:

- To plan the work of the section
- To check the work of other people in the section
- To perform the task personally

The overall function of the task can be documented in the task structure record:

- The purpose of this position is to provide a pleasant and efficient welcome to strangers visiting the plant for the first time.
- The function of this position is to make sure that no object or person enters the premises without leaving an adequate record of identity, purpose, and destination.
- The purpose of this position is to ensure that adequate records are kept securely of all materials of interest to the U.S. Customs Service that enter or leave the bonded warehouse.

Planning Human Resources

An organization is made up of organizational units, such as departments, teams, groups, and projects. It's displayed as an organizational chart.

Organizational units have jobs, with one job for each job title in the SAP R/3 classification. For example, secretary, programmer, and clerk are job titles for jobs. A job can have too much work for one person; there might be several positions for a job. There might be shift-working, which increases the number of positions to be filled for the same job, and there might be several equivalent positions for that job in each shift.

The arrangement of positions is represented by an organization diagram (*organigram*), which shows the conventional hierarchical organization chart, with the added feature that the number of positions at each job is also represented, usually graphically.

The scope of the HR-PD Personnel Planning and Development functions is illustrated by the following structures to which the planning procedures can be applied:

- Multiple reporting paths up and down the company hierarchy from any position selected on a display of an organization chart or organigram
- Organizational structure of any specific project
- Diversified responsibility organizations represented by the matrix methodology

Using HR Plan Versions and Status Control

When you allocate values to a structure of planning objects, you can be testing or simulating a tentative plan that you don't want to release for the moment, so you can store it as a plan version and retain control over its status. Changes can be effected only in a planning object with the status of "planned." Every planning object must pass through the following status stages:

- Planned
- Submitted
- Approved or rejected
- Active (in use)

Rejected data can be returned to the planned status for revision. You can also introduce other status control stages during customizing.

Creating Job Charts and Staffing Schedules

The system creates a job chart online—in the context of the SAP R/3 PD-Personnel Planning and Development module—in response to the entry of a search specification determining the scope of the items to be included in the chart. They can be tasks, jobs, or positions, and any displayed items can be selected as the subject for a drill-down operation in which you use the special function keys to direct the system to display particular attributes of the item selected. In this manner, you can access and alter any job data records to the extent that you have authority to do so.

A staffing schedule is an attribute of a job or, if the job entails several different positions, of a position. The following types of staffing schedule are recognized and supported by the SAP R/3 PD-Personnel Planning and Development module:

- The position can be held by two or more persons.
- The position can be held by one person or a substitute.
- The position can be held by two people simultaneously for a fixed period.

The first type of staffing schedule represents the situation in which a job is planned to exist at a position only if there's work to be done. The position can be vacant because no suitable person is available to do the job planned for it. If there's more work than one person can do, more than one identical position can be planned for the same job. If the work isn't enough for the number of positions occupied at the workplace, work can be shared based on the percentage of material or the number of hours worked.

If a person at a position is expected to be absent for a long period, a substitute person can be assigned to that position for the anticipated length of the absence. The substitute doesn't replace the person who is on long leave of absence.

Having two people occupying the same position can occur when one of them is seconded to the other for training. The trainee might be intended as the successor, or the intention might be to create a second identical position for the same job when the training is completed. This form of simultaneous occupancy is usually of fixed duration, although the end of training can depend on the trainee reaching a defined standard for a formal qualification or for an internal award that's recorded as some kind of "authority to operate unsupervised."

The staffing schedule data for the jobs you select for display will be generated automatically. The persons allocated to the positions on your display will be identified from the master records. Their personal details, where relevant, will be available from the personnel master records.

If one position on your display is determined to be vacant, you can call for the system to suggest suitable people based on their qualifications and personal profiles. The system will try to match the people available with the personal requirements specified for the vacant position. The system will operate with any set of personnel attributes that you define: formal qualifications, previous experience, geographical location, and so on.

This process is a planning activity and, as such, can take place within any time frame. You can ask for a person to fill a vacancy as soon as possible. For example, you might have an overload in a telephone sales function and be seeking someone who is in the building or on the computer network and who can be diverted from other work until the overload situation passes, or at least until an extra position is created and filled permanently.

On the other hand, you might be looking at the staffing schedule for a planning period in the future. In such cases, the system will offer you suitable people for the position who likely will be available when you plan to use them.

If the system can't locate any existing personnel who could be assigned to a position that you plan to have filled by some specified date in the future, the HR-Human Resources system will create a vacancy specification based on the information it has about the job. The processes of filling this vacancy from external sources or recruiting activities can then go ahead when this course of action is submitted for and granted approval.

All this automatic action depends absolutely on your having assembled an accurate job description.

Describing Jobs and Workplaces

The system accepts various conventions regarding the use of the concepts of jobs, tasks, and positions. This discussion won't seek to draw any firm distinctions between them.

SAP R/3 has a defined data object type designated as *task*. An SAP task is made up of any number of tasks and task complexes in any arrangement. The elements of this structure are task structures themselves or individual tasks. A *task structure* can comprise a block of tasks with no particular interrelationship except that they might have to be time-shared by the person holding the position. For example, the receptionist might have to operate the security procedures and the telephone switchboard and the visitors' coffee machine. Only the last would be regarded as a single task rather than a task structure.

For some workplace positions, there might be good reasons the job description should specify quantities or percentages allocated to the different tasks.

During the elaboration of a system of job descriptions for a newly designed work complex, it might be convenient to begin with a rather general job description that becomes progressively more detailed as the necessary information is revealed. During this process, it might become apparent where and on what basis one job should be allocated to more than one position. This approach is reasonable, and the SAP R/3 PD-Personnel Planning and Development module supports it flexibly.

The task descriptions at the lowest level of detail of a task structure can be merely titles that serve as references to a job procedure manual, or they might be rough descriptions of a job element that will be taught by an instructor or by someone who's doing the job already. In other cases, it might be legally required that the details of a task element be formally documented. The system will support all varieties of job description.

Administering Organizational Plans

The PD-OP Organization and Planning component develops actual and proposed personnel scenarios as models in which you can project the possibilities of downsizing, expansion, and corporate reorganization. When a model is built, it can be used to control the collation of information for reporting. The scenario and its associated data are referred to as an *organizational plan*.

Defining an Organizational Plan

The organizational plan is the fundamental structure in the PD module from which all its activities are structured. The organizational plan serves to collate the information necessary to present a complete and dynamic model of the company in the past, the present and, with assumptions, the future.

Although the minimum requirement for an organizational plan is simply the company's organizational structure, the following additional information can be included:

- Individual positions
- Reporting structure (chain of command) of the positions
- Types of jobs performed
- Work centers as physical locations where jobs and positions are carried out
- Different types of tasks performed

In addition to these plan components provided by PD, the following types of information can be associated with the plan if their parent applications are integrated with the PD module:

- Cost centers
- Employees
- Materials

Each information class is represented in an organizational plan by an object type. For example, there will probably be several objects of the type "work center." Each object will be linked in various ways to other objects in the organizational plan as a work center is linked to its parent department and to plant items such as tools needed for the work performed there.

A position can be defined by reference to a number of tasks or responsibilities. Tasks and positions can be linked to work centers. A position also can be linked to a named person who is the current holder.

These objects that appear in the organizational plan are each assigned a life span or validity period. Thus, a position's history can be compiled by listing the employees who held that position with the dates of their occupancies.

Because an object in an organizational plan must be linked, a plan can cover an entire global enterprise or be limited to any section of it. If the information is present in the database, the Human Resources Information System can be used to extract the plan objects for any substructure or selective subset of objects.

The following PD components are also based on organizational plans so that they can be used to control and report on an established plan:

- Personnel Costs
- Qualifications
- Career Planning
- Workforce Planning
- Training and Event Management

If information elements from any of these components are referred to by an organizational plan, the precise details can be maintained as a plan version.

Developing Organizational Plans

It's possible to develop an organizational plan by working on the details of single objects by using the appropriate infotypes. The data for all the relevant infotypes can be presented in list format. By contrast, the Simple Maintenance procedure handles an organizational plan as a tree structure so that objects can be created quickly and simply, although not all PD functions can be used in this method.

Structural Graphics is a system for developing an organizational plan using graphical objects that represent organizational plan objects on which you can also work in detail alongside the graphics presentation. Structural Graphics is discussed in Chapter 11, "Using the HR Information System."

Preparing an Organizational Plan

Building a successful and meaningful plan entails thorough investigation of the following aspects of the organization concerned:

- The organization structure
- How the different areas work together
- The different types, or categories, of jobs performed
- How many individual positions fall within the different job categories you've identified
- If your plan will use tasks, each task should have an intelligible task description
- Tasks routinely performed together should be cataloged as a task group
- If your plan will use work centers, determine any special restrictions or requirements associated with any of them

Identifying the Components of Organizational Plans

An organizational structure is created by documenting relationships in Relationships infotype 1001 between organizational units created previously. The structure might have the form of a hierarchy or a matrix.

Organigram is the name for a reporting structure or matrix management structure associated with an organizational plan to represent the chain of command or authority structure. Relationships infotype 1001 creates relationships between positions created previously. A matrix is distinguished from a hierarchy because the matrix contains at least one position that reports to more than one superior. If your organizational structure requires this feature, settings must be made in customizing.

A job index of the different jobs is developed by creating and maintaining the separate job records. A work center index is developed by creating and maintaining the separate work center records. A task catalog is developed by creating and maintaining the separate task records. Task groups are established by using Relationships infotype 1001 to link the separate tasks.

An organizational plan must contain at least one organizational unit, but there's no upper limit. The units can be subsidiaries, divisions, departments, groups, or special project teams. In fact, any identifiable entity can be an organizational unit, although companies usually want to choose units that perform a particular set of functions within the company.

The function or role of an organizational unit doesn't have to be permanent; a project team, for instance, will have its own life span.

Units can have their own cost centers or can be combined under a single cost center.

Infotypes Relevant for Organizational Units

When an organizational unit is created, a wide variety of infotypes is available to record and store the unit's details. The following standard infotypes might be needed for some or all of your organizational units:

- Object (1000)
- Relationships (1001)
- Description (1002)
- Department/Staff (1003)
- Account Assignment Features (1008)
- Work Schedule (1011)
- Cost Planning (1015)
- Standard Profiles (1016)
- PD Profiles (1017)
- Site-Dependent Info (1027)
- Address (1028)
- Mail Address (1032)
- Sales Area (1037)
- Work Schedule/Shift Group (1039)
- Override Requirement (1040)

Separating Jobs and Positions

A job is defined in SAP R/3 by the records that have been created in the following infotypes:

- Object (1000)
- Relationships (1001)
- Description (1002)
- Department/Staff (1003)
- Planned Compensation (1005)
- Vacancy (1007)
- Authorities/Resources (1010)
- Work Schedule (1011)
- Employee Group/Subgroup (1013)
- Obsolete (1014)
- Cost Planning (1015)
- Standard Profiles (1016)
- PD Profiles (1017)
- Address (1028)
- Mail Address (1032)

The Chief Executive Officer is the only person with the job of that name, but many other jobs can be held by more than one person.

Not all infotypes for a job have to be completed in full. For example, you could enter a long-text description of the job. You also could link jobs with work centers and tasks to create a more detailed job description. Recording the job's cost to the company might be helpful.

As soon as you identify a person as a holder of a specific job, all the infotype data on that job will be associated automatically with that person. The person "inherits" the job's infotype settings, attributes, and properties.

The normal way to create a position is to take a copy of the job—its job specification—and attach it to a position so that it can be edited to redefine any particular aspects of that job as it's performed at that position.

N O T E The system lets you create a position without referring to the job to be performed there, but the experts advise against it because you could generate a vacancy that would be impossible to fill because the work to be performed had not been defined. ■

There are some shortcuts. For example, if several positions entail the same set of tasks, these tasks are best linked to a job you have perhaps invented for the purpose. This job can then be associated with each position without having to assign the tasks to each position individually. Then you can proceed to add other tasks or jobs to each position to define its unique characteristics.

Jobs can be associated with particular work centers, and tasks can be specified for each work center. This will locate the task in the plant and possibly identify the equipment used.

A well described and defined job can be a useful element in building an operational definition of a qualification. Records in the Qualifications infotype are used to record jobs of this kind.

A *position* is an object in an organizational plan and a named assignment in a company, such as CEO and head gardener. A plan can refer to any number of positions.

A reporting structure (chain of command) is defined when you specify relationships between positions. You expect to find that a finished organizational plan shows that everyone reports to somebody. Some positions, such as junior gardener, might have no other positions reporting to them.

Some functions are associated with positions that require specific infotype records to exist. For example, a Vacancy infotype record must exist for a position if PD's Personnel Costing module is going to refer to it. The Cost Planning infotype must also be maintained, either for the position itself or for the job performed there.

When it comes to the operation of maintaining a position, there are three possibilities:

- ■ *Detail Maintenance*, in which each infotype is maintained individually
- ■ *Simple Maintenance*, in which the tasks and jobs of a position are maintained under the control of a simple hierarchy
- ■ *Structural Graphics*, in which the detailed maintenance formats are available in synchrony with a comprehensive system of graphical tools (this is described in Chapter 11)

Using Reporting Structures with an Organizational Plan

A system of reports arranged as a hierarchy is automatically available to extract information that's identified in an organizational plan. However, the reporting structure can be arranged to meet the needs of the organization it's documenting. The report structures don't have to mimic the organizational structures.

Most firms want to be able to see who reports to whom and how the command chains are deployed. A matrix management structure is available to handle complex relationships between positions and managers. The structural graphics technology is particularly helpful in depicting the various structures in a company and the reports that can be collated on them.

Structuring the Chain of Command

The obvious way of mapping the chain of command, or the delegation of responsibility, is to follow the organizational structure. Head Office controls subsidiaries who control departments and so on. Another possibility is to have a reporting structure that relates to particular business interests, which might be the customer groupings or even the individual orders where these are large and complex.

The PD facilities allow the organizational plan to use any combination of methods. For example, "relationship A/B 002" is an entry in the Relationships infotype that signifies that there's a relationship between the organizational units and the leading position of each unit. A section's head is explicitly related to that section.

A report is assembled by following an evaluation path through the relevant records. If you ask for a report based on the chain of command, an evaluation path mapped to this chain must be available.

A chain of command can be represented by using disciplinary relationships:

- *Relationship A 002*, between position X and position Y, signifies that the holder of X reports to the holder of Y.
- *Relationship B 002*, between position Y and position X, signifies that the holder of Y supervises the holder of position X.

A non-disciplinary reporting structure, such as a technical association, can be represented as follows:

- *Relationship A 005*, between position X and position Y, signifies that the holder of X reports to the holder of Y in a non-disciplinary sense.
- *Relationship B 005*, between position Y and position X, signifies that the holder of Y supervises the holder of position X in a non-disciplinary sense.

The Detailed Maintenance procedure enters and maintains chain-of-command information or non-disciplinary reporting relationships at this level.

The Simple Maintenance procedure accepts two positions and automatically infers or suggests the appropriate Relationships infotype entries.

Developing Matrix Management Structures

The matrix management structure represents the reporting situation in which one position reports to more than one supervisory position, possibly from separate areas of the company. There might be several separate types of relationship, for example:

- Disciplinary relationships
- Subject-matter relationships
- Geographical authority relationships

Normally, there won't be a complex matrix on disciplinary matters, even if there's a complex interaction in technical or project activities. If you call for a list of relationships that exist for selected positions, the display will show all types of active relationships. This information will be gathered from records in Relationships infotype 1001.

Using Work Centers in an Organizational Plan

A *work center* can be a physical workstation with a specific set of tools and equipment that handles only a certain type of material. Several such workstations can be represented in the records as a single work center. A work center can also define an organizational or geographical selection from the physical locations of your company, such as a plant or all the premises in a specific region.

There are no limits to the ways in which you define or describe a work center. For example, you might want to record accessibility for disabled persons. You could require an annual eyesight test for position holders at a certain work center.

The following infotypes are available for describing the significant characteristics of a work center:

- Object (1000)
- Relationships (1001)
- Description (1002)
- Planned Compensation (1005)
- Restrictions (1006)
- Health Examinations (1009)
- Authorities/Resources (1010)
- Work Schedule (1011)
- Employee Group/Subgroup (1013)
- Obsolete (1014)
- Cost Planning (1015)
- Address (1028)
- Mail Address (1032)

One way in which work centers are used is to build a job description by using Relationships infotype 1001 to link particular jobs, tasks, and work centers. The job performed in an identified work center will specify the job classification, and the tasks listed for the job will particularize the types of duties carried out there.

Defining Tasks

SAP Business Workflow can use the concept of a task to refer to the activities of more than one person; for example, a team can jointly perform a task. However, the HR system uses the PD module to support the concept of a task as a defined activity carried out by a single person, although many people might separately perform a similar task. Thus, different types of tasks are differentiated by these codes:

TS	Standard task, predefined in the system
T	Task, defined by the user organization in customizing
WF	Workflow task
WS	Workflow templates

All these task types are available in SAP Business Workflow, but HR uses only standard tasks (TS) and tasks (T).

Within the context of HR, a *task* is defined as an individual duty, a set of responsibilities, or an assignment. There's no limit to the complexity of a single task. There can be as many tasks as necessary.

Selections of defined tasks can be used in defining jobs and positions through Relationships infotype 1001. Tasks can also be used in PD's Qualifications module. However, it's not necessary to define tasks at all, although it might be convenient, because a defined task can be used to focus related information defined as task attributes in the following PD infotypes:

- Object (1000)
- Relationships (1001)
- Character (1004)
- Standard Profiles (1016)
- PD Profiles (1017)

A *task group* is a collection of conveniently associated tasks, perhaps because they're usually performed by the same person. A task group can be used to quickly relate many tasks to a job or to a position.

The relationships between tasks are portrayed in the Task Catalog, which lists all the tasks that exist during a specified time period.

A decision obviously needs to be made when relating a task to the context in which it's performed. Should a task be permanently linked to a job or a position? A useful guideline is to link a task to a job if there will be several occasions when the task will be automatically considered part of the job. If the task is performed by a few people as an extra duty in addition to a job that many people have, the task is best linked to just those positions where it's performed. By following this guideline, a specification of the duties of a position can be precise, and the person selected for assignment to this position can be chosen more accurately.

If you define a position by a judicious linkage of jobs and extra tasks, this structure can be copied to generate replicas of this position.

Building Task Profiles

A *task profile* can be a list of the individual tasks that have been assigned to a specific object. The list of tasks collectively defines an object's purpose, role, or action in the R/3 system.

The concept of a task profile is applied in the R/3 Basis system and its application modules in three related ways:

- In PD-Personnel Planning and Development, a task profile provides a highly detailed description of a job or position.
- In SAP Business Workflow, a task profile determines the tasks that a user is allowed to perform in the system.
- In the SAP Session Manager, a task profile determines the areas of the system a user sees when she logs on.

Within HR, a task profile includes normal customer-defined tasks and standard tasks. Within SAP Business Workflow, a profile can also include workflow tasks and workflow templates that can refer to many workflow tasks. Within SAP Session Manager and SAP Business Workflow, the task profile can include activity groups.

If a task is included as an item in an activity group, the other items in this group will be included automatically whenever the task is assigned to a task profile.

Although the concept of a task originated as the activity of a single person, the following R/3 objects can be assigned their own task profiles:

- Organizational units
- Positions
- Jobs
- Work centers
- Users

There are some differences in the procedures for maintaining task profiles according to whether you're using Simple Maintenance, Detailed Maintenance, or Structural Graphics. There are also some differences in the procedures for maintaining the status indicator of an object according to whether you're using Simple Maintenance, Detailed Maintenance, or Structural Graphics.

In essence, the procedural differences arise because Structural Graphics assumes default values for all objects that might be changed later, whereas Detailed Maintenance requires all the data to be entered record by record as it is created, although it's possible to prearrange a default status. Simple Maintenance applies the Active status to all objects and infotype records as soon as they're created.

Changing Statuses in Organization and Planning

After an object or infotype record is created, the following procedures will change the status of the selected items:

- Run the report RHAKTI00, Change Object Status for Selected Objects or Infotype Records
- Change the status of objects and infotype records one at a time in Detail Maintenance

During the use of Simple Maintenance or Structural Graphics, it's not possible to change the status of an object or infotype record.

Manipulating Infotypes in PD

All the data in the PD application is held in infotype records that adopt the format and processing defined for the specific infotype. Thus, knowing the infotype name or ID number tells you what the records will likely contain and how to interpret their various fields and indicators. There's normally no restriction on how an infotype record is used, but each infotype was probably designed to serve a particular set of system functions.

Creating a New Object in the Object Infotype

The Object infotype 1000 has only one real purpose: to enable users to create data objects that didn't exist in R/3 when it was delivered. Typically, it's used to represent physical objects, events, or organizational entities that are unique to the user company.

Creating a new object is controlled by infotype 1000 because there are certain mandatory fields:

- A validity period for the object, which is copied to any infotype records appended to this object
- An abbreviation to represent the object, which can be used to mark the object in a list, for example
- A brief description of the object

Almost any details about an object can be subsequently changed except the validity period, although you can delimit the validity.

Having declared to the system by a record in infotype 1000 that a certain object is created, you can then create records in other infotypes to specify what this new object will be used for. For example, you can record a detailed description of the new object as a record in Description infotype 1002. You probably want to link the new object with existing objects by using Relationships infotype 1001.

If you create an object by mistake, you can delete it, but you wouldn't normally delete an object that had acquired many infotype records because these would also be deleted. It might be better to edit the object or its records.

Linking with the Relationships Infotype

A link between two objects is defined by a record in the Relationships infotype 1001. A set of standard relationship codes is provided so that you can relate tasks to jobs, jobs to positions, positions to work centers, work centers to departments, and so on. The chain of command and responsibility is represented by relationships between positions.

If you're using Simple Maintenance or Structural Graphics, the system automatically creates certain Relationships infotype records. In Detailed Maintenance, you have to create all the links yourself.

Various types of relationships are coded by using relationship subtypes or categories. Some link types aren't intelligible if applied to certain pairs of objects. If you run report RHRELATO, Allowed Relationships of Object Types, it will document the relationships that are applicable for different objects. If you click the Allow Relationships button in the Relationships Infotype screen, a dialog box reveals which relationships are possible.

There's no limit to the number and variety of relationship records that can be maintained for a single object. If the standard set of relationships doesn't suffice, you can create new relationships.

The standard syntax of a relationship is A/B 000. A indicates the passive side, B indicates the active side, and the relationship is assigned a unique three-digit number. For example, relationship A 002 between positions X and Y signifies that the holder of X reports to the holder of Y. X is the passive party. Relationship B 002 between position Y and position X signifies that the holder of Y supervises the holder of position X. Y is the active party.

The relationship A/B 002 is about supervision. A/B 005 is about reporting in a non-disciplinary sense. A/B 003 is about ownership.

When you create a position and assign it to an organizational unit such as a department, the system automatically creates two infotype records:

- The department gets a Relationships infotype record showing B 003 because it's on the active side as the owner of the position.
- The position gets a Relationships infotype record showing A 003 on the passive side because it's owned by the superior department.

Two objects in a relationship can deploy themselves in one of three structural senses:

- *Hierarchically*, as in superior over subordinate
- *Laterally*, as between equals
- *Unilaterally*, as in a one-sided or unidirectional relationship between a position record in PD and an external object such as a cost center in the CO-Controlling application

The lateral or flat relationship is A/B 041 and uses the passive/active coding, although the two sides are equal and can substitute for each other. For example, a job record and a position record can be related by A 041 and B 041, although they are equivalent if that job is what's performed at that position.

Copying Objects with Inheritance

An object in PD automatically inherits the attributes of another object if the two are related in certain ways:

- Positions inherit the attributes of the job to which they're related.
- Objects placed below other objects in a hierarchical tree structure inherit from above.

Automatic inheritance can be used to your advantage when creating large numbers of similar objects.

Reporting with the Relationship Construct

A *relationship construct* is a set of relationships. This construct can be used as an evaluation path when assembling records to make a report. "Unit>Position>Employee" is a relationship construct that can be used to collate employee records under positions that, in turn, are grouped by parent unit.

Documenting in the Description Infotype

The optional Description infotype 1002 is intended to hold lengthy text descriptions of the objects to which it's related. Any information can be included.

Each infotype record in 1002 must be assigned a subtype from the list your company established during customizing. For example, you might want to identify description subtypes for general and technical information and perhaps have a subtype to document safety or environmental concerns. Description subtype records can also be maintained in different languages. There's no limit to the number of description records that can be associated with an object.

N O T E   The Description infotype shouldn't be used for job or position descriptions. These are best assembled by creating relationship records between the constituent jobs, positions, and tasks. This allows a vacancy to be defined in terms of the work to be performed. A search of the records linked by the Description infotype could yield information that is not relevant to personnel management. ■

Flagging with the Department/Staff Infotype

Infotype 1003 is used when a system has integrated PA and PD modules. It has the function of flagging certain departments or units that would otherwise be documented and accounted as operational when they have a specialized function.

A separate function of this infotype is to flag particular organizational units or positions as "staff" in order to exclude them from the normal departmental reporting structures. Examples would be the CEO's personal secretary and an internal audit department that reports directly to the board of directors.

Report RHXSTAB0, Staff Functions for Organizational Units, lists any flagged organizational units. RHXSTAB1, Staff Functions for Positions, lists flagged positions.

Prioritizing with the Character Infotype

Character infotype 1004 is an optional refinement to the HR task catalog. Infotype 1004 accepts records that describe a task using up to three categories named as follows:

- Rank
- Phase
- Purpose

Just how these categories are defined and used is a matter to be established in customizing.

Rank can be used to classify tasks such as planning, completion, or control tasks:

- A *planning task* requires employees to design, arrange, and anticipate future requirements.
- A *completion task* starts with a defined method or procedure that fulfills a precise function, although the employee might have to discriminate between situations that call for variations to the routine operations.
- A *control task* requires employees to manage, oversee, or guide activities that are carried out mostly by other people.

Phase is a category in the Character infotype that can be used to classify how tasks fit into a business process:

- A task classified with the Decision phase would probably require an employee to make judgments that must be researched to determine the range of options and the kinds of information that would be critical when deciding which one to adopt.
- A task assigned the Execute phase would probably depend on following a predesigned procedure, although a great deal of effort and talent could be needed to perform well.
- A task identified by the Purpose phase could be so recognized because it directly contributes to the particular products and services offered by your company that define its niche in the market.

Purpose is a category of the Character infotype than can be used to differentiate between tasks that contribute directly to the goods and services produced by your company and tasks regarded as administrative. It might be quite difficult to arrive at a rational system of task description if a task's character is to be taken into consideration in setting remuneration and premium payments. For example, some decision-making tasks might be highly paid, even though they don't require original thought. Some routine "craft skills" might entail high-level decision-making to deal with variations in the raw materials and perhaps the place where the work has to be carried out.

Report RHXIAW04, Character of Tasks in Organizational Structure, lists the tasks in the selected organizational units. Report RHXIAW05, Character of Individual Tasks, displays the characteristics of selected tasks. Both reports rely on Character infotype 1004.

Compensating Positions Using the Planned Compensation Infotype

Planned Compensation infotype 1005 identifies salaries or wages assigned to particular positions. Benefit details and bonus arrangements aren't recorded in infotype 1005; however, the records of salaries or wages aren't consulted by the payroll. Therefore, this infotype isn't mandatory.

Report RHXSOLO0, Planned Labor Costs, uses infotype 1005 to calculate the planned compensation for all positions from selected organizational units. If this calculation isn't satisfactory—because it excludes any projections of the costs of benefits, health insurance, and bonuses, for example—the PD-PC Personnel Costs module is required.

A single position can relate to several Planned Compensation infotype records if they're documenting the compensation and taxation implications of this position being active in various countries or regions of legal force.

The compensation entries can be made as amounts or ranges of amounts. If the remuneration depends on such factors as wage bands and pay scale grades, the system can consult a table of pay classification data.

Particularizing Work Centers with the Restriction Infotype

Restriction infotype 1006 identifies any restrictions applicable to employees assigned to a work center. For example

- The work center has no wheelchair access.
- The work center requires heavy lifting.
- The work center exposes workers to alcohol and therefore might be unsuitable for employees under 18 years of age.

Table T778C is set up with restriction categories during customizing; table T778X contains the corresponding reasons.

Report RHXIAW01, Single Work Centers with Restrictions, shows the restrictions applied to selected work centers. Report RHXIAW00, Work Center with Restrictions in Organizational Structure, allows work centers to be identified according to organizational structure and lists the applicable restrictions. This report uses Relationships infotype 1001 to determine which work centers are related to each organizational structure.

Detecting Vacancies in Positions with the Vacancy Infotype

Vacancy infotype 1007 identifies position vacancies, both current and those due to arise in the future. The Personnel Costing component can consult the records of the Vacancy infotype to make cost projections. The Career Planning component can identify current or future vacancies from Vacancy infotype records. If your system is integrated with PA-Personnel Administration, the PA Applicant Management component consults Vacancy infotype records when seeking suitable positions for a prospective or current employee.

The system recognizes a distinction between occupied, unoccupied, and vacant positions unless you set a switch to ensure that all unoccupied positions are treated as vacancies. In this circumstance, it's not necessary to maintain Vacancy infotype 1007.

If you mark a vacancy record as an historical record after it's filled, it can be consulted but not changed.

Streamlining with the Account Assignment Features Infotype

The Account Assignment Features infotype 1008 can create records about organizational units and positions. Cost centers can be assigned to cost objects with infotype 1008 so that they can provide data for the PD-PCP Personnel Cost Planning module.

Infotype 1008 also accepts default account assignment settings used by PA to facilitate integration with PD.

Account Assignment Features infotype 1008 records the default assignment of organizational units and positions to cost centers. Such assignment information also suggests defaults for associated cost objects.

Inheritance applies—that is, all the account assignment defaults set for an organizational unit are passed on as account assignments to all lower level objects defined by Relationships infotype records. These default account assignments are inherited by positions assigned to the organizational units or their underlying organizational units.

N O T E In customizing, you can set up a single default account assignment for all organizational units, in which case you don't need Account Assignment Features infotype 1008. ■

Applying the Personnel Area Defaults

A *personnel area* is a convenient grouping of places where people work. A personnel area can suggest default values that are inherited by records being created in connection with an organizational unit or position or for a person assigned to them.

Each personnel area has a company code assignment, which will affect how cost centers are associated. Thus, the entry of a personnel area code on a record might well obviate the need to complete the rest of the infotype.

Stipulating Health Requirements of Workplaces with the Health Examinations Infotype

Health Examinations infotype 1009 identifies any health requirements for employees intending to work at workplaces in a particular work center. Two standard logical conditions are available in the form of subtypes:

- *Health exclusions*, which depend on specified medical history factors
- *Health examinations*, which have to be carried out regularly

Additional subtypes can be defined in customizing. The maintenance of this infotype isn't mandatory.

The requirements can be consulted by calling report RHXIAW02, Work Centers Requiring Health Examination Along Organizational Structure, or report RHXIAW03, Single Work Centers Requiring Health Examinations.

Controlling with the Authorities and Resources Infotype

Authorities and Resources infotype 1010 is associated with positions or work centers to limit their authority and to nominate particular resources over which they have control.

Authority could pertain to the value of contracts that can be signed at a position. Authority can also be used to define access to particular physical areas in your company.

Resources and equipment, such as production and administrative machinery or a company car, can be associated with a particular position or work center.

When a record is created in Authorities and Resources infotype 1010, the information must be assigned to one of the following subtypes:

- Authorities subtype
- Resources subtype

The maintenance of this infotype isn't mandatory.

Report RHXHFMT0, Authorities and Resources, can be run to inspect the stored information.

Interpreting the Work Schedule Infotype

Work Schedule infotype 1011 holds a definition of a work schedule that includes the average number of hours worked. A work schedule record in infotype 1011 can be created for organizational units, work centers, or positions. Work schedule groups based on employee groups and employee subgroups also can be assigned a particular work schedule.

In the Organization and Planning module, a work schedule is treated as a reference source for a policy or guideline regarding working hours. The work schedule values aren't used by payroll. The maintenance of this infotype isn't mandatory, but it can be useful if there are recognized exceptions to the default company-wide work scheduling information that's maintained in customizing separately from the Work Schedule infotype records.

Complex work schedules can be planned and implemented in PD-WP Workforce Planning.

If the PD-CP Personnel Cost Planning module is installed and configured, the system consults the work schedule and the Cost Planning infotype.

If you define a specific work schedule for an organizational unit, any lower-level units attached to it inherit this work schedule unless they are assigned specific work schedules. To process work schedule information, the system starts at the bottom and most specific level of the inheritance structure and consults infotype records in the following order:

- Work centers
- Positions
- Work schedule groups via organizational units
- Organizational units according to their structural position in the company hierarchy
- Default work schedules

Report RHXSBES0, Staffing Schedule, displays the work schedules of organizational units, positions, and employees according to your specification. If your PD module is actively integrated with PA, this report can also be configured to show absentee statistics and other personal data.

Because a work schedule group isn't an object, it can't be directly assigned a work schedule. The work schedule group is located within an organizational unit object, which can be assigned a work schedule by an infotype record. You have to deselect the Gen. Work Schedule indicator and complete the Work Schedule Group field. If an organizational unit includes several work schedule groups, you have to complete an infotype record for each.

Assigning Positions with the Employee Group/Subgroup Infotype

Infotype 1013 assigns a position to an employee group/subgroup. When PA and PD work together, the effective conceptual link between them is the employee group and employee subgroup structure. The system can cross-check employee and position data by confirming that the employee and his position belong to the same employee group and employee subgroup.

Furthermore, the system can automatically confirm that the employee is assigned work times in PA that are consistent with the work schedule assigned to his position and to the employee group and employee subgroup to which he belongs.

Marking Positions with the Obsolete Infotype

A position might become obsolete when the company is downsized or merged. The same might apply to a work center. PD's Career Planning module looks for positions marked as obsolete so that the system can help the holders find other jobs. If the holder of an obsolete position leaves or obtains another position, the system prompts you to delimit the validity period of the obsolete position record in Obsolete infotype 1014.

Developing Scenarios for the Cost Planning Infotype

PD's Personnel Cost Planning module consults Cost Planning infotype 1015 because it contains scenarios for personnel cost targets and projections. The scenarios can also be transferred to Controlling (CO) for budget planning purposes.

Costing scenarios can be developed from projected pay, payroll results, and basic pay. Infotype 1015 stores labor cost information needed to compute projected pay—for example

- Employer contributions to pension plans
- Employee benefits
- Wages and salary

Records in infotype 1015 can be appended to positions, individual jobs, work centers, or organizational units. The principle is normally to associate a Cost Planning infotype record with the most appropriate level of object. For example, a sum assigned for a social fund would be entered at the level of the organizational unit whose employees would benefit from it.

Each Cost Planning infotype record can hold up to seven wage element entries. A *wage element* is defined in customizing and is held in wage table T77KL. When a wage element is nominated in an infotype record entry, the following information must be supplied:

- Name of the particular wage element
- Amount of the element suggested from the wage table, edited if necessary
- Currency
- Time frame, such as monthly contribution or yearly adjustment

These wage elements identified in the Cost Planning infotype record become cost elements in Personnel Cost Planning.

Linking Authority Profiles with the Standard Profiles Infotype

Standard Profiles infotype 1016 links standard R/3 authority profiles to organizational units, jobs, positions, tasks, or standard tasks (in Workflow).

An authority profile controls the types of activities a user is allowed to perform in R/3. The separate authorizations in a profile can allow access to a business area such as accounting or personnel records, and they can also specify which types of infotypes a user can access in all the installed modules of the R/3 system.

Authority profiles are created in customizing and are normally applied to R/3 users individually. If you create Standard Profiles infotype records that are associated with organizational units, jobs, positions, or tasks, the authorizations can be automatically applied to all employees linked with these objects.

This linkage between objects and employees is put in place by running report RHPROFIL0, Generate Authorization Profiles.

A Standard Profiles infotype record can be used to nominate more than one authority profile as necessary for users such as system administrators.

If it's necessary to restrict some users from looking at certain organizational plans held in PD, the PD Profiles infotype 1017 can be used. Alternatively, table T77UA can be maintained manually to control authorizations.

A standard authorization profile can be applied to an organizational unit if all the employees should have the same access. However, individual subunits or employees might have been assigned particular profiles. These will be taken into consideration in addition to the higher level profile. This confirms the principle of inheritance for profiles.

Authorizing with the PD Profiles Infotype

The PD Profiles infotype 1017 maintains authority profiles that pertain specifically to PD users.

PD authority profiles are designed specifically for the PD environment because it contains organizational plans and personnel records that aren't open to general inspection and editing. A PD profile comprises a list of authorizations. Any object listed in the profile can be accessed and the nominated activities are allowed.

Records in infotype 1017 can be applied by running report RHPROFL0, Generate Authorization Profiles, or by maintaining table T77UA manually.

A user with PD authorization must also have basic authority privileges defined by the Standard Profiles infotype because they are necessary to log on to R/3, for example.

Linking a Calendar with the Site Dependent Info Infotype

A calendar is essentially a list of non-working days such as civic or religious holidays, Saturdays and Sundays, and work holiday shutdowns. Each company has a default factory calendar, but particular units might adopt a different calendar. Site Dependent Info infotype 1027 is used to link a specific calendar with an organizational unit or with a location.

By consulting records in the Site Dependent Info infotype, PD's Training and Event Management and Shift Planning modules can check calendars to ensure that business events and shifts are planned for working days only.

Infotype 1027 can also be used to record the currency and the language normally used at the site.

Attaching the Address Infotype

An object in PD can be assigned a particular address by a record in Address infotype 1028.

Records in infotype 1028 might be assigned to objects in the Organization and Planning component for reference purposes. This applies to organizational units, work centers, and positions.

A location has to have a record in infotype 1028 for its address. This address is used for such items as business event confirmation letters. If the Seminar and Convention component is used, the Address infotype could be needed for resources, external persons, contractor companies, kitchen facilities, and so on, in addition to the location address of the business event itself.

Notifying with the Mail Address Infotype

Mail Address infotype 1032 is typically a record of the organization that should be informed by email if a significant event occurs. For example, PD's Room Reservation Planning module sends room reservation confirmations and other notifications by using the email system. The mail address record will include the details needed, such as user IDs.

If Mail Address infotype records are attached to a room reservation event, the system automatically sends SAPmail to all persons or organizations involved if, for instance, there's a change of venue or a cancellation. The list of relevant addressees is assembled in customizing by nominating the types of person or organization, all of which are defined as data objects.

The mail address record must contain the following information:

- Name of the electronic mail system used (SAPmail)
- User ID of the employee responsible for coordinating mail communications in the organizational unit, company, work center, or user ID of the external employee or position holder
- Owner or creator of the distribution list for the organizational unit, company, or work center (If you're working with an external employee or position, this information isn't required.)

If you want to assign a mail address to any objects other than organizational units, positions, or work centers, you must use transaction PP01, PP02, or PP03.

Invoicing with the Sales Area Infotype

Sales Area infotype 1037 is needed when the SD-Sales and Distribution application is integrated with PD's Training and Event Management module. The idea is to have SD manage the tasks of generating invoices and receiving payment for business events. Infotype 1037 allows you to attribute the revenue earned from business events to SD sales areas, which are typically groups of products or services handled by similar sales procedures.

There are two ways of using infotype 1037:

- Apply infotype 1037 to an organizational unit in Organization and Planning that has been identified as the organizer of business events.
- Apply infotype 1037 to selected business event types in the PD-SCM Seminar and Convention Management module if the organizer will depend on the event type.

A sales area must be identified as follows in records of infotype 1037:

- Sales organization code
- Distribution channel code, which indicates whether products or services reach a customer via wholesale, retail, or direct sales, for example
- Division code to categorize products and/or services into product lines

Shift Planning with the Shift Group Infotype

Shift Group infotype 1039 assigns a shift group to an organizational unit for use by PD's Shift Planning module. A *shift group* is a user-defined collection of individual shifts recorded in Shift Planning.

This infotype associates the attributes of a shift group and the requirement types with an organizational unit. The system can then check automatically that shift plans contain the correct shifts and requirements for the organizational units for which they're intended.

Defining Exceptions with the Override Requirement Infotype

Override Requirement infotype 1040 is used by PD's Shift Planning module to process exceptions to normal staffing requirements. (A temporary work shutdown would be an example.) A separate record in infotype 1040 is needed for each exception or override applicable to an organizational unit.

Administering Organizational Personnel Structure

If your system doesn't have the HR Planning and Development module integrated with PA-Personnel Administration and Payroll Accounting, you have to define jobs, positions, and organizational units as elements in control tables. The following definitions apply:

- *Job*, a standard description of the function to be performed and tasks to be dealt with by an individual person
- *Position*, an organizational grouping of work that can be performed by one person
- *Organizational unit*, an organizational grouping of employees

A department can be an organizational unit or a larger aggregate. The status of an organizational unit depends on the position it occupies within the company hierarchy.

If your PA system is integrated with HR-PD Planning and Development, the tables detailing company structure must be set up and maintained in PD. When you assign an employee to a job, position, and organizational unit, the system automatically takes you from PA maintenance to a PD Planning transaction.

Integration with PD offers a number of significant advantages that stem from the possibility of associating a set of personnel requirements with a position and thus being able to look for suitable employees to hold that position.

In PD, the Position data is linked to the following data objects:

- Employee group
- Employee subgroup
- Personnel area
- Personnel subarea

- Company code
- Business area
- Cost center
- Job
- Organizational unit

You see the effect of all these links when you run a personnel event such as hiring an employee and organizational reassignment. The following benefits are apparent:

- Because a position is nominated for hiring in Events infotype 0000, the system automatically suggests entries for Personnel area, Employee group, and Employee subgroup, and the system validates any entries you might edit.

- If PD is integrated, the position-staffing schedule supplies a value for the planned working hours for the position. In the Percentage field, which appears in Organizational Assignment infotype 0001, the staffing percentage is displayed. If the position is offering less than 100 percent employment, a pop-up window suggests other positions to which the employee also can be assigned.

Planning Shifts in PD

PD's Shift Planning module schedules the appropriate type and number of human resources at the appropriate time. A shift plan is intended to embrace all factors, including employee preference, that affect workforce requirements. One factor is the workforce actually available—in particular, the skill sets of the employees.

Information maintained in PA's Time Management module includes employee sickness, vacation time, and training days. This can be interpreted to yield accurate estimates of employee availability, which are automatically embodied in the shift plans.

When shift assignments are specified in Shift Planning, they can be transferred to Time Management. Thus, the dependent processes, such as running payroll, can use the most up-to-date information.

Customizing defines and structures the shift patterns for your company. From this prerequisite, the shift planning sequence follows this order:

1. Define human resource requirements for the organizational units in your organizational structure.

2. Open a target shift plan for a selected organizational unit or set of units.

3. Inspect the work schedule information that is automatically imported from Personnel Administration's Time Management module for each employee assigned to the selected organizational unit(s).

4. Consult the Requirements Matchup window and adjust the target shift plan until human resource requirements are met.

5. Save the changes made to the target shift plans. Changes to employee working times are automatically recorded as substitutions in Time Management.

6. Mark as complete each target shift plan that's satisfactory to make it the actual shift plan.

A copy of the target shift plan is recorded for comparison in the PD database.

Defining Shift Groups

A *shift group* is a collection of individual shifts and requirement types. A *requirement type* is a classification of calendar days, such as weekday, weekend, and public holiday. For example, the following information can be defined as a shift group:

- Morning Shift 06:00 to 14:00
- Afternoon Shift 14:00 to 22:00
- Evening Shift 22:00 to 06:00
- Morning Shift 06:00 to 12:00
- Requirement types: Weekdays, Weekends

Such a shift group can be assigned to one or many organizational units by records maintained in Shift Group infotype 1039. A lower-level unit inherits the shift group from its superior.

A *shift* is a specific range of dates and times. During this time period, certain tasks must be performed, including being on call or working flexible hours.

The ID of a shift is its text name (Morning Shift) or a two-character abbreviation (MS), which is used in displays. Shifts can be assigned to a shift group, such as Weekdays, which can include morning, afternoon, and evening shifts.

Specifying Requirements

A human resource requirement for an organizational unit must be specific and quantifiable:

- Types of jobs that need to be performed
- Number of employees required to perform each different job
- The period of time over which the requirement exists

The requirements must be defined to correspond with the shift groups assigned to the organizational units in customizing. This includes any calendar-dependent variables in the shift requirements, such as weekend versus weekday working.

Using the Explode Switch when Creating or Changing Requirements

Human resource requirements are created or changed by the same procedure. The *explode switch* is a control mechanism over the following options:

- Enter or change shifts, types of jobs, and numbers of employees per job
- Enter or change only the numbers of employees per job

The explode switch was probably so named because it makes such a difference to the amount of information displayed. The following steps set the explode switch:

1. From the R/3 main menu, choose Human Resources>Planning>Shift Planning.
2. Select Current Settings.
3. From the Select Activities screen, select Specify Job Requirements.
4. On the Shift Planning: Requirements - Initial screen, identify the organizational unit that contains the requirements with which you want to work.
5. Select Job Requirements>Edit Requirements.
6. Select Settings>Requirements Entry.
7. Set the explode switch in the pop-up window.
8. Select Transfer.

The explode switch setting is active during the current work session only. You can change the default through customizing.

After the explode switch is set to allow or prohibit changes to the details of requirements, the following steps create or change requirements:

1. From the R/3 main menu, select Human Resources>Planning>Shift Planning.
2. Select Current settings from the Shift Planning screen.
3. Select Specify Job Requirements from the Current Settings: Select Activities screen.
4. The Shift Planning: Requirements - Initial screen appears.
5. Identify the organizational unit that contains the requirements you want to work with.
6. Select Job Requirements>Edit.
7. From the Shift Planning: Edit Requirements - Overview screen, mark the type of requirement you want to work with.
8. Select Job Requirements>Edit.
9. A pop-up window lists the different shifts that occur at the organizational unit, the different types of jobs performed, and the number of employees required to perform each type of job. Use the scrollbars to move up and down the list of shift requirements.
10. Enter the requirement details as appropriate.
11. Select Transfer requirements, and the system will save the requirements.

Similar steps display rather than edit the human resource requirements.

Reporting on Requirements

The following steps report on the human resource requirements for a selected organizational unit:

1. From the R/3 main menu, select Human Resources>Planning>Shift Planning.
2. Select Current Settings.

3. Select Specify Job Requirements.

4. Identify the organizational unit you want to report on.

5. Select Utilities>Weekly or Utilities>Daily.

6. Adjust and print the report as required.

Selecting Data for Shift Plans

A shift plan can be built for individuals working in many different departments that varies from the rest of the employees in each work center. There are three ways of identifying the employees for a shift plan:

- Select employees by organizational unit
- Select employees by job classification
- Select employees individually by personnel ID

Selecting Shift Data by Organizational Units

If you identify an area in the company by selecting one or more organizational units in your organizational plan, the system will trace the relationships between these units and their underlying subunits until all the employees in scope are identified. This employee list can then be used in shift planning.

If you're working with only one organizational unit, the Shift Planning component will automatically work with all employees in this unit. If you want to work with more than one organizational unit, you must identify a root organizational unit that's at the highest level in your organizational plan.

The following steps access Shift Planning and display the area of the organizational structure defined by the unit named in the Organizational Unit field:

1. From the R/3 main menu, select Human Resources>Planning>Shift Planning.

2. From the Shift Planning screen, select Shift Planning>Shift Planning Extras.

3. Select Employee Selection>Restrict OrgStruc.

4. From the display of the structure, select the organizational units you want to work with.

5. Select Continue to return to the Shift Planning Initial screen, which displays only the selected employee data.

The following steps select data by jobs:

1. From the R/3 main menu, select Human Resources>Planning>Shift Planning.

2. From the Shift Planning screen, select Shift Planning>Shift Planning Extras.

3. Select Employee Selection>Restrict Jobs.

4. From the list of the types of jobs performed within the selected organizational unit, select the jobs you want to work with in the shift plan.

5. Select Continue to return to the Shift Planning Initial screen, where the data is displayed for the employees holding the selected job types.

Opening and Changing Shift Plans

You can work on a target plan until it's marked complete. From then on, the only plan you can work on is the actual shift plan.

After you select the employees, you select the time frame of the shift plan you want to work with, such as the current or subsequent month. After you opt to work on the target plan or the actual plan, the Requirements Matchup window appears automatically. This window indicates the extent to which the shift requirements specified for the organizational units in a shift plan are met in the shift plan you're working on.

The summary view shows a percentage for each day. This indicates the extent to which all requirements have been met for all shifts on that day. If you select the detailed view, the information is displayed shift by shift. A tree structure is used for the different days so that you can expand or collapse the scope of the view.

Each different job type is shown for a given shift, with the number of employees required for each job and the percentage to which that requirement has been met. You can identify the individual employee for each job and call for a list of other employees who will be available and suitable for any requirement that hasn't been met in the shift plan.

The Requirements window provides separate information for each organizational unit if there is more than one in the shift plan.

Saving Shift Plans

Selecting Save after changing a shift plan records the changes in Shift Planning and in Time Management, from where they can be used in Payroll and other components.

> **CAUTION**
>
> Don't save experimental shift plan data; otherwise, it might be used in Payroll and elsewhere.

Completing Target Shift Plans

After you finish adjusting a target shift plan and have met all reasonable requirements, select Shift Plan>Complete. This will store a copy of the target plan and change the status of the shift plan from Target to Actual. To reverse this action, select Actual Plan>Undo Completion.

To change the shift of an individual employee, mark the shift in the plan, overwrite with a new shift code, and save.

The Copy Shifts function conveniently assigns a shift to other employees.

Finding Alternative Employees

From the detailed view of the Requirements Matchup window, you can mark a shift for which there is insufficient coverage and select Alternatives. This will identify employees who match the job class. Those who are available are highlighted. Then the Shift Plan window can be used to enter the shift abbreviation on the required day against one of the available employees.

If the requirement originates from an organizational unit that's not the same as that of the alternate employee, it's necessary to assign that person temporarily to the unit where the shift is worked. This doesn't affect the employee's job classification as recorded in the company organizational plan.

The following steps assign an employee to another unit that's already part of the shift plan:

1. Open the shift plan you want to work with.
2. Double-click the understaffed shift.
3. In the Works Temporarily For field, identify the organizational unit where the employee is to be assigned.
4. Select Continue.

The following steps assign an employee to another unit that's not already part of the shift plan:

1. Open the shift plan you want to work with.
2. Select the employee who should be reassigned to another organizational unit.
3. Select Edit>Employee>Temporarily Assign.
4. Use the Transfer To field and press Help F4 to identify the organizational unit where the employee is to be assigned.
5. If necessary, use the Temp. Payment field to redirect costs for the employee to another cost center.
6. Use the Time Period fields to identify how long the temporary assignment should be valid.
7. Select Continue.

The system will remove the employee's previous shift assignments from the shift schedule.

Temporarily Assigning Employees to Different Jobs

It might happen that a person with the correct job classification can't be found for a particular shift. The following steps temporarily assign an employee to a different job classification:

1. Open the shift plan you want to work with.
2. Double-click the shift.
3. In the Employee list box, use the Works Temporarily As field and press Help F4 to identify the job classification to be assigned to the employee.
4. Select Continue.

Recording Employee Preferences

Within the Shift Planning component, an employee preference is a preferred shift. The system automatically implements this preference, although you can override it.

The following sequence implements an employee preference:

1. Open the shift plan you want to work with.
2. Select the menu options Goto>Employee Preferences.
3. Inspect the shift plan for preferred shifts displayed in a different color.
4. To implement a preference, locate the employee you want to work with and enter the preferred shift on the appropriate day. Repeat this step for each employee preference you want to enter.
5. To return to the target shift plan, select the Goto>Target Plan.

If a shift plan shows shifts highlighted to indicated that preferences have already been implemented, the following override steps change the shift:

1. Double-click the shift you want to override.
2. In the Shift Time list box, use the Shift field to identify the shift.
3. Select Continue.

Unlocking/Locking Master Data

If a shift plan is being worked on, the personnel master data of each employee involved is locked so that other users can't change the data in Time Management during the process. However, other users might need to update an employee master record for payroll or other purposes. The following steps unlock employee master data:

1. Open the shift plan you want to work with.
2. Select the employee whose master data should be unlocked.
3. Select Edit>Employee>Unlock. An icon indicates that the employee's master data is unlocked.

Before any new shift changes can be made to the employee's master records, they have to be relocked. The following steps return the master data to locked:

1. Open the shift plan you want to work with.
2. Select the employee whose master data needs to be locked.
3. Select Edit>Employee>Lock.

Displaying Shift Plans

The following steps display the shift plans of an individual employee for the period indicated in the Shift Planning Initial screen:

1. Open the shift plan you want to work with.
2. Select Extras>Personal Shift Plan.

The following steps generate a report containing employee names, job classes, shift abbreviations, and shift times for all shifts covered by the shift plan, or to a single day in that plan:

1. Open the shift plan you want to work with.

2. Select a day and then select Extras>Attendance List, or select Extras>Attendance List without marking a day to report on all days in the plan.

Adjusting Shift Plan Views

A shift plan display is normally presented in alphabetical order by the employee's last name. One extra column can be included to show one of the following fields:

- Job classification
- Organizational unit
- Personnel number

The following steps add the selected column to the shift plan display:

1. Open the shift plan you want to work with.

2. Select Views>Information Column.

3. Select either Jobs>Organizational Unit, or Jobs>Personnel Number.

Requesting Additional Employee Data

If you need to see other information—such as address, organizational assignments, qualifications, leave entitlement, and so on—about the employees in a shift plan, it can be requested from PA and PD with the following steps:

1. Open the shift plan you want to work with.

2. Select the employee whose additional information you want to display.

3. Select Edit>Employee>Disp. Employee Data.

4. Select the type(s) of information required.

5. Select Details to see the information.

 You also can double-click the name of an employee to see his data.

Planning Personnel Costs

PD-PCP is the Personnel Cost Planning module of PD-Personnel Planning and Development. It supports the following activities:

- Determine current or actual personnel costs
- Preview future personnel costs
- Project future personnel costs

The projection of future personnel costs is based on the anticipated organizational changes and pay structure changes. Vacant positions are taken into consideration, and some functions factor in progressive changes such as staffing reductions or increases.

Cost planning relies on data undergoing predefined calculation scenarios that use the following sources according to the plan's intention:

- Projected pay
- Basic pay
- Payroll results

The scope of cost planning is defined in terms of the organizational structure from which units can be selected to define scenario groups processed with their own scenarios.

After a cost planning scenario is created, you can experimentally edit the details because the system immediately recalculates the scenario after each batch of changes is entered. The figures can also be downloaded to a Microsoft Excel spreadsheet format or to SAP Business Graphics, in which a three-dimensional bar graph display is available. When such experiments yield a satisfactory scenario, it can be transferred to CO-Controlling and then take part in overall budgetary planning.

Defining Cost Elements

The Personnel Cost Planning component depends on cost elements that represent the different categories of costs that arise from maintaining staff, such as wages, salaries, and employer contributions to pension funds.

Cost elements are differentiated according to the R/3 application module in which they're set up and maintained:

- Cost elements derived from *wage elements* that are set up in PD-Personnel Planning and Development
- Cost elements derived from *wage types* that are set up in PA-Personnel Administration and Payroll Accounting

Projected pay scenarios use wage elements from PD to form cost elements.

Basic pay or payroll results scenarios use wage types from PA and possibly also wage elements from PD to form cost elements.

No action in Personnel Cost Planning will alter any PD wage element records or PA wage type records.

Attributing Personnel Costs to Cost Objects

A *cost object* is any R/3 object to which costs can be assigned or attributed. In the HR context, a cost object is an object to which salaries, benefits, and other personnel-related costs can be assigned. For example, the following objects can be used as cost objects:

- Organizational units
- Work centers
- Positions
- Jobs
- Employees

Two procedures associate costs with cost objects:

- If the cost object originates in PD, such as a work center or a job, wage elements are assigned to the cost object by using the PD Cost Planning infotype 1015.
- If the cost object originates in PA, it represents an employee, and wage types are assigned in PA.

Determining Current or Actual Costs

Either basic pay or payroll results are used to compile the current costs of personnel because they represent the actual costs recorded in the system. Scenarios are used to calculate the actual personnel cost data using work schedules and data recorded by Time Management.

Previewing Future Costs

Future personnel costs can be estimated or previewed by extrapolating from current or actual costs. The term *preview* tends to be used for a calculation of future personnel costs that assumes that the number of employees and the pay structures will remain the same over the period being previewed. By contrast, a *forecast* tends to be reserved for a projection of future costs that factors in one or more changes to the cost structures. A projection also usually tries to include an allowance for all personnel-related costs likely to arise in the nature of overhead costs additional to the elements used in a preview based solely on basic pay or payroll results. Thus, training costs will usually figure in a forecast.

Somewhat in between a preview and a forecast is the use of a simulated payroll run that embodies some anticipated developments in personnel costs. This technique can be useful in making comparisons of actual and target personnel costs in the middle of a period before the final period-end costs are cumulated.

Comprehensive planning of personnel costs entails projecting pay costs according to the activities of the company. Thus, where new equipment and procedures are anticipated, the projected costs of retraining the staff might well constitute a major item. If organizational changes are anticipated—perhaps in the work centers or the job requirements—these should be included in personnel cost planning. Vacancies might well have to be factored into the projection using the Cost Planning component.

Administering Personnel Costing Scenarios

Scenarios are identified by the following data elements:

- Plan version code, which identifies the data to be used.
- Scenario abbreviation, which is a unique two-character alphanumeric code assigned by the user.
- Scenario period or planning period defined by a start date and an end date. All objects valid at any point during the scenario period are included.
- Short-text description of up to 25 characters.

The system extracts information for the scenarios by following evaluation paths set up by customizing in Personnel Cost Planning.

Setting Up Scenario Groups

A costing scenario is subdivided or *modularized* into one or more separate scenario groups. Each scenario group is a self-contained calculation covering a specified area of your company, such as a particular division or department. This area is defined by nominating the organizational units when the scenario is started.

The whole company can constitute a single scenario group. However, multiple scenario groups are convenient if decentralized cost planning is in operation and if personnel costing scenario results are to be transferred to CO-Controlling. If you require both an overall consolidation and multiple scenario group cost planning, it's best to create two scenarios: one for the entire company and one modularized into scenario groups. Passwords can control access to scenario groups.

Scenario groups are created by building one scenario at a time, but giving each the same scenario abbreviation to ensure that they are all affiliated. The first scenario group to be created will have to be entered with a code and short text description in the Plan Scenario field, which then applies to other member groups in the scenario if the shared scenario abbreviation is also entered.

Extracting Projected Pay Data from PD

Project pay scenarios cull their data entirely from the following PD source records:

- *Cost Planning infotype 1015* stores personnel costs as wage elements for positions, jobs, work centers, and organizational units.
- *Work Schedule infotype 1011* stores the average number of hours worked by organizational units, work centers, positions, and work schedule groups based on employee groups and employee subgroups.

If you use only Cost Planning infotype 1015, the system assumes that the full work schedule will be worked throughout the planning period. If you also use Work Schedule infotype 1011, it's possible to use entries in the Percentage field to adjust the personnel cost planning calculations. Thus, you could take account of any partial weightings anticipated for the planning period because of reduced workload, for whatever reason.

In summary, projected pay scenarios are appropriate if your system doesn't use the PA-Personnel Administration and Payroll Accounting application, or if you're expecting changes of a strategic nature, such as reorganizations, pay structure changes, personnel training, and development changes.

Understanding Wage Elements

A *wage type* is an object in PA; a *wage element* is an object in PD. Personnel records use wage types to record basic pay information and calculate payroll. PD's wage elements differentiate the various cost categories that are totaled to form the overall cost of maintaining staff.

The different wage element categories—such as wages and salaries, employer contributions to pension plans, and employee health and insurance benefits—are set up during customizing. Each wage element is assigned a default amount, which can be inspected in the Wage Element table T77KL.

There are no restrictions on how the user defines and uses wage elements. They're typically defined for each personnel-related cost that can't be traced through the payroll. A staff training and education facility, for example, could be costed in this way.

Wage elements are associated with particular objects, such as organizational units, work centers, positions, and jobs, using the Cost Planning infotype record in PD's Organization and Planning module.

An object can have more than one Cost Planning infotype record. Each record can accept up to eight different wage elements. The amount for each wage element can be determined by indirect evaluation using the default set in customizing, or by direct evaluation using an amount entered manually on a specific infotype record.

The Personnel Cost Planning component consults the Cost Planning infotype records to calculate projected pay.

Starting a New Projected Pay Scenario

If you need to calculate costs over a different period of time or work from a different organizational plan, you have to start a new projected pay scenario by following these steps:

1. From the main Personnel Cost Planning window, select Plan>Create>Projected Pay.
2. In the Planning Basis for Projected Pay window, complete the relevant fields.
3. Select Execute.

The main Personnel Cost Planning window shows the calculation results for the selected organizational units, with the original cost calculations in the Reference Value column.

Personnel Cost Planning with Basic Pay Scenarios

An essential requirement for a basic pay scenario is a selection of basic pay records from PA. Data is also required from PD.

Basic pay is defined as the amount paid to an employee. It's assigned as a wage type to an employee record held in PA in Basic Pay infotype 0008. Wage types also can be used to represent any other type of cost incurred by the company to employ a person.

Stored wage type values take no account of any variable costs such as overtime or bonus payments. These are obtained from payroll results.

If a position is vacant, a PD record will exist that can be consulted. Thus, the planning system can improve on payroll data, which doesn't use wage types for any vacant positions because no employees will be holding them and expecting to be paid.

The system consults PD records in Cost Planning infotype 1015 and Work Schedule infotype 1011. Costs for the vacancy period can thus be computed for planning purposes.

The advantage of using a basic pay scenario is that it determines actual results without waiting for payroll results. If your master data in PA already includes details of a planned pay raise, a basic pay scenario can be used over the period as a method of projecting future pay.

Personnel Cost Planning with Payroll Results

After it completes a payroll run, PA automatically writes the payroll results to database PCL5 in PD. This database is reserved for use by Personnel Cost Planning when integration between PA and PD is active.

The payroll driver procedures and personnel calculation schemas are discussed in Chapter 5, "Administering Payroll." It's possible to use payroll results as the basis for cost planning scenarios. Schema x500 in payroll driver RPCALCx0 is used for actual payroll results; the combined payroll and evaluation schema x400 is used if the payroll run is for simulation with integration with PD Personnel Cost Planning.

A simulated payroll run isn't helpful if your planning period includes major changes in pay structures or organizational assignments. Payroll results scenarios can take a long time to process, but they provide the most accurate planning data.

The following steps start new payroll result scenarios when you want to work with a new set of figures:

1. From the main Personnel Cost Planning window, select Plan>Create>Payroll Results.
2. In the Planning Basis for Payroll Results window, edit the fields to define the scope of the plan.
3. Select Execute to inspect the calculation results for the selection organizational units and positions.

The system automatically displays the original cost calculations in the Reference Value column.

Deleting Simulated Payroll Results

If you want to remove payroll results from the designated Personnel Cost Planning database PCL5, you can nominate a selection period to allow the system to delete payroll data that overlaps this period. You must also identify the personnel numbers of the employees whose data should be removed.

Opening Existing Scenario Groups

Scenarios groups are stored in a tree structure from which they can be identified, one at a time, for editing. The following steps open a scenario group from the Personnel Cost Planning window:

1. Select Planning>Change.
2. In the Change Planning Group window, click the tree of existing scenario groups at the name of the scenario group you want to edit.
3. Select Planning Groups>Change.
4. Modify the costing figures and save.

A tree structure can include branches that can be opened or unfolded to reveal the underlying structures. From the Planning Scenario Administration window, click the item and select View>Expand Sub-Tree. The display is compressed behind a marked item by View>Compress Sub-Tree. Details are displayed by choosing View>Detail Information.

Released and unreleased scenarios are highlighted with different colors in the Planning Scenario Administration window.

Comparing Scenarios

By using the figures arrived at by different personnel cost planning scenarios, it's possible to discern ways to improve a personnel plan. The Personnel Cost Planning function allows you to work with a single scenario in which the original (Reference) and adjusted figures are displayed for comparison. It's also possible to work with two scenarios together.

Every time you change the figures, the system recalculates the scenario(s). At any stage you can save the adjusted figures to become a new scenario. SAP Business Graphics can be used to portray the results of one or two scenarios in bar graph format.

Comparing Scenario Results with External Salary Surveys

A salary survey can collect any type of salary, wage, benefit, and other workplace pay statistics from various external sources and collate them for analysis and distribution. In particular, survey results can be retrieved into Personnel Cost Planning to use in comparisons with costing scenarios.

Four techniques are available to utilize salary survey information:

- Enter survey data manually to Cost Planning infotype 1015 as a subtype or subcategory for each survey source, with a record for each position, job, organizational unit, and work center. Create a record for each position by using the wage element to record the actual situation.

■ Create a costing scenario by using the survey data and store it in the Survey subtype of the Cost Planning infotype. Specify the correct Cost Planning subtype in the Salary Surveys field of the Planning Basis for Projected Pay window.

■ Use the Load Reference Scenario option to retrieve a second costing scenario to use for comparison.

■ Create two separate plan versions: one containing the real cost planning information, the other the salary survey information.

The following steps retrieve a reference scenario:

1. From the main Personnel Cost Planning window, select Planning group>Load Ref. Planning.

2. From the Select Reference Plan window, click a scenario's name.

3. Select Planning Group>Load.

The reference scenario display mode includes a special overall calculation feature that combines calculation results from a scenario's different scenario groups. Costing figures can be presented according to cost element or cost object or given in overall totals. All three formats can be specified to appear in the Display Planning Group window.

Percentages or absolute figures can be specified for the values in reference scenarios.

Transferring Personnel-Related Cost Planning Data to CO-Controlling

If your PD application is integrated with CO, a transfer of personnel-related cost planning data can be initiated from within the CO module. This will succeed only if the following conditions are satisfied:

■ Integration between CO and PD is active.

■ Cost centers in PD are assigned to the organizational units and, if required, to the positions in your organizational plan.

■ The appropriate personnel cost scenario is marked as released because the cost center and general ledger account assignments are valid.

The following steps initiate the transfer:

1. From the R/3 main menu, select Accounting>Controlling>Cost Center Accounting.

2. Select Planning>Planning Aids>Transfers>Personnel Costs.

Assigning Cost Centers in PD

Although an organizational unit is the obvious locus for a cost center for assigning personnel costing scenarios, it's possible to assign particular positions to cost centers not necessarily within the same parent organizational unit.

Any organizational unit "inherits" the cost center assignment of its parent organizational unit unless you specify another cost center. By default, positions also inherit the cost center assignments of the organizational units where they're assigned unless you specify otherwise.

A cost center must be specified by a cost center code and a controlling area code when it's defined by a record in the Relationships infotype. You can establish a default controlling area code that is automatically assigned to all new cost centers, unless you specify differently in an Account Assignment infotype record or a Relationships infotype record. Another procedure is to select some objects and use the Account Assignment Features infotype during Detail Maintenance to specify the default controlling area.

A controlling area specified in a record in Relationships infotype 1001 takes precedence over a default controlling area set in a record in Account Assignment Features infotype 1008. The controlling area assigned as the default in table T77S0, item PPINT is used if no infotype record overrules it.

Releasing Scenarios

A scenario isn't used to alter the database until it's released. At this point, the system automatically checks the validity of all cost center assignments and blocks the scenario if any errors are detected. The following steps check a scenario without attempting to release it:

1. From the main Personnel Cost Planning window, select Plan>Release.
2. In the Release Plan Scenario window, mark the scenario whose cost center assignments you want to check.
3. Select Plan Scenarios>Check.

Using the Long-Term Manpower Planning I Component

The long-term planning of the company's manpower requirements includes the distribution of planned amounts to each workplace on the basis of guideline figures that you enter, such as the following:

- Planned turnover per product
- Planned output per product
- Planned turnover per location

The employees and their qualifications are taken into account, along with the number of employee-hours available in the planning period. The hours available are first distributed to take account of shift schedules and overtime planning. A second operation adjusts these hours to take account of nonproductive hours arising from a range of causes.

Using the Short-Term Manpower Planning II Component

Manpower Planning II improves short-term planning by ensuring that business needs are covered by sufficient personnel.

The SAP R/3 Basis system provides full integration of your system so that Logistics data relating to the workplace and time data from PA-TIM Time Management are normally available to PD Personnel Planning and Development. Your company might elect to keep the PD Personnel Planning and Development system separate from the following integrated logistics application modules:

- SD-Sales and Distribution
- PP-Production Planning
- MM-Materials Management
- PM-Plant Maintenance
- QM-Quality Management

The manufacturing data transferred from the Logistics modules is concerned with the following aspects of short-term manpower planning:

- The general amounts of work planned and in progress
- General data from the work plans of your company, including the plant locations in relation to the addresses of the personnel who might be employed there
- The patterns of qualifications, formal and in terms of experience, needed throughout the planning period

It's necessary for the Manpower Planning II component to call on the PA-TIM Time Management component for the following types of information:

- Company time models
- Shift schedules
- Personal calendars of individual employees, which will yield information on employee hours that can't be planned for normal work activities because they've already been assigned to such activities as vacation, education, training, or business trips

The PA-TIM Time Management component is also important in this context because it initiates manpower planning, and hence possibly redeployment or recruitment if it should happen that the number of suitable employees at a workplace at any time falls below the minimum required or is forecast to do so.

The Manpower Planning II component requires certain PD Personnel Planning and Development components to be installed and configured, regardless of whether there's direct transfer from the Logistics modules. PD-OM Organizational Management and PD-WP Workforce Planning are required to provide the data on workplaces, the activities that need to be performed, and the employees assigned to them on specific dates and times throughout the planning period. These components are also needed to supply the job specifications of workplaces and the qualifications held by the employees in these positions, as well as their suitability profiles.

HR's PA-Personnel Administration module also must be installed because it contains the employee master file required to gain access to the personnel data.

The emergency role of the Manpower Planning II component is to enable you to deal effectively and swiftly with unplanned staff shortages. You want to locate the right people to fill the gaps. The right person is the one with all the requirements of the vacancy and no disadvantages. This statement is true of the aim but is difficult to realize in practice.

The approach taken by this component is to assemble and make readily available all the information that might help you cover the staff shortage. For example, you might want to have records of the following types of information about employees:

- Whether a person is incompatible with another and shouldn't be assigned to work with him
- How a particular work team should be made up from a specific mixture of person types and capabilities
- Which persons have registered preferences or requested limitations on the working hours or working days of the week assigned to them

Workplaces should be assigned master records carrying data on factors that could help or hinder your efforts to fill an unplanned vacancy there:

- Minimum number of positions that should be occupied at the workplace
- Maximum number of positions that could be accommodated at the workplace
- The optimum number of people to be located at this workplace
- Preferred staffing arrangements for the different shifts or other working patterns that sometimes or regularly occur at the workplace

The solutions that the Manpower Planning II component proposes to you must include the schemes and arrangements your company has discovered or developed over the years, plus any new possibilities that can be conceived of now that you have a flexible integrated manpower planning system in operation. The list probably includes such tactics as the following:

- Assigning a person to be on call in case her expertise or work capacity is needed at the workplace suffering a staff shortage
- Assigning standby duty
- Effecting a temporary transfer from another workplace or from another section of the plant
- Engaging outside personnel through a placement agency
- Engaging a person who was previously an employee
- Engaging a freelance worker
- Engaging a seasonal worker directly or via a seasonal worker agency

The component extensively uses the standard SAP graphical display facilities to make the operation of the functions easy for inexperienced users. As of R/3 release 3.0, these facilities are controllable over the Internet. See Structural Graphics in Chapter 11.

Planning for Personnel Development

In this chapter

Developing the HR Data Models

During the research and development phases for R/3, it became apparent that the SAP standard business software approach could be extended to the data manipulation areas associated with human resource management. The most significant technical development was in the matter of handling more complex data structures concerning, for instance, qualifications and job requirements. In particular, it's obviously essential to be able to store information about the positions in a company that its personnel might occupy.

If a person doing a job is to be replaced—by a substitute during the employee's absence, for instance—the knowledge and skill needed for that job should be specified so that the replacement can be chosen and prepared by training to do that job with the absolute minimum loss of performance due to the changeover.

You might assume that the replacement person knows nothing and has to be trained in everything. If that person already works in your company or in a similar job, however, that assumption would be wrong. Furthermore, you would waste resources and probably squander the goodwill of the trainee if you made him take a full training course.

It's therefore necessary to specify the starting qualifications and experience of anyone about to undergo training or about to take over a job they haven't performed before. This is true for a fresh applicant outside your company as well as for internal applicants.

SAP has adopted an extension of its data model approach to cope with this requirement to record the jobs and skills of the staff. The standard system of information types (*infotypes*) includes several hundred that have been defined for various purposes in the SAP R/3 system.

Several additional data models have been introduced to help cope with the complexities of personnel data. The result is an extensive object-oriented data scheme. The scheme requires that a clear distinction be recognized between methods of representing structural relationships among planning data objects and other information about them. You can allocate several workplace positions to a cost center; the master records will show this "ownership" as a relation, and your graphical display can draw an arrow to represent it.

Accountants need to know who will pay for work done in a workplace and may want to analyze this in relation to a system of cost centers. This kind of information, however, doesn't help the Personnel department when it comes to filling positions. This is the kind of other information that must be associated with positions and people, and it must be done flexibly if it is to be of any use.

The standard system of infotypes associates sets of data elements with the attributes of data objects. During customizing, you can define which infotypes are required for each attribute of each type of data object, and how they should be displayed on user-interface screens. Infotypes can be assigned directly to planning objects independently of the object type.

The benefits of this approach stem from the standard methodology being used to identify and link objects and to evaluate them. It also means that planning can be installed step by step; a set of planning objects is no longer defined during system design, but rather during the actual installation and customizing of the system. The set can be extended later.

The method is used to establish extra data models in HR-Human Resources.

Introducing the Personnel Planning and Development Functions

The purpose of personnel planning is to determine who will be required, and when. Personnel development ensures that the aspirations of the personnel planners can be realized by selecting suitable applicants and giving them the broad educational qualifications and specific training requirements. Those things ensure that sufficient suitable staff will be available to do the jobs when they are required.

The functionality of the PD-Personnel Planning and Development module is embodied in the following standard business program components:

- PD-OM Organizational Management
- PD-WP Workforce Planning
- PD-PD Personnel Development
- PD-RPL Room Reservations Planning
- PD-SCM Seminar and Convention Management

Each component includes software functions that extend the component's scope. For example, PD-OM Organizational Management includes extensive functionality devoted to the description of jobs, positions, and workplaces. The same component includes personnel cost planning programs.

The SAP standard business software in the Human Resources domain is under continuous development because this aspect of business grows in complexity and becomes increasingly critical as the productivity of individual workers is increased by technological improvements in production and communication methods.

N O T E   The R/3 Human Resources components are so complex that successive releases haven't always been able to maintain a consistent letter coding for the subsidiary functions. There's a tendency for the HR product associated with R/3 release 4.5 to be titled as the SAP R/3 Human Resources System.

Developing Company Personnel

If the aim is to provide a comprehensive human resources service to your company and the people in it, the place to start is with a set of clear job descriptions. These descriptions not only portray what is done, but they also must show how these results are to be achieved. In some form or other, the necessary knowledge and skills have to be identified. There are two obvious methods:

- Identify people who can do the job and then find out how their knowledge and skills are different from people who have just been recruited.
- Identify people who can do the job and find out how they came to be in that position.

Neither method solves all the problems of getting good people into jobs they do well. The approach of personnel development is to assume that you've recruited at least some good people who will want to stay in your company, and then provide them with a job trajectory so that they can acquire not only the necessary knowledge and skill, but also confidence in their own ability, which is essential to good performance.

Interpreting Requirement and Qualification Profiles

The logic is simple: A person is suitable for a position as long as her qualifications match the requirements of all the jobs that will be her responsibility if she takes the appointment. A person can be more or less suitable; she also can be suitable in some respects and not in others. Put this data on a scale, and you have a *suitability profile*.

Some job requirements can be documented, and some can be set up in the form of admission tests. Some requirements can be described in general terms, such as "resourceful" or "sociable." The difficulty with using these types of words to describe the appropriate response to an unknown future situation is that, by definition, there's no way of knowing whether a specific individual can cope. For some personnel selection assignments, it may be best to concentrate on the negative side. For example, a person who has had no practice at first aid shouldn't be placed in a position where it might be needed. A person who has shown no sign of being friendly to strangers shouldn't be in charge of crowd control in cases of emergency.

Where you can define what's needed in terms of the amount or weighting of each of several characteristics, you can draw a job requirement profile. Some requirements will be absolute and admit no leniency; some will be desirable but not essential. In some positions, the lack of one good quality can be compensated by an abundance of another—for example, a very good memory can serve as well as intelligence in some circumstances.

If you have a personnel selection procedure, even if it's just an interview, you might arrive at a measurement of each applicant's capability in each dimension of the job that you've used to build the job requirement profile. Put this data on a scale for a qualification profile.

If you are bold enough to compare the qualification profile of a person against the job requirement profile, you can derive the data to yield a suitability profile of this applicant for this job. If you were to carry out this profile matching for all applicants for all your vacancies, you would arrive at a list of people in rank order of suitability for each vacancy. This function is available through the PD-WP Workforce Planning component, along with the following functions:

- Manage the requirements for jobs, positions, workplaces, and tasks, and set priorities and weightings if required
- Manage the qualifications of applicants and the quality or level of these qualifications
- Mediate the substitution of qualifications in relation to job requirements when compiling a short list of suitable people
- Create job requirements profiles
- Create applicant qualifications profiles
- Carry out matching of requirements and qualifications profiles and produce suitability profiles

■ Maintain a catalog of exemplary qualifications and requirements

Refining the Catalog of Qualifications and Requirements

A catalog of exemplary or model qualifications and requirements is supplied as standard in the PD-WP Workforce Planning component and is available as the Qualifications/Requirements component. You can attach items from it to persons, positions, workplaces, and specific tasks. You can extend or adapt the catalog to suit the type of work carried out in your company.

The quality parameter of a qualification record can be interpreted as the proficiency level attained by the person holding it. It can be assumed that this proficiency is at least adequate for the job. If this same qualification, perhaps with an entry in the quality parameter, is associated with a position, it serves to define a requirement. The level can be used to indicate what's regarded as an acceptable proficiency for that position.

Requirement weighting is a percentage applied to a requirement; it represents the level of knowledge and skill needed to effectively perform the task(s) assigned to a particular workplace or position. Requirements and qualifications can also be applied to work breakdown elements in networked projects.

Using the Decay Meter

Some qualifications represent knowledge and skills that can deteriorate over time, through disuse or by becoming out of date. The PD-Personnel Planning and Development module provides the ability to enter a half-life value for a qualification; a half-life is the period of time taken for the skill to deteriorate to half its proficiency if it's not required by the job and if it's not kept up to standard by refresher training. The Decay Meter function will compute the exact degree of deterioration to be assumed for any other period under consideration if you've specified a value for the half-life.

If you're looking at a person who has performed a job that demands the exercise of the skill or other requirement corresponding to the qualifications he possessed on appointment, there's no reason to suppose that proficiency has deteriorated.

The qualification data object is established by infotype records that can be assembled to build a profile or list of qualifications associated with another object. In particular, an employee can have a qualification profile. The elements in a qualification record are linked explicitly during customizing as requirements of particular jobs, positions, or workplaces. Thus, a person with a match between his qualifications and the requirements of a vacant position is recognized as a suitable candidate for assignment to that position.

You can assign a percentage value to record the degree to which a candidate's or holder's qualifications match the requirements assigned to the particular position. As of R/3 release 4.0, ranges of suitability can be defined and named by users as "somewhat suitable" or "highly suitable." A suite of functions is available under the title of Qualifications Management, in which the user company can apply a customized scale of appropriate quality to persons and positions to refine the assignment process.

Furthermore, the requirements of a job, position, or workplace can be given priorities as well as requirement weightings. This again refines the way in which the match of a person's qualification profile and a position requirement profile can be managed. Alternative or substitute qualifications can be defined in a job's requirements profile.

When all the qualification records held in the PD database are assembled, the list constitutes a qualification/requirements catalog. It may then be consulted when defining a new job's requirements profile or a new applicant's suitability profile. As of release 4.0, the qualifications catalog can be freely structured to group qualifications according to their content.

For each quality scale, you can customize the number of points and the descriptions of each point. One or more alternative qualifications can be assigned to each qualification. The qualifications and requirements catalog is consulted by users of personnel development, recruitment, shift planning, training, and event management.

The exact allocation of functions within a team may well change frequently according to the details of the particular task in hand. Team requirements profiles are under development in which a team task is assigned requirements as qualities. Someone with one or more of these qualities could be deemed suitable for assignment to a team. Thus, a person could be assigned a suitability profile for team work.

Planning Careers and Succession

The logical extension of the system of matching vacancies and employees is to repeat the match for the same employee when some additional qualifications are acquired. The result is a potential career path. Thus, a *career path* is a list of positions.

The system can generate a career planning hitlist of employees sorted in order of suitability. The display shows suitability percentages and ranges such as very suitable to partially suitable. You can view the formula used and apply adjustment settings to refine the hitlist.

Release 4.0 includes the capability to provide potential career paths for individual employees.

Position-related succession planning begins with a search for a second person to fill a vacancy. You could perhaps delete from the position requirements profile a qualification that could be acquired by a suitable candidate in the period that the person appointed is expected to hold the job. Alternatively, you could add an attainable qualification to the pool of potential appointees. You can simulate succession planning to test out the propagation of vacancies and qualifications by using different suitability formulas.

Career and succession planning can be carried out independently of career models. For example, you could apply a career model that limited the search to the organizational unit to which the employee belonged as well as that employee's technical or personal qualifications. By contrast, you could define a career path that entailed a wide variety of positions, possibly in many different organizational units within the enterprise. Developments in this component are expected to extend the range of career planning and refine the identification of the training and educational events that would be beneficial.

The Profile Matchup function depicts person profiles and position profiles graphically. It can show over- or underqualification and thus suggest where further training measures might be advantageous. Release 4.0 has elaborated this functionality and provide enhanced user navigation during career and succession planning.

Users may well want to define certain appraisal systems in customizing. This entails specifying such information as the appraisal type, the procedure, the criteria, the evaluation scales, and the persons needed to perform the appraisal. An appraisal model would comprise a set of definitions of all the potential criteria and criteria groups that could be used in an individual appraisal. Any particular appraisal of a person or a position could then be carried out by using elements selected from the model. If the actual data has been collated according to the model, the compilation of hitlists could then take place.

Developing Career Models

Again, a career path is an ordered list of particular positions to which a person could be assigned if a reasonable amount of experience and training had been encountered in each before moving on. A career model extends the concept of career path by referring to position types or levels rather than specific positions.

A *career model* is an ordered list of the opportunity types open to someone in your company or someone you want to recruit. Clearly, each step in the career model is taken only if the person is suitable and willing to move, and if the target position has a vacancy.

The same general approach is used for assigning new recruits, selecting suitable successors for existing positions, and managing individual career paths.

The HR-Human Resources module PD-PD Personnel Planning and Development provides the following functionality:

- Representation of careers
- Association of the career potential assessments taken from the selection procedure with the steps of potential career models
- Determination and representation of further training needs of individuals embarked on career paths
- Representation of further training programs
- Graphical editing of profiles and profile comparisons

Representing Career Potentials

The first candidate potentials are derived from the assessment procedure, whether formal or informal. For every position for which the candidate is likely to be considered, his or her assessed potential is stored.

As time passes and experience is accumulated, these potentials can be adjusted on the basis of new information coming to light. Alternatively, the assessed potentials can be stored with their original values intact and a set of current potentials maintained separately.

Planning Careers

The planning of an individual career begins with a discussion with the person concerned and the identification of one or more positions for which this person wants to be considered. This data is entered under the organizational structures established in the PD-OM Organizational Management component, and the suitability profile of this candidate is computed.

The integrated PD-Personnel Planning and Development module lists all the positions for which the candidate would be suitable and provides a sublist of vacancies or positions likely to be vacant on a future date suggested to the system.

The system can be run in simulation mode to analyze any domino effects in which the appointment of one person can release or block the progression of another, and so on throughout the network of career pathways. If the career candidate elects to accept an offer of a position change, a vacancy will be created elsewhere, and so on. When a transfer or recruitment actually takes place, the system suggests all the vacant positions in succession, so that the planner can be sure that the subsequent transfers are processed.

Planning Succession for a Position

Whereas career planning is the employee's viewpoint, *succession planning* is concerned with who will maintain the company's work by succeeding to a specific position if and when it becomes vacant.

Several candidates may well be suitable successors. This matter can be illuminated by considering their qualification profiles in relation to the position's requirements profile. Even so, there may be no real differences in the suitability profiles of several candidates. Other factors must be considered:

- Time served with the company
- Time served in the present position
- Staff association membership
- Educational background as a potential for further career development

Discerning Training Needs

It can easily happen that no candidate can match qualifications with requirements for recruitment or career progression. Your company will have to weigh the costs and other considerations to decide whether to look again, perhaps elsewhere, for someone with the right qualifications, or whether to accept one candidate and make up the difference by having that person trained.

The system will tell you what qualifications are lacking and to what level of proficiency they are required by the vacancy. If the training course database is accurate, the system will also tell you where and by what method the additional qualifications can be obtained.

This functionality enables you to create an education and training plan for an individual by reference to the qualification deficits discovered by the career planning activities. You can also modify these plans before they are released for processing.

Reporting on Qualification and Requirements

An employee may have several individual qualifications and perhaps more than one profile. A list of employees who have a specific qualification or profile may therefore be culled from the PD database.

An alternative report is of the qualifications and suitability profiles of the employees in a group selected individually or by organizational unit.

A flexible selection pattern of qualifications and other attributes can be defined and used to identify employees or potential employees who qualify.

Administering Education and Training

You might want to adopt the convention that *education* is the process of drawing out the best that a person can do, whereas *training* is the process of arranging for a person to acquire a skill that most people could acquire, given suitable coaching and instruction. Of course, you may stumble on the practice of demanding ever more difficult training exercises until you discover a person's limitations.

However, SAP R/3 knows nothing about education or training. There's a database of records. Some functions read these records and write fresh records. Some records serve the purpose of linking others. An *infotype* is a class of record used to assemble a collection of related records so that users can inspect and perhaps alter some recorded entries. You can build and manage an education and training system via these infotypes. For example, a training course needs a data structure with data elements to represent the start date, the finish date, the location, the account settlement arrangements, and so on, all of which can be assigned standard infotypes that can be used to build data entry and display screens using the standard SAP R/3 methodology.

A *training program* is the sequence of course types needed by one person to qualify for a specific position within a stated time period. It's assumed that each course of the same type is equally effective and covers the same content, even though the venue and teachers may be different.

A *course type* requires one or more resource types, such as teachers, premises, and equipment. A course type may impart one or more qualifications, which are defined in terms of the positions they are preparation for. A course type may impart one or more task requirements, which may exceed the skills necessary for qualification, or fall short of this. A course type is defined by an entry in the catalog of course types. The course type is therefore a very flexible planning entity.

A *course* is a specific instance of a course type held for specific attendees on a particular set of dates. It uses one or more resources of one or more resource types. A *course group* is a set of courses. A course needs one or more instructors and one or more attendees. An *instructor* is someone internal to the company or an external person. An *attendee* is either an internal person or an external person—in other words, anyone for whom a personnel record has been created.

Administering Training Events

The following functions are available through the PD-Personnel Development component:

- Manage internal and external training events.
- Manage and plan all the resources required for internal and external training events, such as rooms, instructors, course materials, and equipment.
- Process all correspondence in connection with training events.
- Check the prerequisite courses or other qualifications of the employees or external people who intend to enroll.
- Automatically update the qualification master records of those who pass the course standards.

The concept of an educational or training course has been refined to focus on events. These are the elements from which training can be built. They are referred to as *business events* because they can include any interlude in normal work that's authorized and funded. A business event is considered to contribute to the attendee's education or training.

PD-SCM Seminar and Convention Management manages the booking of internal and external participants at events. The following facilities are provided:

- Automatic creation of waiting lists
- Automatic sequential processing of waiting lists
- Booking with priorities
- Booking from lists
- Canceling from lists

All training events can be processed without regard to their time dependency, if necessary. For example, the component can be asked to create a complete catalog of all further training events scheduled throughout the company.

The system ensures that a participant isn't booked on the same course twice and isn't destined for two courses that overlap in time. If you've installed the PA-TIM Time Management component, employees identified automatically by the system as suitable to act as instructors on a course won't be assigned to it if, for example, their vacations will make them unavailable.

Events can be linked to specific locations if this is necessary—for instance, if a particular resource is available nowhere else. A specific language for the conduct of a course can similarly be dealt with. Different calendars can be invoked to ensure that the courses aren't planned for statutory holidays.

Pre-booking for a general course topic or theme, delimited by a range of dates, can be later confirmed by the release of firm booking for specific training events. Booking priority is covered by the following standard scheme:

- Essential for the good of the company
- Normal, first-come, first-served
- Waiting list for places not filled by participants with higher priority

The system will propose a redistribution to subsequent courses of those remaining on the waiting list after the event takes place.

Education and Training Planning

Included in the PD-Personnel Planning and Development component, PD-PD Personnel Development is a suite of functions that carries out quantitative planning of education and training events and makes optimum use of time.

The requirement for planning arises in the form of data on the estimated numbers of courses made up from the requirements per subject and per calendar quarter. Alternatively, the requirements can be expressed as pre-bookings for each course type that specifies the subject or theme of interest. Career and succession planning functions in the PD-OM Organizational Management component provide a source of pre-bookings. These functions can identify the needs for further training in connection with career planning and the preparation of successors for those who are moving on.

The education and training requirements are serviced by the following functions:

- Scheduling numbers of different training events
- Optimizing event schedules with respect to the resources available
- Scheduling sequences of training events for individuals or groups of participants

Overall scheduling depends on the following factors:

- Preset limits on the number of events each year
- Number and timing of events according to the pre-bookings
- Education and training budget
- Demands from career and succession planning

Optimized event scheduling must take account of the resources required and their availability:

- Suitable rooms according to the PD-RPL Room Reservations Planning component
- Instructors available according to the PA-TIM Time Management component
- Course materials and equipment

The detailed procedures for creating training programs and managing educational assignments are discussed in Chapter 10, "Managing Business Events."

Recruiting, Changing Jobs, and Leaving

Introducing the HR Recruiting Activities

The functions in the R/3 HR Recruitment component have evolved from the modules introduced as part of the PA-Personnel Administration and Payroll Accounting application. Additional functionality was added in the PD-Personnel Development application. The most recent designation of the system, R/3 Human Resources, should be assumed to include full integration of the PA and PD components.

A Recruitment module is available for use as a standalone system from which data can be transferred to PA in an R/3 system. Recruitment and Personnel Administration can be implemented as a combined system, with or without integration to the PD-Personnel Planning and Development application.

Within the Recruitment module, a separate applicant database is maintained in the PA-APP Applicant Management component to which the functions of the PA-Personnel Administration module may be applied. The data on any hired applicant can automatically be transferred to an integrated HR-Human Resources database under control of the PA-EMP Employee Management component.

HR's Recruitment component is designed to reduce the cost of recruiting and hiring new employees with the right skills and education. The following key processes are supported:

- Managing open positions and requisitions
- Screening, selecting, and hiring applicants
- Managing correspondence
- Reporting
- Analyzing costs

The data already collected about an applicant is made available for use by other HR components if the applicant is hired.

A *personnel event* is a procedure that ensures that all infotype records needed for a particular purpose are created or updated in an orderly fashion. Standard SAP R/3 HR provides the following procedures as personnel events for updating the HR master database:

- Hiring an employee
- Organizational reassignment, used for recording promotion, demotion, and lateral transfers
- Early retirement or normal retirement
- Leaving
- Re-entry into company (rehire)

A personnel event should always be used in preference to manually selecting and updating individual records.

Job openings are represented as open positions for which the following kinds of information can be maintained:

- Position open date
- Location
- Management reporting specifics
- Job descriptions
- Skills and education requirements or qualifications

The same information is used for internal job postings and external advertisements with newspapers, magazines, colleges, recruitment agencies, and Internet notices. Costs incurred during advertising and interviewing for each open position can be recorded and analyzed.

Selection is supported by facilities to match employee and applicant qualifications with the requirements of the job.

HR Recruitment interfaces directly with Microsoft Word for Windows to generate standard applicant letters. The SAP Office Communication link is available for sending email messages to internal applicants.

Representing Workforce Requirements

A *vacancy* is a position that can or must be staffed (either completely or partially). If you're using Recruitment as a standalone system, you must manually enter all data on a vacancy.

If Recruitment is integrated with Personnel Planning and Development, it's only necessary to mark the positions vacant on a structured list compiled by the PD system. These vacancies are said to be created in PD and can't be maintained except for the following fields:

- Personnel officer
- Line manager
- Percentage reserved

Vacancies are normally maintained by a line manager or personnel officer. A typical arrangement is for the line manager to decide who is suitable and for the personnel officer to manage the data. Any person recorded as an employee in the PA database can be defined as a line manager for applicant processing.

A vacancy record contains the following information:

- Eight-digit vacancy number
- Vacancy description
- Date from and to
- Personnel officer responsible
- Line manager
- Percentage approved
- Percentage reserved
- Staffing percentage
- Staffing status

Relating Applicants to Advertisements

When an applicant responds to an advertisement, the recruitment procedure must assign that applicant to the specific advertisement. The system may later propose a likely vacancy assignment for the applicant. If the application wasn't solicited by an advertisement, the line manager or personnel officer has to assign the applicant to a vacancy.

If the applicant has been identified with an advertisement, he or she is assigned to a recruitment instrument and a medium as well as to the particular advertisement. This information is then available for evaluating advertising materials.

Creating a Vacancy in the Recruitment Application

Follow these steps to create a vacancy in Recruitment:

1. On the initial Recruitment screen, select Advertising>Vacancy>Maintain.

2. Enter any relevant selection criteria to identify vacancies and click Execute.

3. Click Create Vacancy in the Maintain Vacancies screen.

4. Examine the Create Vacancy screen for a position that already exists for the vacancy you want to create. Enter and save the details.

N O T E If there's no position, it must be created in customizing.

The system automatically determines the staffing status by using your entries in the Percentage Approved, Percentage Reserved, and Staffing Percentage fields.

Creating a Vacancy in Personnel Planning and Development

If there's an active integration between PA and PD, follow these steps to create a vacancy in Planning and Development:

1. On the initial SAP screen, select Human Resources>Planning>Organization.

2. Select Detail Maintenance>Position.

3. Maintain the administrative fields.

4. Check that the Plan Version field contains the integration plan version.

5. Select the vacancy infotype.

6. Select the status Active.

7. Click Create Infotype to display the vacancy infotype 1007 create screen.

8. Select Vacant and then select Save to display the Recruitment system's Create Vacancy screen.

9. Complete the details in the fields.

10. Save your entries.

These vacancies created in Planning and Development are marked with a P in the PD field of the vacancy view (V_T750X). They can't be maintained in Recruitment, except to alter the following fields:

- Personnel officer
- Line manager
- Percentage reserved

Changing a Vacancy

A vacancy created in Recruitment can have any of its fields edited, but a vacancy created in Planning and Development can be altered only for the personnel officer, line manager, or percentage reserved. The following steps change a vacancy:

1. From the Recruitment screen, select Advertising>Vacancy>Maintain.
2. Enter any relevant selection criteria and click Execute.
3. Position the cursor on the vacancy you want to change and click Change Vacancy.
4. Overwrite the entries on this screen.
5. Save your entries.

Select Display to view a vacancy and follow a similar procedure.

Creating Vacancy Advertisements

A recruitment instrument is assigned a vacancy advertisement characterized by the following data:

- Eight-digit number
- Recruitment instrument and medium
- Publication date and costs
- Advertisement text, if applicable
- Vacancies published in the advertisement

The advertisement won't be accepted by the system unless the vacancy and the recruitment instrument exist.

Hiring a New Employee

The successful applicant or employee to be hired first needs to be incorporated into the company structure and the personnel structure. The data needed and suggested as default values is controlled by entries in organizational assignment infotype 0001. If PD is implemented, the employee's organizational assignment data is linked to the employee's position records held in PD. An administrator is also assigned to the new employee.

Under control of the hiring personnel event, the following information must be entered:

- Personal data
- Payroll-relevant data
- Contractual and corporate agreements
- Time data, including the employee's planned working time and other information required by Time Management

A personnel number is either assigned automatically or entered manually. This won't be the same as the applicant number that may have been held in the Recruitment component or in an external recruiting system.

The hire date is taken as the start date of the validity period of the personnel number, and this is used elsewhere to determine seniority and in payroll accounting. The *entry date* refers to the date of formal entry to the company and usually is the same as the hire date.

If the required information isn't available, a personnel event such as hiring may be interrupted and resumed. Individual infotypes may be skipped in the sequence defined for the event. When the event is restarted, the system prompts for the missing information.

Interpreting the Recruitment Infotypes

The following infotypes from PA are used in Recruitment:

- Organizational assignment (infotype 0001)
- Personal data (infotype 0002)
- Addresses (infotype 0006)
- Education (infotype 0022)
- Previous employment (infotype 0023)
- Qualifications (infotype 0024)
- Bank details (infotype 0009)

The following infotypes are stored in the Recruitment database:

- Applicant events (infotype 4000)
- Applications (infotype 4001)
- Vacancy assignment (infotype 4002)
- Applicant's personnel number (infotype 4005)

Transferring an Applicant to PA

An applicant must be transferred to PA to enjoy a place in the payroll run. This can be arranged from the Recruitment module or during the running of the hire applicant personnel event.

If you're hiring an employee without Personnel Planning and Development integrated, the hiring event will allow you to assign the employee a personnel area, an employee group, and an employee subgroup. Events infotype 0000 is used for the records, with the other infotypes set up for this personnel event. As you save the entries for one infotype, the next one is displayed until the last, when the initial events screen is redisplayed.

If you're hiring an employee when Personnel Planning and Development is integrated, the hiring event accepts your entry to the Position field in events infotype 0000. This is linked to a personnel area, an employee group, and an employee subgroup. These elements therefore don't have to be maintained for each new employee because they are entered automatically.

The system retains the position data as defaults for successive hiring events unless you change it. You can overwrite the fields Personnel Area, Employee Group, and Employee Subgroup, but the system accepts your entries only if they are valid for the position you've assigned.

If Personnel Planning and Development is integrated, the Percentage field appears in organizational assignment infotype 0001. The percentage refers to the planned working hours stored in the position-staffing schedule in PD. If you assign less than 100 percent, you are asked to assign additional positions to this employee when you save the organizational assignment infotype record. PA won't take account of any positions assigned after the first.

Deleting a Personnel Number

Almost the only occasion for deleting a personnel number is if you've entered it twice. When a person leaves, the personnel number remains valid so that his records may be accessed later.

Another reason to delete a personnel number is if you've been using the test system and want to remove test employee records. You need authorization to delete a personnel number and must also have authorization to display and maintain all the infotypes that contain data concerning the personnel number you intend to delete. The relevant infotype records are offered for deletion.

If you want to delete a personnel number that already is included in a payroll accounting run in the test system, you must change payroll status infotype 0003 for this number. You must delete the date of the last payroll run and save the record.

Changing an Employee's Entry Date

If an employee's entry date is wrongly entered, the mistake might not be noticed until the payroll run reveals the error.

If the employee hasn't yet appeared in a payroll run, there's an auxiliary function to change the employee's entry date in events infotype 0000, where it's recorded as the start date for the validity of the record. You need special authorization to alter this infotype. The system automatically changes the date on all infotypes containing the erroneous date.

However, repairing the records after a payroll run takes place is more complicated. If the wrong entry date is earlier than it should be, you must run the incorrect personnel entry and corrected entry events to initiate a payroll correction. The system assigns an employment status of 0 "left" for the period of the error and a deduction from pay will take place on the next retroactive payroll accounting run.

On the other hand, if you've entered an employee on a date after work actually began, you again need special authorization to change the payroll status infotype by altering the validity date so that an extra payment can be made in the next retroactive payroll run.

Administering Selection Procedures

Every action must be logged when dealing with applicants for jobs. The Recruitment system maintains records of the activities' sequence as Applicant Actions, each action differentiated by the following characteristics:

- Action type, such as mail confirmation of receipt of application
- Planned/completed status
- Performance date, the date by which or the date when actually carried out
- Employee responsible for the action being completed by the deadline, who may or may not be the person performing the action

The following procedures are available for monitoring the dates of applicant actions:

- Report planned actions for personnel officer (monitoring of dates), which extends to the date specified
- Display planned actions sorted by personnel officer
- SAPoffice (Reminders), which are standard mailings to the persons responsible at each level, according to the customized settings
- Structured evaluation (overall monitoring)

The overall monitoring functions provide structured reports as follows:

- Overall applicant statistics throughout the company, from which subsets can be selected and applicant actions maintained
- Applicant statistics for each vacancy, from which subsets can be selected and applicant actions maintained

The applicant statistics for a vacancy include reports on the actions for each applicant and therefore provide a progress report.

Using the Recurring Tasks Facility

As part of customizing, you can arrange for an applicant event to automatically create a corresponding applicant action. For example, the Initial Entry of Basic Data event can trigger mail confirmation of receipt and set the indicator for recurring tasks.

The Recurring Tasks facility allows various tasks to be performed by a report program. This can be repeated as often as required and also run in test mode. After each successful run, a second report marks the planned tasks as Completed so that the action isn't repeated. The following tasks can be managed this way:

- Printing of letters in bulk processing
- Transfer of applicant data to Personnel Administration

Setting Individual Access Protection

A personnel officer or line manager is normally allowed access to personnel data only within a restricted sphere of responsibility. Access protection can be controlled according to organizational assignment, the employee's assigned duties, or both. Thus, a personnel officer may be allowed to enter applicant data but not take selection decisions. The scope could be limited to just one personnel area.

Reviewing the Selection Procedures

Vacancy assignment entails associating an applicant from the applicant pool to a vacancy, perhaps to more than one. If the Recruitment module is integrated with Personnel Planning and Development, the system reviews the applicant's qualifications and the requirements of the available vacancies. Thus, the system seeks suitable vacancies for an applicant and seeks suitable applicants for a vacancy.

The system also supports decision making by presenting a short profile and archived facsimiles of the application documentation for any candidates selected for a short list. The selection can be entered directly on the list display and follow-up activities can begin immediately.

Entering Basic Data on an Applicant

The following services are provided by the integrated HR-Human Resources system:

- Management of internal and external applicant data
- Recognition of multiple, repeated, and duplicate applications
- Determining vacancies automatically from the HR planning components
- Triggering job advertisements automatically from the HR planning components, using job description text and a detailed breakdown of media and recruitment instruments in each
- Assigning applicants to advertisements to check cost effectiveness
- Processing correspondence
- Applying the PA-TRV Travel Expenses component to process job interview costs and to reimburse interviewees
- Automatic data transfer to PA-EMP Employee Management

All these activities depend on a database of applicant data. This may be held in a separate Recruitment system for external applicants from which only the successful candidate records are transferred. Internal applicants may be nominated by simply entering their personnel number if the PA system is part of the network.

Using Fast Data Entry for External Applicants

Fast data entry is carried out in two stages, perhaps by different employees:

1. Run the Initial Entry of Basic Data Applicant event, which may include optical archiving of application documents.

2. For applicants in which your company is still interested, run the Enter Additional Data Applicant event, which includes assignments to one or more vacancies, education, training, qualifications, and previous employer.

Entering Basic Data on an Internal Applicant

The following steps enter basic data on an internal applicant:

1. On the initial Recruitment screen, select Applicant Master Data>Initial Data Entry.
2. Enter the applicant group, applicant range, personnel area, personnel subarea, and personnel number.
3. Complete the Advertisement field if the applicant is linked to a job advertisement.
4. Complete the Unsolicited Application Group field if the candidate is an unsolicited applicant.

Applicant class P is entered as the applicant group for internal applicants. Class AP flags external applicants.

When you press Enter to confirm your entries, the system determines whether this applicant has applied before or is a former employee, in which case the system accesses the New Application event and completes the fields for the personal data and addresses infotypes and suggests the personnel officer. The check for multiple applicants and former employees is carried out automatically once for every second and first name entered. If you want to check further, click Check Ex-Applicant/Ex-Employee on the Initial Entry of Basic Data screen.

The defaults for organizational assignment are taken from the candidate's previous application. You can overwrite the entries as necessary.

If you're entering basic data on several applicants in succession, the system retains your entries as default values in certain fields unless you click Clear Fields in the Edit menu.

If you've signified that the applicant has responded to an advertisement, the system automatically proposes the vacancies mentioned in the advertisement.

Changing an Applicant's Address

If you've detected an error in an applicant's address, you can overwrite the entry by following these steps:

1. On the initial Recruitment screen, select Applicant Master Data>Maintain.
2. Enter the applicant number.
3. Select the addresses infotype.
4. Click Change to display the Change Addresses (infotype 0006) screen.
5. Make the necessary changes and save.

An applicant may have moved or may intend to move. In these circumstances, you must not change the address record. Instead, you have to create a new record in the addresses infotype as of the appropriate date. The system automatically delimits the validity of the existing record and issues a warning message.

Storing an Applicant's Bank Details

If your company intends to reimburse an applicant for the expenses incurred, you have to create a record of her bank details. Follow these steps:

1. On the initial Recruitment screen, select Applicant Master Data>Maintain.
2. Enter the applicant number.
3. Select the bank details infotype.
4. Click Create to display the Create Bank Details (infotype 0009) screen.
5. Enter the applicant's bank details and save.

If you're dealing with someone who has applied several times, you may want to see his previous applications. The following steps display all applications filed by an applicant:

1. On the initial Recruitment screen, select Applicant Master Data>Display.
2. Enter the applicant number.
3. Select the applications infotype.
4. Click List.

Deleting an Applicant

The following steps delete an applicant:

1. On the initial Recruitment screen, select Applicant Master Data>Delete.
2. Enter the applicant number.
3. Click Execute to display a second Delete Applicant Data screen.
4. Click Select All to select all infotype records stored on this applicant.
5. Click Delete and then confirm your intention by clicking Delete again when prompted.

Administering Selection by Applicant Actions

An *applicant action* processes applications, classified as follows:

- Action type, such as mail invitation to interview
- Action status, planned or completed
- Performance date or target date
- Person responsible for action

The following tasks are controlled by applicant actions:

- Administration of Applicant Correspondence
- Transferring Applicant Data to Personnel Administration

Actions are created and maintained for each application, although actions common to all applications are normally created automatically. The names of the action types are set up in customizing.

An action can be created afresh or copied from an existing action. The system can be set up to propose likely follow-up actions after the first action is processed.

The Maintain Applicant Actions screen comprises a list of all planned and completed actions for a selected applicant. The following steps create the Appointment for Interview applicant action:

1. Select Edit.
2. If Appointment for Interview is to be created as a planned action, choose the function Create Planned Action. If Appointment for Interview is to be created as a completed action, choose the function Create Completed Action.
3. Enter the key for the Appointment action type for interview in the Action Type field.
4. Enter the desired performance deadline in the Performance Date field.
5. Make any other necessary entries.
6. If automatic mail isn't preconfigured, select Send Mail.
7. Choose Maintain Notes from the Function Key menu.
8. Use the Change Notes on Action: Appointment for Interview Language E screen to maintain the notes.
9. Save your entries.
10. Click Back; the Notes field will be flagged.
11. Click Transfer.
12. Save your entries.

If you decide to create an applicant action by copying an existing one, select the planned or completed action you want to copy and click Copy Action. You can overwrite the default values.

If you mark an existing action and click Follow-Up Actions, the system offers some suggestions that can be adopted as planned or completed actions.

Maintaining References Between Applicant Actions

If an appointment action contains data needed by the Mail Invitation to Interview action, the Appointment for Interview action is defined as the reference action for the mailing. The data is automatically included in the text where a reference has been established.

Each applicant action may have only one reference action.

A reference can be created between two existing applicant actions, and between one action and its follow-up.

Managing Selection Procedures

Selection entails two stages: global selection into the company and selection for individual vacancies. There are two corresponding status indicators: overall status and vacancy assignment status. Each status may be customized to accept values such as Processing, On Hold, and To Be Interviewed. Each vacancy assigned to an applicant is maintained with its own status.

Overall status control ends when an applicant is assigned Rejected or To Be Hired.

Processing Applicants with the Procedure Options

The Recruitment system can handle individual applicants and a list of applicants as well as statistics. The lists and statistics are created by running reports that generate displays that can be used directly to process applicants.

When you've generated a list, you can use the following functions to work on several applicants at once:

- Enter additional data
- Maintain actions
- Maintain applicant master data

The listed applicants can be processed in sequence or simultaneously, provided their Overall status or Vacancy Assignment status is part of the display. By working with the status, you can reject all or several applicants at the same time, put them on hold, or make any other assignments.

Grouping Applicants

The following classification criteria are applied to applicants when their records are first considered:

- Personnel area/personnel subarea
- Personnel officer
- Overall status
- Internal/external applicants, including former employees, recorded as applicant class as a subdivision of applicant group
- Unsolicited applicants/candidates who applied in response to an advertisement
- Applicant group, according to the type of contract
- Applicant range, freely defined according to functional or hierarchical principles

Applicant Screening

A position can be marked as vacant, which allows it to be released for filling. If an unoccupied position isn't so marked, it is ignored. If a position is subject to a long notice period, it can be marked as vacant although still occupied.

The applicant screening process can be used to find all applicants suited by their qualifications for any set of positions. You can screen for all positions in the company, for those on a particular set of career paths, or for those marked as vacant.

The ensuing hit list for each position contains those applicants whose qualification profiles most closely match the position's requirement profile. There is an automatic estimation of the possible training needs of any applicant who doesn't have each requirement to the degree required by the position.

As of release 4.0, qualifications recorded in the HR qualifications catalog can be distributed via ALE to Logistics. A Logistics work center is represented as an external object in the HR entity relationship model (organizational model). This enables links between a work center in Logistics and a work center held in the HR model.

Qualifications can be entered for work centers and for orders such as in PM, PP, and PS. Thus, a qualification profile can be identified as a requirement for the order and the Logistics work center where it's processed.

Personnel data is also distributed to Logistics via ALE, so that persons can be assigned to orders by using various criteria.

Making Decisions

The system expects decisions on applicants to be made in two stages. The line manager will inspect a list of applicants for a vacancy and consider the short profile of each. Some applicants can be marked and have their status in the vacancy assignment infotype changed from Processing to Invite. It may be necessary to consult the archived application documents. The rest of the applicant pool for this vacancy is marked Rejected or On Hold.

The second stage is for the personnel officer to carry out the follow-up activities by working on a list of all applicants marked Invite. These activities include maintaining the applicant actions such as Appointment for Interview and Mail Invitation to Interview. These actions are automatically created when the vacancy assignment status becomes Invite.

Finally, the line manager consults the short profile and archived application documents and reviews the interview notes so that he can mark no more than one applicant as Contract Offered, the rest as Rejected or On Hold. The personnel office then changes the successful applicant's overall status to Contract Offered and creates an employment contract for the applicant. When the signed contract is returned, the personnel officer runs the applicant event Preparing to Hire.

If the selected person turns down the job offer, applicants marked with the status On Hold can be processed. A standard sequence of actions can be planned in customizing to allow rejected applicants to be reconsidered in addition to those on hold.

Offering a Contract

Offering a contract to an applicant entails setting to Contract Offered his overall status and assignment status for the vacancy. A contract must then be printed.

The following steps set an applicant's overall status and vacancy assignment status to Contract Offered:

1. On the initial Recruitment screen, select Applicant Master Data>Bulk Processing>Vacancy Assignment List.

2. Enter * in the Status (overall) field.

3. Specify the vacancy for which the applicant is to be offered a contract in the Vacancy field.

4. Click Execute; a second Vacancy Assignments screen appears.

5. Position the cursor on the applicant who is to be offered a contract and click Change Overall Status.

6. Enter 5 (for Contract Offered) in the Overall Status field and click Continue.

7. From the Maintain Vacancy Assignments screen, select the vacancy for which the contract is to be offered and click Change Status (Vac.).

8. Enter 5 (for Contract Offered) in the Vacancy Assignment Status field and click Continue.

9. If the applicant is assigned to more than one vacancy, select all other vacancies for which the applicant is to be offered a contract and click Change Status (Vac.) for each.

10. Enter the desired status (usually 3 for On Hold) in the Vacancy Assignment Status field and click Continue.

11. Save your entries. The Change View Vacancy: Detail screen appears.

12. Maintain the Percentage Approved, Percentage Reserved, and Staffing Percentage fields.

13. Save your entries.

Printing an Employment Contract

The standard contract stored in the system for the applicant action Mail Offer of Contract can be printed out for an individual applicant or by bulk processing by using the Printing Letters Using Recurring Tasks facility.

Supporting Vacancy Assignment

You can create a list of all applicants in the applicant pool, which is defined as applicants with On Hold status. From this list you can assign individual applicants to one or more vacancies.

If Recruitment is integrated with Personnel Planning and Development, you can also initiate a search based on user-definable qualifications profiles. These qualifications are listed in a qualification catalog and may be freely combined to form a profile. Most positions will have a preassigned requirements profile.

Follow these steps to find applicants for a vacancy by using requirements profiles for positions:

1. On the initial Recruitment screen, select Selection Procedure>Applicant Pool>Via Positions.

2. Enter any selection criteria you require and click Execute.

3. Position the cursor on the vacancy you're trying to fill and click Find Candidate.

The screen displays Persons for Qualifications and/or Requirements. It is sorted according to the number of required qualifications they possess.

If you mark an applicant and click Profile, the system makes a profile comparison of the specifications or values of the applicant's qualifications and the specification of each qualification required by the position.

Evaluating the Applicant Pool

An evaluation group can be identified according to any data fields held in the applicant database. There are two types of standard evaluations in Recruitment:

- Analysis reports (which are essentially lists of applicant data)
- Statistics reports (which are essentially numerical reports on applicant numbers in relation to job advertisements)

Analyzing Applicant Data

The following applicant data analysis reports are available as standard:

- Applicants by Name
- Applications
- Applicants by Event (Receipt of Application)
- Vacancy Assignments
- Maintain Vacancy Assignments

To access the selection screen for the evaluation reports, choose Applicant Master Data>Bulk Processing.

The following steps access the report Applicants' Education and Training:

1. Select Info System>Report Selection.
2. Explode the Applicant mode by marking it with the cursor and selecting the Explode button so that the system will display the available information.
3. Select the appropriate evaluation.

To access the selection screen for the Vacancies report, choose Advertising>Vacancy>Evaluate. To access the selection screen for the Planned Actions for Personnel Officer report, choose Action>List Planned Actions.

Most reports can be accessed by using the reporting tree; choose Info System>Report Selection.

From the list screen, you can call the Refresh function to update all the data analysis reports with any changes that have occurred in the applicant data. If Status is a field in a report's output list, the Bulk Processing function allows you to select several applicants and assign them the same status, such as Rejected or On Hold.

Transferring Applicant Data to PA

Hiring entails transferring applicant data from the Recruitment module to the Personnel Administration module, where it's placed in the employee database. The process can be controlled in three ways, according to the system configuration:

- Using an integrated system starting from Recruitment

- Using an integrated system starting from Personnel Administration
- Saving the data from Recruitment to a local data carrier from which it's imported to Personnel Administration because the system isn't integrated

Each method is managed as a personnel event in which the predefined infotype group and set of infotypes are scanned for relevant applicant data. This information is proposed for transfer and can be overwritten, if necessary. Missing data can be entered at this stage.

The applicant must be assigned the planned actions of Transfer Applicant Data and Hire Applicant, both of which are set to Completed when the actual transfer takes place.

Changing Jobs

The Organizational Reassignment personnel event is run to document any changes in an employee's position in the company structure and personnel structure. This personnel event ensures that all relevant infotypes are brought up to date by creating new records. The validity of the existing records is delimited to allow the system to compile a history of the changes for later analysis.

For example, an employee may be transferred to a different work center, be promoted, or both. The reason for an organizational reassignment is recorded via a set of indicators defined in customizing.

An employee's payroll accounting area can be changed only for a period that hasn't yet been subjected to a payroll run.

N O T E The Organizational Reassignment event is a business procedure that documents a movement or promotion that has to be taken into account by payroll and the costing functions. You must not use it to make corrections for mistakes made during the running of other personnel events.

If the Personnel Planning and Development component is integrated, the employee is assigned to a position during hiring. Organizational Reassignment offers any related infotypes for maintenance. Planned working time infotype 0007 and basic pay infotype 0008 are often edited as a result of organizational reassignment.

If there's a change of administrator, you may have to reassign or return objects on loan. Automatic reminder messages can be arranged for this type of situation during customizing.

The following steps run the Organizational Reassignment event for an employee:

1. Select Human Resources>Personnel Admin.>HR Master Data>Personnel Events.
2. Enter the employee's personnel number.
3. Enter the begin date for the event.
4. Select the Organizational Reassignment event.
5. If the Personnel Planning and Development component is integrated, maintain the Position field in events infotype 0000.

6. Maintain the information on the personnel area, employee group, and employee subgroup if PD isn't integrated.

7. Either select the Choose function or press Enter.

8. Maintain the infotype records sequentially for the reassigned employee.

9. Press Enter when you've entered the data.

10. Save your entries for each infotype in turn.

Leaving the Company

The Leaving personnel event is designed to ensure that all necessary infotypes are delimited with the correct date so that the payroll run or retroactive accounting run is successful. Some records are retained in the system to form a history and be available for consultation if the employee applies for a position in the future.

> **CAUTION**
>
> Don't delete the personnel number of an employee who is leaving the company because she may be due additional payments or benefits.

The following distinctions are made between employees who have left the company:

- Employees who have retired
- Employees who are absent for a long period of time, for example, due to maternity leave or military/civil service

Specific absences are documented when maintaining time data by using absences infotype 2001.

The reason for leaving and the leaving date are recorded by the Leaving event in events infotype 0000. The employment status is set to 0 so that the payroll will omit this employee from the next run. If the Personnel Planning and Development component is integrated, the employee who leaves is automatically assigned to position 99999999. An additional dialog box assists in managing the position vacated by the leaver.

The following infotypes have to be delimited in the list screen because they aren't automatically delimited during the Leaving event:

- Recurring payments and deductions (0014)
- Additional payments (0015)
- Time recording info (0050)

Organizational data, personal data, addresses, and basic payroll data remain in the system; their infotype records must not be delimited. This data is required if the employee receives a back payment, such as overtime or leave compensation after the last payroll accounting run is performed. Basic pay infotype 0008 must not be delimited in case it's needed for retroactive accounting.

Maintaining an Inactive Work Relationship

A work relationship can be inactive because the employee isn't reporting for work because of maternity protection leave, parental leave, military or civil service, and so on. Your company may want to pay (or may be legally required to pay) such items as a Christmas bonus or vacation allowance during the period of the inactive work relationship.

If an employee doesn't actually return to work after an agreed period of an inactive work relationship, you must run the Leaving event to terminate his contract.

There may be differences in the legal requirements for payments during a period of an inactive work relationship depending on the region of legal force covering the contract. SAP suggests that an inactive work relationship should be represented via absences infotype 2001, in which you can record whether the employee is to be paid over this period.

An extended period of inactive work will be classified with employment status 3 (Active). This automatically includes the employee for all personnel functions. If you intend to employ this person—perhaps on a part-time basis during parental leave—you should hire this employee under a different personnel number without terminating the original inactive work relationship.

Managing Business Events

Creating a Training Program from Business Events

A *training program* is a sequence of business event types. A successful training program leaves the trainees more knowledgeable and with more skill than they had before. A PD component known as Training and Event Management is being developed by successive R/3 releases in order to extend the functions of PD-SCM Seminar and Convention Management. The following activities need to be supported:

- Creating training programs for employees' further training needs
- Making potential attendees aware of the benefits
- Booking places
- Costing and charging
- Evaluating the effectiveness of the events

Creating a Business Event

The creation of a new business event, such as a training program, begins with entry of a training program number or acceptance of the system-determined internal number, together with the start date for the validity period of the event data object that represents the training program. Selecting Create establishes this object and displays the data-entry screen, which can be supplied the necessary information and saved.

If a similar object already exists, it can be entered in the Copy From field as a reference. All the data already in the reference object will be suggested as defaults for copying or editing. An object created by manual entries can also be used as a model for the rest of the objects to be created in the same session. If you choose Fast Data Entry, the system retains the data-entry screen for the number of objects you want to create. Select Back to leave fast data-entry mode.

The standard R/3 system as delivered includes many predefined data objects needed by the system itself. Also, many standard objects are likely to be immediately useful in the company's implementation. When a company installs and configures the standard R/3, the particular system of software is classed as an *instance* because it's a logical instantiation of the original R/3.

If you then decide to create a new type of data object that will replace the standard object, it's classed as an *instance object type*. For example, a standard instance object of type R is recognized as a resource type, of which there may be several objects of type G that represent examples of different resources.

In training program design, one key resource is the instructor. You can define an object of type H (an external person) as the instance object type that's to be taken as a resource.

The *controlling area* is an object that identifies a self-contained, organizational unit within a group, for which cost accounting can be performed.

Cost center is an object that represents an organizational unit within a controlling area. The cost center object represents a separate physical location in which costs are incurred. The cost center concept can be extended to cover situations in which the following kinds of costs are incurred:

- Cost centers based on functional requirements
- Cost centers based on allocation criteria
- Cost centers that differentiate activities or services provided
- Cost centers defined by location or area of responsibility

A training program is always assigned to a cost center for billing purposes.

Setting Up a Business Events Catalog

The business event catalog's fields display the availability of a training course and include the following elements:

- Prerequisites
- Contents and objectives
- Additional information (notes)
- Time schedule
- Allowed number of participants
- Internal and external planned costs

The business event infotype 1026 stores the following additional information:

- Internal/external flag
- Flag indicating a session
- Business event language in which the event is held
- Lock flag (to inhibit further attendance bookings)
- Deletion flag to signify that the event has been canceled

Assigning Courses

The course assignment serves to identify the persons or organizations responsible. Teaching may be provided by an external organizer and also have internal organizers spread across more than one course location. There's also provision to record the following information about the administration of the resources generally required:

- Capacity of rooms and so on
- Availability features (how many per unit?)
- Assignment of resource types to course types
- Assignment of individual resources to courses
- Assignment of individual resources to locations

Creating Resource Types

A *resource type* defines a group of resources with the same characteristics that are normally interchangeable, although the following resource types have special characteristics that can render them unique:

- *Rooms* because they have a specific capacity.
- *Instructors* because they may have particular qualifications. External instructors have to be associated with an external company or contractor.

If you have several seminar rooms similarly equipped, you can designate them as a resource type because any one of them is suitable for a seminar. One or more resource types can be assigned to a business event type to create utilities, which can then be assigned to individual business events.

The following data is normally recorded for resource types:

- Capacity, such as maximum, optimum, and minimum number of places
- Costs subdivided into cost elements that can be used to calculate a price proposal for a business event
- Availability indicators to determine who is allowed to use the resource
- Alternative resources

After you create or select by reference a typical object—such as a business event or a resource—you can call, create, and maintain similar objects from the catalog by using the Maintain Master Data via Catalog function.

Resources are classified as follows:

- Rooms, in particular, with details of the building owner, room number or name, and any resource types that are always provided, such as projectors, telephone, fax
- External instructors not recorded in HR master data, with their company affiliation and administrative details, including the type of business event they normally supervise
- Other resources

A resource data object can be subjected to the status cycle:

active -> planned -> submitted -> approved/rejected

This normally isn't necessary for established resources.

Creating a Business Event Group

Creating a business event group and then assigning business events or business event groups to it can link courses and other business events into a hierarchical structure. The hierarchy can be viewed selectively to determine events offered in a specified period.

This assignment is conveniently accomplished by assigning business event types as "belonging to" when creating the business event type. The hierarchy should be built from the bottom up.

Creating a Business Event Type

An actual business event is a specialization of a business event type assigned to a particular time. Each business event type is defined by the following parameters:

- Capacity in terms of minimum, optimum, and maximum number of attendees
- Internal and external prices
- Decay meter, to control the minimum time before a person can attend the event type again
- Additional information, such as indicators to signify that the event is a convention and whether it should be included in the business event brochure
- General description comprising contents, notes, and extended business event texts that can be used in a brochure
- Schedule model, which nominates the main time schedule from infotype 1042 and, optionally, an alternative schedule from infotype 1035
- Business event demand, which shows how often this business event type has to be run per quarter and per language
- Procedure, which specifies the mechanisms for double booking checks, double prebooking checks, attendance prerequisites, attendance qualifications, and arrangements for following up on this event
- Costs subdivided into cost elements
- Sales area (to control billing)
- Relationships

The following relationships are defined for each business event type by entering the necessary information:

- Belongs to business event group
- Requires resource type(s)
- Is held by person (the normal instructor)
- Imparts qualification
- Presupposes business event type
- Presupposes qualification(s)
- Is organized by organizational unit (internal event)
- Is organized by company (external contractor)

Business event type info infotype 1029 stores additional information about a business event type in the following check boxes:

- Inclusion in Business Event Brochure
- Convention, which is defined as a multisession business event comprising one main business event and one or more sessions

Planning a Catalog of Course Types

The definition of a course type or other training event type is specified in a catalog of course types maintained by the HR-Human Resources application. The data attributes and elements of this catalog are as follows:

- Prerequisite courses or other qualifications for attendance at this event
- Qualifications provided by this course
- Contents of the training event
- Methods of this training event
- Dates and time patterns of this event
- Planned internal costs of this event, including currency, hours, and persons absent from normal work
- Minimum or maximum critical numbers for this event
- Technical resources of equipment and instructors required
- Course description in text form for use in brochures

If you have a model or have created one in the form of a business event group or type, you can use it to build a set of business event records. The only element you can't create or delete from a catalog is a training program.

The catalog display differentiates different objects by the colors of the backgrounds, and you can access a key to interpret them. The catalog's structure is indicated as a hierarchy using line indents and bullet styles.

Placing Qualifications in the Organizational Model

The following object types are used in the PD-OM Organizational Management component's data model:

- Organizational unit
- Position
- Workplace
- Job
- Task

Two anchor object types are accessed by the PD-OM Organizational Management component:

- Person as defined in the HR-Human Resources, PA-Personnel Administration module
- Cost center as defined in the CO-CCA Cost Accounting component

These anchor object types aren't managed in the PD-OM Organizational Management component. Their data can be accessed via relationships that are master records which record the permanent association of a data element of a record in one database with a data element of a record in another.

A cost center specified in CO-CCA Cost Accounting has allocated to it one or more organizational units, which can be all on the same level in a flat structure or arranged into hierarchies, parts of which may be flat structures.

A person defined in the HR-Human Resources, PA-Personnel Administration system holds or occupies a position and a workplace. The position is attached to a particular workplace, and the workplace is defined as having room for only one person. For example, a machine operator is a position. A position may be unoccupied, in which case it takes up no space in the workplace. Several positions can occupy a workplace, each held by different peoplemd]but not at the same time. They would have to be shift workers or those engaged in job sharing. Also, one person can have positions in more than one workplace, but again, not at the same time.

The position is part of an organizational unit.

A *job* is a description of what's entailed by a positionmd]what the person holding that position must achieve. There may be more work than one person can do, in which case there will be more than one position for the same job.

A *task* is what has to be done to carry out part of a job. One job might entail several different tasks, or separate tasks can be repetitions of a basic task, perhaps with occasional minor variations due to variations in the material being processed or in environmental conditions. The distinction between task and job is a matter established to suit the individual company.

A position may entail a specific personnel requirement, as may a specific workplace or one or more of the tasks entailed by the job to be performed there. For example, high tower crane driver requires a person who is reliable and patient. This particular workplace couldn't be occupied by a person who was afraid of heights. The task of controlling the swing of the load on the crane as it's being moved needs to be done by somebody with the knowledge and the eyesight to judge the situation. The crane driver also must have good hand/eye coordination to operate the crane precisely and quickly so as to cancel the tendency for the load to swing past the point where it's to be placed. Each crane comprises one workplace. A person with the position of crane-driver could be qualified to occupy any of them.

A person appointed to a position may have some requirements, but not all; in that case, there's a requirement for a training program and (certainly in the case of the crane driver) a period of personal supervision by an experienced operator, perhaps leading to a formal certification of competence. The SAP R/3 system needs the Qualification object type recognized to support the Qualification and Requirements component of the PD-OM Organizational Management module.

Using Dynamic Data-Driven Menus

The functionality of the data-driven menus in Training and Event Management is focused on a structure that links all the application module's individual functions and data objects. The following dynamic menus are used to create and edit objects: Attendance, Business Event, and Information.

At the top of a structure you might have a type of course represented as a business event group. This top-level group would have individual members represented also as business event groups. This arrangement of classifying business event groups could have any number of levels. Thus, one level could be a specific type of course—in a technical specialty, for example.

The next level would represent specific planned business events that executed this type of course at specific locations to a schedule. In each location there can be several equivalent seminars at the same time for which specific persons are booked.

A menu is said to be *dynamic* because you can expand the structure until you're working in the level that suits your purpose. In the Attendance menu, for example, you could expand the structure down to the level of a specific business event. The following functions would then be available and automatically primed with the relevant data:

- Book
- Prebook
- Replace
- Rebook
- Cancel

You can arrange through customizing for the dynamic menus to adopt the data collation and display arrangements most suitable for your purposes.

The Selection Criteria function opens a dialog box that offers the following criteria for selecting the business events you intend to work with:

- Status
- Number of attendees
- Business event type (internal/external)
- Historical record
- Deletion flag
- Lock flag
- Business event location

The structure can be used to display business events with vacant places by selecting just the criterion Available (business events). Each user can set the special access to limit the display to a chosen root object and its lower-level associates. This substructure then remains as the default special access for the user who set it. The total overview is always available as an option.

The display can overlay a Color Legend dialog box to reveal how the various object types are presented with different color backgrounds.

Planning Business Event Dates and Resource Reservations

Planning the date of an internal business event needs at least the following information:

- Status firmly booked/planned
- Location
- Language
- Schedule
- Number of attendees
- Price and cost assignment
- Organizer

The planning of external events is obviously a matter for the contractor company.

The following steps initiate business event date planning:

1. From the Training and Event Management menu, select Business Events>Dates>Plan.
2. In the Business Event Type field, specify the business event type for which you want to plan a business event.
3. Enter or accept a business event number.
4. If necessary, edit the Planning Period fields by specifying start and end dates.
5. Select Data Screen>Firmly Booked or Planned Status.
6. Enter the business event location, if necessary.
7. Copy from the schedule model or create one.
8. Select Transfer if the schedule is acceptable.
9. If you want to plan your business event date without selecting resources, click the Save w/o Resources button. If you want to plan the business event date with the required resources, select the resources.
10. If you want to transfer the date proposal output by the system, skip to step 14. If you don't want to transfer the date proposal, click the Previous Date icon or Next Date icon.
11. If none of the proposed dates suits you, change the start and end dates of the planning period.
12. If no suitable date can be found, you can remove the planning conditions by deselecting either Take Account of Days Off or Take Account of Start Day.
13. Make a resource selection and repeat the sequence until a suitable date can be found.
14. Click Transfer.

Planning with the Availability Indicators

Availability indicators infotype 1023 stores the conditions that apply to resource types required for planning or preparing a business event. Availability indicators specify the following resource details:

- The type of resource
- Any location-dependent factors

- The reservation characteristic of the resource (obligatory, single, or multiple)
- The amount available
- The resource priority
- The instances

If a resource is obligatory, the amount available is taken into consideration in relation to the number of attendees and the amount they each require.

Checking Booking with the Procedure Infotype

Infotype 1030 specifies how the system should check up on potential attendees for each business event type. In customizing, a standard online processing procedure is assigned for business event types. Individual business event types can be assigned their own checking procedures.

The attendee checking procedure includes the following programmed actions:

- Check for bookings on business events of the same type
- Check for prebookings on the same business event type
- Check for attendance prerequisites in the form of business events already attended
- Check for required qualifications for attendance at this business event

Procedure infotype 1030 also specifies follow-up activities, including the following:

- Transfer the business event objectives to the attendee's records in the form of qualifications.
- Delete the relationship between the business event and the attendee.
- Set up a relationship between the attendee and the business event type that can be used to check the attendee's attendance prerequisites when making a later booking.

Specifying Business Event Type Prices

Infotype 1021 records the price that an attendee has to pay for attending a business event of a particular type. The price is quoted in the appropriate currency and may be an internal price for cost allocation or an external price for billing an external business event organizing company. A booking may be processed free of charge, or the default price suggested from the infotype may be overwritten. Each attendee may be charged a different price, if necessary. Choose Business Events>Price Proposal to call the Maintain Prices report to update the prices infotype.

Interpreting the Resource Type Indicators

A group of resources with the same characteristics can be identified as *members* of a resource type. Rooms are recorded as a resource type with special characteristics because they have a particular capacity. External instructors are also a resource type with the special characteristic of being provided by an external contractor company.

Resource types can also be characterized by the following reservation characteristics:

- *Multiple* if more than one business event can reserve the individual resources at the same time, such as a suite of similar rooms
- *Obligatory* if resources of this type must be considered in planning
- *Critical* if an obligatory resource type is in short supply over the period

Interpreting the Decay Meter

The *decay meter* is an infotype record used in personnel planning to record the interval of time in years and months after which the value of a qualification is reduced to half its original value.

In Training and Event Management, the decay meter infotype record specifies the time between attendance at a business event and the need to re-attend the business event.

The decay meter record is used to control rebooking an attendee on a business event attended previously.

Operating with Schedule Models

A *schedule* is a record in infotype 1035 that specifies a time plan of business events. A schedule model contains a business event type time plan in infotype 1042 that can be copied and edited if necessary. A schedule needs the following information:

- Day number for each day with date, start and end times, and flag indicating days off
- Duration in days
- Duration in hours
- Number of dates (one date or several dates)
- Start day

Schedule models are differentiated according to their components:

- Schedule model with pattern
- Schedule model without pattern
- User-defined schedule model
- Day number with start time and end time
- Duration in days
- Duration in hours
- Number of dates (one date or several dates)
- Start day

The following schedule model subtypes have already been set up in the standard SAP system:

Subtype 0001	Main schedule model
Subtype 0002	Alternative schedule model
Subtype 0003	Temporary schedule model

You can create further schedule model subtypes in customizing. These subtypes can be used to arrange business events that vary only in their scheduled deployment over the calendar and hence in the way they may encounter weekends and public holidays.

A *schedule pattern* is a standard specification for the time structure of business events. It can be used as a model for copying. The pattern takes the form of a sequence of day descriptions, each of which comprises a day number and a time block ID. A time block can comprise a maximum of three time blocks, each defined by its start and end times.

A schedule may include a flag to indicate that a generalized schedule is to be applied, whereby each day starts at 00.01 and ends at 23.59.

Marketing Business Events

The following functions are available to assist in marketing and publicizing business events:

- Customer and address management sorted by branch region
- Administration of agreements and conditions including discounts and service contracts
- Customer history
- Mailing actions
- Business event planning
- Quota and budget administration

Recording Business Event Demand

The demand for business events of a particular type is expressed as the number of events needed in a given period. This is normally a calendar year, optionally divided into quarters. Infotype 1020 records the demand for events of each business event type.

The validity period of a business event type is normally set or left to default within the calendar year. Validity periods of records of the same business type may not overlap.

Weighting with the Booking Priority

The *booking priority* is a two-digit number used to apply weightings to bookings in order to sort them into priority intervals that relate to the following booking priorities:

- Waiting list
- Normal booking
- Essential booking

Applying Capacity Rules

Capacity infotype 1024 accepts values for the minimum, optimum, and maximum capacity for resource types such as rooms, resources, business event types, and business events. The system will suggest canceling an event if the minimum capacity hasn't been reached when firm booking is attempted. Optimum capacity is used in calculating the resources required and the expected costs.

The following rules calculate the capacities of a business event:

- The minimum capacity of a business event is the highest of the minimum capacities of the resources involved and the business event minimum.

- The value of the optimum capacity of a business event is the lowest of the optimum capacities of the resources involved and of the business event optimum.

- The value of the maximum capacity of a business event is the lowest of the maximum capacities of the resources involved and of the business event maximum.

If neither resources nor business event has capacity infotype records, the business event type capacity values are taken.

If the value you enter as the minimum capacity exceeds the value specified for the optimum capacity, the system automatically reduces the minimum capacity to the value of the optimum capacity.

If the value you enter as the maximum capacity is less than the value specified for the optimum capacity, the system automatically increases the maximum capacity to the value of the optimum capacity.

Assigning Booking Priorities

Normal or *attendance* booking is assigned if attendance of a business event is guaranteed and if the optimum number of attendees isn't reached.

Essential booking is assigned if attendance of a business event is considered absolutely necessary, even if the optimum number of attendees has already been reached.

Waiting-list booking is assigned if attendance of a business event isn't possible because all places on the business event have already been booked up. Rebookings or cancellations can allow a waiting-list booking to be converted into an attendance booking.

Differentiating Attendee Types

An individual attendee can be identified as any of the following attendee types:

- Person
- User
- External person
- Applicant
- Contact person

A group attendee is defined according to its affiliation:

- Company
- Organizational unit

- Customer
- Interested parties

Group attendees can be booked in the form of a number of persons, an N.N. (no-name) booking. Alternatively, a group can be booked by first booking individual attendees and booking them as group attendees.

Firmly Booking Business Events

The following steps firmly book a training event for which there are some attendance bookings:

1. From the Training and Event Management window, select Business Events>Firmly Book/Cancel.

2. In the Editing frame, choose Firmly Book (optimum) or Firmly Book (maximum).

3. If necessary, edit the proposed current date in the Rebooking As Of field in the Additional Data frame.

4. Select Data Screen.

5. If the number of attendance bookings is less than the minimum capacity, decide whether you want to cancel the business event.

6. If there is no waiting list of unplaced attendees for the business event, select Save Without Rebooking. If there are unplaced attendees and you want to revise the attendee list, select an attendee on the list of Firmly Bookable Attendees to be replaced on the waiting list.

7. Under Unplaced Attendees, select an attendee to be included in the attendee list.

8. Click the Swap Selected button.

9. Select Save.

Arranging Correspondence

The "set up user-specific output control" and "output control based on attendee type" customizing steps allow you to determine the documents to be used for business event notification. A default choice of media is also predefined. Notifications for a business event can be output selectively according to priority, attendee type, and individual attendee.

Following Up Business Events

You can arrange various follow-up activities for a business event that has reached the Firmly Booked status, hasn't been canceled, and hasn't already been marked with a historical record flag.

From the attendees' viewpoint, one important activity after a business event is for the business event objectives to be recognized as qualifications. The following actions are also part of follow-up:

- Deleting all attendance bookings
- Creating a relationship between the business event type and the attendee, which includes storing a value that initiates the transfer of qualifications to the attendee's records
- Setting a historical record flag for the business event
- Outputting confirmation of attendance notifications

Control of the follow-up activities is organized by entries in procedure infotype 1030 for the business event type. Actions for each attendee type are determined in this way.

The stored relationship between a business event (or any instance of a business event type) and a particular type of attendee can be used to check whether the attendee meets the prerequisites for attending other business events.

A default procedure for each business event type is established when customizing Training and Event Management in the "set up control parameters for follow-up processing" step of the implementation procedure.

When a business event is marked with the historical record flag, you can't make any changes to the data—the event will no longer be offered. However, the business event objectives are transferred to the attendees as qualifications.

The following steps follow up a business event:

1. From the Training and Event Management window, select Business Events>Follow Up.
2. Enter the business event on which you want to follow up.
3. Complete the Valuation of Qualifications field as appropriate.
4. Select an execution mode as Online or Background.
5. If you want to historically record the business event, click the appropriate option.
6. If you want to run the follow-up in test mode first, click the Execute button to start the program in test mode. To start the program immediately, deselect the Test Mode check box.

Arranging Appraisals

Standard appraisals are provided as models for business events and attendees. You can edit copies of these models or create new appraisals in customizing. The main appraisal parameters are as follows:

- Appraisal type
- Assessor
- Appraisal criteria
- Criterion values as the number of points on an evaluation scale for each criterion

NOTE Standard SAP defaults to a criterion value scale from 1 to 6. ■

An evaluation path between the assessor and the object type being appraised must be defined by a series of linking relationships.

The following steps create a business event appraisal:

1. From the Training and Event Management menu, select Business Events>Appraisals.
2. Specify the type of assessor by clicking the down arrow button and selecting an object type.
3. Specify an assessor that corresponds to the object type you chose.
4. Accept the default object type and specify the business event to be appraised.
5. Change the selection period, if necessary, from the default of three months ending with the current date.
6. Select Continue.

You now have to choose the business event to be appraised by selecting the appropriate check box in the initial screen and selecting Data Screen. The default validity period of the business event appraisal is the date of the business event. You can inspect previous appraisals for this business event by selecting Existing Appraisal. You must enter a value for each criterion before saving the appraisal you've created.

An *attendee appraisal* appraises attendees at a particular business event. A sample is provided in standard R/3. The procedure begins by choosing Attendance>Appraisals from the Training and Event menu. Thereafter, follow the steps for creating a business event appraisal.

Billing and Allocating Business Event Costs

You can bill individual and group attendees with the fees for a business event by issuing an invoice via the billing interface; this can be done only if you've set this up in customizing. The billing document number is stored in the relationship infotype against the Takes Part In link between attendee and business event.

Assigning Sales Areas with the Billing/Allocation Info Infotype

Infotype 1037 records an association between a business event organizer and a sales area. You must also assign sales areas to business event types if you intend to carry out billing for business events. A sales area billing specification includes three characteristics:

- *Sales organization*, identified as the organizational unit responsible for the sale of particular products or services
- *Distribution channel*, indicating how the goods or services reach the customers
- *Division*, which groups materials, products, and services

If you're using internal cost allocation, you can specify an activity type for each business event type or organizer. A cost allocation specification is formed in customizing from activity types used in cost accounting to valuate the various services and activities performed in a cost center.

Costing Business Events

Business event costs are computed from the cost elements stored in costs infotype 1036. Separate records can exist per business event type or business event and per resource type or resource.

The following business event type costs are compiled from cost elements that are customized with default values:

- Instructor costs
- Training materials
- Marketing costs
- Resource type costs such as equipment rental, electricity, and stationery

The costs can be calculated per time unit, per business event, or per attendee. The costs can be used for a price proposal based on the optimum number of attendees. A price proposal is stored as a record in prices infotype 1021.

If the costs are transferred to Cost Accounting, the system lists the individual costs of the cost elements, the activity type, the resource, and organizer cost centers as well as the overall costs per business event. The system also outputs an error log that lists the business events whose costs weren't transferred.

Budgeting and Funds Management

If you've created a budget for an organizational unit, you can compare it with the attendance and cancellation fees recorded in Training and Event Management. The comparison period is for the current fiscal year up to a key date that you specify.

The following steps create a budget:

1. In the Training and Event Management menu, choose Business Events>Budget>Create.
2. Specify an organizational unit.
3. Accept or edit the current date as the date.
4. Select Data Screen to see the organizational unit, along with any subordinate organizational units it might have.
5. For each organizational unit, specify the budget value for the fiscal year that corresponds to the date you entered.
6. Select Save.

The value displayed in the Distributed field is the budget value cumulated from the budget values of the subordinate organizational units.

Comparing Budgets

From the Training and Event Management menu, you can choose Business Events>
Budget>Comparison and then specify one or more organizational units. You can then inspect
the structure of these units and elect to include or exclude cancellation fees.

When you execute the program, the system displays the budget value and the actual value for
each organizational unit. The display uses the predefined currency and covers the period from
the first day of the current fiscal year up to the key date that you specified.

Using the HR Information System

In this chapter

Placing HRIS in the Center of the Company

The SAP HRIS (Human Resources Information System) provides relevant HR information to those who need it to make decisions. Because HRIS extends across the enterprise, it can extract pertinent information from the other business applications such as Financial Accounting, Controlling, Product Planning, Plant Maintenance, Logistics, and the Project Systems.

Some ways in which HRIS can be used are as follows:

- Strategic staffing using shift planning that meets the capacity requirements by deploying staff according to their qualifications, availability, and shift preferences
- Comparative staffing options costing that offers the best costing data to assist in decisions
- Staffing for particular customers
- Performing a simulation to explore the HR needs of company restructuring and resizing
- Anticipating the HR costs of new products, customer partnerships, and acquisitions
- Assessing the costs of absences, substitutions, and overtime
- Allocating training costs according to instructors, rooms, materials, and equipment
- Calculating costs of plant maintenance from time management information
- Monitoring assets such as company vehicles, personal computers, credit cards, security badges, keys, tools, and other equipment on loan to employees
- Automatically consulting payroll information and generating payments to benefits providers
- Sending garnishments to third parties by using Accounts Payable
- Invoicing customers who attend training events

Techniques of linking HRIS to the Internet and to the internal company intranet are improved by browsers that are easy to use because they adopt control modes familiar to users from many different systems. Given proper attention to authorization and the privacy of personnel information, this extensive linkage can be exploited to provide employees access to relevant business-critical data and to their own records, which they might need to manage their careers and their finances.

For personnel managers, the HRIS system can provide the central utility for managing personnel and their careers. The networked nature of the extended HR community allows vacancies to be widely advertised and inquiries to rapidly return useful responses. When applicants are given a personal ID or password, they can monitor the progress of their bids.

From the company's viewpoint, the HRIS provides a valuable directory of employees and their supervisors, complete with all relevant details and perhaps even a photograph. Selective searching can track down any mix of work experience or qualifications.

The function of business workflow is to distribute tasks automatically at the right time to the right employees. In particular, the following tasks can be distributed to mailboxes and supported as needed by automatic mail and optical archiving:

- Submission of application forms
- Planning and holding interviews
- Drawing up contract offers
- Preparing new appointments
- Monitoring rejected applications

HR Employee Self-Service components are based on intranet scenarios that enable employees to display and selectively update their own personnel data from their Internet browsers. The following functions illustrate the type of interaction that is possible:

- Updating address and dependents' data
- Checking entitlement and submitting leave requests that will be delivered to the leave controller by workflow
- Reviewing own benefits data online
- Consulting regulations and entering expense account data online; monitoring progress of expense claims
- Calling up Certificates of Employment

Data that an employee changes is automatically sent to the Human Resources department for checking and confirmation.

Reporting Master Data

A *master data list report* takes the form of an employees list, with each employee associated with data fields that are specified online or as defaults in the report's design.

A *master data statistical report* gathers numerical information about employees according to the search specification and processing instructions assigned for the report. The display format can be a list or, in some cases, graphs that use SAP business graphics.

The reports most likely to be needed are arranged as a hierarchy known as the *report tree*, from which a selected report can be initiated.

A *log record* documents all changes that are made to Master Data and Applicant Data infotype records. Log records can be inspected for a specified period by using the Logged Changes in Infotype Data report. The change records for a personnel file include the ID of the user responsible for the changes.

The HR system compiles a data history by collating all records in the order of their validity periods, which can extend into the future.

ABAP/4 Query is a software component that allows authorized users to set up specific reports of the following types:

- Basic lists
- Statistics
- Ranking lists

These reporting types can be combined to specify more complicated reports through the ABAP/4 Query component.

N O T E Familiarity with the ABAP/4 programming language isn't essential for using the ABAP/4 Query component. ■

Using the General Report Tree

The menu path you follow to select a report using the general report tree begins at the highest level by selecting an application integrated with the R/3 system. The next subnode comprises a component from the application nominated at the top level. Successive subnodes refine the report target and scope according to the data objects most often used to collate data. Thus, a stock report would appear under Materials Management>Inventory Management>Material, and so on.

Depending on the application, reports can be available at several levels.

The following steps execute a report from the report tree:

1. Select Information systems>General report sel to display a report tree.
2. Expand the Human Resources subtree.
3. Expand, if necessary, an additional subtree that might have been added to Human Resources.
4. Start the chosen report by clicking it.
5. View the selection screen for the report and enter the selection criteria.
6. Select Execute.

Interpreting the Report Selection Screen

The HR Report selection screen shows a list of selection criteria, each with two data-entry fields: From and To. A single value would be entered in the From field. The report output can comprise data of specific employees or numerical (statistical) analyses.

You can configure the structure of the Report selection screen. The following functions are available from this screen:

■ *Further Selections* allows a customized extension to the default selection criteria list. It can include reports and concatenated fields made up from standard data elements. Unnecessary criteria can be eliminated from a search specification.

■ *Sort* controls the order in which employees are presented in a list report.

■ *Matchcodes* are fields to receive information that's to be used with selection criteria specified in the selection screen.

■ *Variant* is used to identify a collection of data field entries and additional attributes that have been saved for rapid report specification.

■ *Complex Selections* allows selection criteria to be more complex than a simple range of values by including or excluding particular values and subranges.

■ *Selection Options* extends the scope of the Complex Selections function.

Generating Master Data Reports

The following master data list reports are standard:

■ List of Employees, with personnel number, job title, and entry and leaving dates

■ Employees and Their Family Members

■ Bank Connections for Payments to Employees

■ Service Anniversaries, including date of entry into the company and years of service

The following steps generate a list report:

1. Select Human resources>Personnel admin.
2. Select Info system.
3. Select an individual master data report, or select Report Selection to display a part of the general report tree.
4. Expand all the subnodes for Employee.
5. Choose a report by double-clicking it.

The following master data statistical reports are standard:

■ Staffing Level Development, including the number of employees in an employee subgroup over the selected time period.

■ Employee Groups and Subgroups, including gender, average seniority, and age statistics per selection unit.

■ Nationalities, including gender statistics.

■ Seniority and Age: Part 1 gives gender and average age statistics for each seniority level, part 2 provides gender and average seniority statistics for each age group.

■ Statistical Evaluations, which is based on user-defined column and row classification features.

■ Salary and Seniority, including projected annual salaries derived from each employee's Basic Pay, Pension Plan, Additional Payments, and Recurring Payments and Deductions infotype records. The average annual salary and number of employees are given for each seniority level. By using the Employee List function, you can see specific information per employee. The report also calculates total salaries paid and the average annual salary.

■ Pay Level, based on the pay scale classification of the employee workforce. Gender and associated years statistics are given for each combination of pay scale area, type, group, and level. Summary information is provided for each pay scale area and type combination.

Reading Log Records

You display log records for a specific period with the Logged Changes in Infotype Data report. The fields are Field Name, Old Value, New Value, and Action. Action reports whether the infotype record is inserted (I), updated (U), or delimited (D).

Log records can be sorted and displayed selectively.

Noting Improvements to the HRIS

As of release 3.1, reports can be generated in HTML format so that they can be directly transmitted over the Internet to any standard browser and be used in email. Most other improvements to HRIS have focused on ways of avoiding the use of the Report selection screen, especially for reports likely to be frequently used.

The ABAP Query function provides a simple means for defining your own reports. ABAP experience isn't needed because data selection and the specification of an output format are menu driven. As of release 4.0, the Ad Hoc Query function requires only a click on the required information as you identify what you need from the organizational diagram.

Portraying Objects with the PD Graphic Tools

Graphic tools in R/3 visually present information and allow users to work from within the display. PD includes the following graphics tools:

- Structural Graphics
- Statistical Graphics
- Business Graphics

The main tasks of Structural Graphics in Organization and Planning are to help you inspect the structures and objects that make up an organizational plan and to maintain these entities and thus manipulate the plan itself. The basic viewing format is the hierarchical or family tree structure.

There are two ways of maintaining organizational plan objects:

- Use the Structural Graphics toolbox with the main graphics window
- Use the menu options behind Utilities and Extras

Although using Structural Graphics is faster than using Detail Maintenance, some PD functionality isn't amenable to management from Structural Graphics, which is mainly focused on creating Relationship infotype records. If you need to maintain other infotypes, you need to exit Structural Graphics before these infotypes become refreshed with your new data.

Structural Graphics is well adapted to working with organizational, reporting, and business event structures.

Statistical Graphics outputs a two-dimensional line graph that's best suited to comparisons, such as the qualifications of an employee with the requirements of a position.

Business Graphics can develop graphs and charts of three and four dimensions suited to depicting breakdowns (of costs, for example) according to organizational unit.

The toolbox presents a collection of options that allow you to perform basic editing on an object that you've identified in the main Graphics window. The toolbox can be customized.

The graphics tools in PD are associated with different modules, although there are routes to each tool from each module. The scope of objects is normally limited by the module from which the graphics tool is accessed. You can enter Structural Graphics for any object by the appropriate procedure.

The following steps start Structural Graphics for Organizational Units so that you can work with related positions, employees, or work centers:

1. From the Organization and Planning window, select Reporting>Organizational unit.
2. Under Organization Chart in the dialog box, double-click the Graphics option that suits your needs.
3. Complete the fields and click Execute.
4. From the window listing organizational units and possible positions, employees, and work centers, select the highest level that includes the units of interest.
5. Select the Structural Graphics button.

The following steps start Structural Graphics for Positions, provided at least one position is in the organizational plan:

1. From the Organization and Planning window, select Reporting>Position.
2. Under Organigram, double-click the Graphics option that suits your needs.
3. Complete the fields and click Execute to display a listing of the selected positions and employees (if this option is chosen).
4. Select the highest position in the list that includes the items of interest and select Structural Graphics.

The following steps start Structural Graphics for work centers, provided that the organizational plan contains at least one organizational unit:

1. From the Organization and Planning window, select Reporting>Work center.
2. Double-click Work Center Per Org. Unit.
3. Restrict the scope of the report if necessary by entries in the Report Request window.
4. Select Execute.
5. Select the highest position in the list that includes the items of interest, and then select Structural Graphics.

The following steps start Structural Graphics when you want to view and work with tasks in an organizational plan, or with the positions and employees involved:

1. From the Organization and Planning window, select Reporting>Task.
2. Double-click the required task profile option.

3. Limit the scope of the report, if necessary, by entries in the Report Request window.

4. Select Execute to view the selected organizational units, positions, tasks, and perhaps employees.

5. Select the highest position in the list that includes the items of interest and select Structural Graphics.

The following steps start Structural Graphics for any object:

1. From the Organization and Planning window, select Tools>Structural Graphics.

2. Complete the appropriate fields in the Report Request window to identify the objects you want to work with.

3. Identify an evaluation path in the Evaluation Path field.

4. Select Execute.

Creating Objects in Structural Graphics

An object in Structural Graphics is defined by a record in the Relationship infotype that links it to an existing object in the organizational plan. You can create more than one object at a time by following these steps:

1. From the Structural Graphics window, select the object that's to become the parent object for the new object you create.

2. Retrieve the toolbox and select Utilities.

3. Double-click Create Object or select Utilities>Create objects.

4. Complete the Abbr. and Name fields for each object. You want to create up to five new objects.

5. Enter a validity period for the objects you create by selecting the Period button or pressing F5.

6. Enter validity periods for the object and the Relationship infotype or accept the default dates shown.

7. Display the Status dialog box for the objects you create by selecting the Status button or pressing F6.

8. Select the appropriate status option or accept the default.

9. Select Continue.

The new objects you create appear in the hierarchical structure shown in the Structural Graphics window. The Utilities>Insert Objects function is available to relate existing isolated objects to specific parent objects in the organizational plan. A dialog box invites you to select the appropriate relationship, enter the validity period, and assign a status indicator.

Moving Objects in Structural Graphics

Moving an object in an organizational plan entails changing the Relationship infotype records of the object and those beneath it. The move won't be permitted unless the new relationships are allowable in the application holding the data. The following steps move an object in Structural Graphics:

1. Select the object you want to move.
2. Retrieve the toolbox and select Utilities.
3. Double-click Move Object or select Utilities>Move objects.
4. Drag the "move" symbol with the mouse to the object that's to become the new parent.
5. Click to have the system move the selected object, as well as any underlying objects, to the specified area of the structure.

Delimiting Objects in Structural Graphics

The following steps delimit the validity period of an object in the Structural Graphics window:

1. Select the object you want to delimit.
2. Retrieve the toolbox and select Utilities.
3. Double-click Delimit Object or select Utilities>Delimit object.
4. Set the delimitation date by pressing the Period button or F5 and complete the Delimitation Date field.
5. Select the Continue button to return to the Delimit dialog box.
6. Select the Continue button to return to Structural Graphics.

Deleting Objects in Structural Graphics

The Delete function is used only on objects created in error. Delimit is used when an object ceases to be current because the records can still be accessed from the archives as necessary.

Using the Structural Graphics Dialog Box Buttons

Although the object types available through Structural Graphics vary according to the installed and configured applications, the following buttons achieve consistent results when they appear in graphics dialog boxes:

- *Continue* saves the entries made and exits the dialog box.
- *Apply* saves the entries made, but the dialog box remains open.
- *Cancel* stops the system from saving the entries made as the dialog box is exited.
- *Help* displays online help that describes the options offered in the dialog box.

Selecting Structural Graphics Objects

The following conventions are adopted for all structural objects, including those in Structural Graphics:

- Click a single object to highlight it.
- Shift+click objects anywhere in the display to select objects randomly.

- Click and drag to create a rectangle that encompasses all objects you want to select, and then release the mouse button.
- Press Ctrl and select the highest level of a branch you intend to work with.
- Hold down Ctrl+Shift until you select the highest level of each branch you intend to work with.
- Select Edit>Select all to highlight all objects in all view windows.

The menu sequence Edit>Deselect releases the objects in all view windows from the selection.

Various functions are available to effectively zoom in and out of a structure and place particular objects centrally in the display window.

The following aspects of individual objects can be changed:

- Background color of an object shape
- Text that identifies an object
- Geometric shape representing the object
- Lines that connect an object to its parent object

Color and shape changes apply only to the current work session, unless the Save Options function is called before leaving the work session. Line styles remain as altered. Design profiles can be established to control the colors of the various elements of a Structural Graphics display.

The Sort function in Structural Graphics controls how the objects on the same level are ordered from left to right. Objects can be given priority numbers that can be used in sorting for display purposes. Each application can apply its own system of keys for sorting objects. The default order is the order of retrieval from the database. Sort doesn't affect the relationships between objects. Sort parameters aren't stored between work sessions unless the Save Options function is called.

The Search for Objects function allows organizational plan objects to be located by using a character string compared with the text associated with the object. Searches can be cumulative and adjusted between runs. The search will include all open view windows.

Controlling View Windows

The Structural Graphics display includes overview and detail modes. Overview mode compresses an entire hierarchical structure into one view window but might obscure some text labels on the objects. Detail mode shows all the text but might not be able to reveal all the structure.

You can have more than one view window open at the same time and use different view modes, if necessary. Goto>Detail<->View or Select>Detail<->View are the control commands for switching view modes.

You can add more view windows to which you can apply different attributes such as color or shape assignments. Select Options>Further view, or select the plus sign (+) in the top right corner of the display area.

To delete a window, use Options>Delete view.

Choosing Options>Arrange views displays a dialog box; use the left side to adjust window arrangements such as side-by-side or stacked. The right side of the dialog box allows you to reorder the windows. These changes are put into effect when you select Arrange>Close.

N O T E Unless you save the options, the view arrangements will last just for the current work session. This default arrangement is established in customizing. If you access the View Options dialog box through the Print dialog box rather than through the menu, the settings you enter apply to the print request only. ▦

The View option accesses the views in numerical order and rotates through the sequence. The Display Level option cycles through 0 for the entire structure, 1 for top level only, 2 for top two levels only, and so on.

The grid over which hierarchical structures are laid out can be shown or hidden by using the check box.

The Display Mode option cycles between overview mode and detail mode.

The knock-on mode, which applies to the previously selected object, provides multiple views of the selected object. The form of these views is determined by using the following radio buttons:

- ▦ *Off.* The system highlights the selected object, but otherwise the presentation doesn't change.
- ▦ *Center.* The system highlights the selected object and positions it in the center of the view window.
- ▦ *Substructure.* The system highlights the selected object and confines the display to the select objected and its child objects.
- ▦ *Parent structure.* The system highlights the selected object and confines the display to the selected object and its parent objects.

The Graphic Type option controls the Structural Graphics presentation format when you mark the corresponding radio button:

- ▦ *Normal.* The system presents the hierarchical structure in a top-down format, useful for the upper levels of a structure.
- ▦ *Feathered.* The system presents the hierarchical structure in a right-to-left format.
- ▦ *Compact.* The system presents the hierarchical structure using a combination of formats.
- ▦ *User-defined.* The system presents the hierarchical structure according to a user-defined format, which is set by using the Define Graphic Type button.

Objects on the lowest level are presented vertically to a default of three levels that can be reset.

The Design option determines which predefined design profiles are used to present the objects in a view window. Thus, the geometrical shape used for objects and the color of the connecting lines, for example, can be stipulated by the design profile. The available profiles are determined by the design group selected by the Change Design option.

Using the Define Graphic Type Button

A user-defined format for presenting hierarchical structures is established in response to selecting the Define Graphic Type button:

- *Alignment.* Radio buttons offer left justified, right justified, or centered.
- *Rotation.* Select the arrows until the correct rotation is shown.

Managing Object Options

Object options apply in detail and overview mode for the active view window. The Object Options dialog box offers the following choices:

- *Text Alignment* applies to the text labels of the objects.
- *Draw* controls the shapes used for objects.
- *Shadow* gives a three-dimensional effect.
- *Solid* fills the shape with a solid color.
- *Line Wrap* automatically "wraps" the text that identifies objects, but only in overview mode.
- *Font* controls the onscreen and printout fonts.
- *Outer Frame* determines the vertical and horizontal dimensions of the cells in the grid used to lay out a hierarchical structure, and hence the number of objects in view at once.
- *Inner Frame* determines the boundaries of the text that can be displayed within the cell dimensions chosen by the Outer Frame option.
- *Font Size* controls the display font size and the print font size if accessed from the Print dialog box.

Using the Line Options Dialog Box

Line options apply in detail and overview modes for the active view window. The Line Options dialog box must be accessed through the Print dialog box. The chosen settings apply only to the current work session and the particular print request, unless you save the options.

The following line options can be selected:

- *Relationship line*—diagonal or straight
- *Relationship indicator*—other aspects of the way a relationship line is presented, such as line thickness

- *Text*—a text determined by the R/3 application that describes the association or relationship between two objects connected by a line
- *Font*—used for the application-specific relationship description in the display and printout
- *Marker*—the system places a small rectangle on the line
- *Arrow*—the system uses an arrow to illustrate the relationship's direction
- *Group same texts*—shows an explanatory text only once for the selected group of objects that share the same relationship to a common parent
- *Font size*—controls the display font size and the print font size if accessed from the Print dialog box

Saving Option Settings

The Structural Graphics system reverts to the last options saved unless you save your current options that you've established in the following dialog boxes:

- View Options
- Object Options
- Line Options

The Save Options function also stores the following parameters:

- Sort options
- Search option settings
- The number of view windows opened
- Color assignments, except those applied to specific objects through the Object menu option

Selecting Options>Delete options clears all settings.

Mailing and Printing Hierarchical Structures

The following steps send a structure through the R/3 main system, SAPoffice:

1. Select Structure>Send.
2. Use the Recipient field in the Send Document window to identify the persons who should receive the hierarchical structure.
3. Select Send.

The Print dialog box of Structural Graphics controls a number of printing outputs. Print Quantity offers the following choices:

- *Completely* prints the entire structure on a single page overview or a set of detail mode pages that can be made into a poster.
- *View* prints the hierarchical structure as it now appears in the active view window, taking as many pages as necessary.

■ *Book* prints each substructure within a hierarchical structure on a separate page or on pages that can be joined to make a poster. The number of levels printed is controlled from the Display level setting in the View Options dialog box.

■ *Frame* offers the settings Solid Frame, No Frame, and Edges Only, which is useful when joining pages to form a poster.

■ *Output* identifies an output device such as a local PostScript printer, System PostScript printer spool, local named file, and Export Filter.

The Export Filter option allows the following choices:

■ *PostScript*—The system sends the structure to a PostScript printer.

■ *CGM*—The system sends the hierarchical structure to a Computer Graphics Metafile (CGM) file used for graphics such as PowerPoint and CorelDRAW.

The following printing options also can be selected:

■ Page Numbers, for print styles Completely and Book

■ Page References, automatically selected with page numbers for Book print style only

■ File, destination, local printers will be PRN or LPT1

Setting Up the Control Mechanisms in HR

In this chapter

Reviewing the Data Structures

The HR application doesn't require intensive programming. Nevertheless, some occasions inevitably will arise in which your background knowledge will help you find some good places to look for solutions to operating problems, and possibly for ways of unlocking your installed system's considerable business data processing capabilities.

> **N O T E** *Sams Teach Yourself ABAP/4 in 21 Days* is a useful introduction to the details of code programming. ■

There are two divisions to HR background knowledge: the database and the functions that access it. They are related in the closest way but are distinguishable because some apparent operating function complexities are necessitated by the way SAP databases are constructed. It's this database design, however, that allows all R/3 applications to work together under a strict control system.

HR master data and time data are stored in the transparent tables designated by the numbering format PA*nnnn*, where the *nnnn* string comprises a four-digit number that specifies the infotype. A *transparent table* is defined in the database but doesn't need to be obviously formatted as a table when you see the data onscreen. Another table type is a *structure*, which doesn't exist in the database but does contain data at runtime. A third table type, a *pooled table*, has the form of a physical data pool from which elements can be extracted.

Transparent tables PA*nnnn* holding HR data can include keys and data belonging to infotype *nnnn*. The keys are codes that identify the following objects:

■ Client

■ Personnel number

■ Subtype

■ Object ID

■ Lock indicator

■ Validity period

■ Sequential number

Exploring the Structure of Infotypes

The Data Dictionary contains a P*nnnn* structure for each infotype *nnnn*.

The Data Dictionary is a subcomponent of the R/3 BC-Basis Component, which is integral to all R/3 implementations. The Data Dictionary constitutes a central catalog containing descriptions of an organization's data. This information is regarded as *metadata* because it is information about data—in particular, the format of the data records and the interpretation to be used when reading the fields.

The metadata in the Data Dictionary also provides information about the relationships between the data and how it's used in programs and screens.

N O T E In this context, the term *client* refers to the code attached to all data in an R/3 implementation instance that belongs to one particular business. The client code ensures that the live production data of one business isn't confused with the data belonging to another that's inhabiting the same R/3 system. A client can be set up for testing or training purposes alongside a production client. They can share functions but not private data. ■

Your software shows interest in an infotype by executing a declare action. The INFOTYPE statement declares the specific infotype. The system then creates an internal table named P*nnnn* with the fields as specified in the structure P*nnnn*. The logical database is searched and copies of all records with the declared infotype structure are transferred to this table; this is done provided that they contain the personnel number of the employee of interest and that their validity accords with the time period being processed.

Using Repeat Structures

Many master data infotypes accept data in table form. Thus, you can enter many items represented by the rows of the table. A separate infotype is repeatedly consulted to define the form of each row. For example, you can enter up to 20 wage types and their amounts into Basic Pay infotype 0008; the line format of five fields is defined in infotype structure P0008.

Similar repeat structures are also used in the following infotypes:

- Leave Entitlement (infotype 0005)
- Cost Planning (infotype 1015)

Authorization Checks in Reporting

Authorization checks in reporting entail a standard check for data read authorization. The authorization group must be R or *.

You can use the RPORGIN and RPABAP objects to allow a simplified and faster authorization check when running reports.

If a report can't read certain personnel data due to lack of authorization, all data for these persons is skipped at the stage when the report is obeying the GET PERNR command to select the next valid personnel number for processing. The system creates a note that appears at the end of the list stating the number of persons who were skipped due to lack of authorization.

Using Specific Commands in HR

Selecting a menu option or entering a direct call for a command normally attracts the attention of a module, a utility, or a function. There is an infinite number of ways to traverse a network of menus and commands, but at least one function module will be called en route.

A function is serviced by a program module that has a defined interface. This interface tests parameters to confirm that they are of the proper type.

Function modules can be associated into function groups. Transaction SE37, which has the task of managing functions, can be accessed by selecting Tools>ABAP/4 Workbench>Function Library. You can branch from report processing to a display of the function module details by the SHOW FUNCTION * editor command. HR function groups adopt the naming convention Rp*xx* or Hr*xx*, where *xx* is an indicator defined by the user during customization.

Using Macro Modules

A *macro module* is a software procedural component. It can be defined in reports or during "includes" by calling the ABAP/4 define command. This technique allows you to change the details of the macro between calls to the report or include in which it's embedded.

Another technique with macros is to define them as TRMAC macros. The source code of these modules is stored in the function section of the control table TRMAC. The first two letters of the macro name indicate the application; the rest identify the particular macro code stored in the TRMAC table.

Customer-specific macro modules should begin with a special character, chosen from the available range by the customer. The macros defined in the control table TRMAC can be used by all reports.

Unlike macro modules, altered TRMAC macros don't automatically cause a regeneration of the report in which they're called. You must regenerate the report manually.

Using Utilities Modules

HR utilities are executed by RMAC modules, of which the following reports are examples:

- RPUACG00, Code Generation for HR Master Data Authorization
- RPUAUD00, Infotype Auditing
- RPINCL10, String Search in Reports
- RPCLSTyy, Display Clusters in PCLx (yy = Relid)
- RPUPxD00, Delete Cluster from PCLx (Single Records)
- RPUPxD10, Delete Cluster from PCLx (Several Records)

Defining LOWDATE and HIGHDATE

The RP-LOWDATE-HIGHDATE function module has the task of defining the following constants:

- LOWDATE TYPE D VALUE 18000101
- HIGHDATE TYPE D VALUE 99991231

These values represent the earliest and latest points on the time line and aren't actual points in time. These dates can be used only in comparisons, not in calculations. For example, an employee's infotype record that's assigned a validity end date that equals the HIGH-DATE would indicate that this person is an ex-employee and his records could be skipped for most purposes.

Selecting the Current Workforce

The function module RP-SEL-EIN-AUS-INIT has the task of setting a default search specification that collates records of events infotype 0000 that don't have 0 in the time period (PN/BEGPS, PN/ENDPS) reported in field P0000-STAT2.

In use, the current date would be entered to define the selection period for the current workforce.

Setting the Key Date

The RP-SET-KEY-DATE function is used to enter the current day's date as the default data selection period when preparing a search. The system will adopt LOW-DATE or HIGH-DATE to define the other end of the time period. However, if you want to use a single date as a key date—perhaps for a snapshot view of the staffing situation on that day—you must define a time period by entering the key date as the begin date and the end date.

Selecting Employees for Whom Payroll Is Completed

Module RP-SEL-CALC selects only those personal numbers where the payroll is completed for the selected payroll period. It should therefore be used in all payroll evaluations with the RMAC module RP-READ-PAYROLL-DIR.

RP-Generating Address in Compliance with Mailing Regulations

The RPC remote procedure call RP-MAKE-ADDRESS is an RMAC module that creates an interface on which to edit an employee's address in order to comply with international mailing regulations. It's used in any report that must generate address labels or address letter texts. In addition to the general address, a fixed short address in a string is generated for special purposes:

- Surname, first name, title
- zip/postal code, city

Transaction SE37 is a standard function module used in address editing. It processes the following IN parameters:

- Infotype P0001, organizational assignment (P0001-BUKRS for T001F)
- Infotype P0002, person data (P0002-ANRED for form of address)
- Infotype P0006, address data
- EDIT-NAME, name in compliance with national regulations (use with RP-EDIT-NAME)
- Number of lines in the address window

The OUT parameters are the specified number of address window lines followed by the short address line.

The address window's coordinates can be defined in table T001F, which contains the company code parameters. Your report can either refer to the following address window table values or you can enter different values as parameters for each report:

- ZEIVN (Line From)
- SPLVN (Column From)
- ZEIBS (Line To)
- SPLBS (Column To)

Reading All Time Infotypes in a Time Period

The function RP-READ-ALL-TIME-ITY collects all time records from infotypes 2000–2999 on the person being processed for the period given. These records are arranged into the corresponding internal infotype tables.

The user must have the correct authorization for a record to be accessed. The following code illustrates the style:

```
DATA: BEGDA LIKE P2001-BEGDA, ENDDA LIKE P2001-ENDDA.
INFOTYPES: 0000, 0001, 0002, ...
        2001 MODE N, 2002 MODE N, ...
GET PERNR.
BEGDA = '19900101'.
ENDDA = '19900131'.
RP-READ-ALL-TIME-ITY BEGDA ENDDA.
IF PNP-SW-AUTH-SKIPPED-RECORD
NE '0'.
 WRITE: / 'Authorization for Time data lacking'.
 WRITE: / 'by Personnel number', PERNR-PERNR. REJECT.
ENDIF.
```

Editing RP-Name in Compliance with National Regulations

RP-EDIT-NAME is an RMAC module that edits names in all RP standard evaluations in compliance with the national regulations of a particular country. Name editing consults table T522N (RP name editing) and takes account of the following information sources:

- MOLGA (company code, personnel area, personnel subarea) from T001P
- The report format from table 522F (Default: '01')
- Personal data infotype 0002
- Family data infotype 0021
- Indicator KNZNM for name editing from personal data infotype 0002

Manipulating Data Files

Data from the different HR application areas is stored in clusters in PCL*n* files (*n* = 1, 2, 3, or 4). These files can contain internal report fields, field strings, and internal tables. Each application area has a relation ID comprising a two-character cluster name and a key structure of up to 40 bytes stored in the SRTFD field.

When a record is exported to the PCL*n* file, the cluster ID is written to the RELID field and the key value to the SRTFD field. The relation ID is followed by the country grouping code letter and a sequential number.

Using Import/Export Files in HR

Files PCL1, PCL2, PCL3, and PCL4 have identical structures and are used as follows:

- PCL1, the database for HR application areas, contains information from time recording such as incentive wage time tickets and supplementary infotype texts.
- PCL2 contains derived information such as payroll accounting results. It also contains all generated payroll schemas.
- PCL3 contains applicant data.
- PCL4 contains the change documents for HR master data and recruitment.

The key element with the highest priority in a file is the client. Data within a client is grouped according to basic relations specified in field PCL*n*-RELID. The type of basic relation is known as a *cluster*. A cluster relation defines data according to its type. Cluster RX contains the payroll results for country X according to table T500L, and cluster TE the travel expenses data.

The structure of PCL*n*-SRTFD, the sort field, depends on the cluster and is defined in the *xx* KEY field string. This key is defined by the software component include RPC*n*xxy0.

Interpreting the Naming Conventions

The designation of include RPC*n*xxy0 is interpreted as follows:

- *n*=1, 2, 3, or 4 (for PCL1, PCL2, PCL3, or PCL4)
- *xx* for the cluster relationship ID
- *y*=0 for international clusters or a country grouping code according to T500L for national clusters

The personnel number is the first component of the *xx* KEY field string.

Importing and Exporting Data

The import/export files PCL*n* are managed with the ABAP/4 IMPORT and EXPORT commands. Fields, field strings, and internal tables are stored in or read from the database.

Data is read from and written to the database via a unique key (*xx* Key). The following RMAC macros call the ABAP/4 commands:

- RP-IMP-Cn-xx for importing data
- RP-EXP-Cn-xx for exporting data

Storing Data in PCLn Files

Data from the different HR application areas is stored in clusters in the PCL*n* files. Each application area must have a two-character cluster name that identifies the relationship between the items in the area.

The application area cluster must have a key structure of up to 40 bytes of the SRTFD field. When a record is exported into a PCL*n* file, the cluster ID is written to field RELID and the key value to field STRFD. For example, if this field structure is specified in the Data Dictionary as PC200, the system will know that a record is to be stored and interpreted as the PERNR personnel number field followed by the SEQNO sequential number field. The Data Dictionary structure specification for Personnel Cluster 200 also includes other internal tables.

To inspect the full range of data clusters available, consult the domain description in the Data Dictionary.

Exporting and Importing via the Data Buffer

When macros are used for exporting, records aren't written directly to the database but to a main memory buffer. After the program runs, the records in the buffer are stored in the appropriate PCL*n* database file.

When macros are used for importing, the system checks the buffer directory to determine whether a record with the same key is available in the main memory. If not, the record is loaded from the PCL*n* to the buffer and then read from the buffer to the report.

Noting the Payroll Cluster Directory Managers

Two versions of the cluster directory are based on different structures and therefore aren't compatible:

- Cluster Directory Manager for the United States, Canada, and Japan
- Cluster Directory Manager for all other countries

Operating the HR Utilities and PA Tools

Personnel calculation schemas comprise functions processed sequentially to perform time and payroll calculations. The main payroll schema is X000, the international schema for the international payroll driver RPCALCXO. It contains internationally valid components for calculating gross pay. Country-specific versions of this schema are available.

The schema has source text divided into several well-structured subschemas:

- 0001 COM Payroll schema INTERNATIONAL
- 0002 COM Gross calculation
- 0003 COM Net payments/deductions and transfer
- 0004 COPY XIN0 Initialization of payroll
- 0005 COPY XBD0 Edit basic data

- 0006 COPY XLR0 Import last payroll result
- 0007 COPY XT00 Gross remuneration (time management)
- 0008 COPY XAP0 Import further payments/deductions
- 0009 COPY XAL0 Monthly factoring and storage
- 0010 COPY XNA0 Cumulation of net amount/net pay
- 0011 COPY XRR0 Retroactive accounting
- 0012 COPY XNN0 Net payments/deductions and transfer
- 0013 COPY XEND Final processing

Maintaining a Schema's Attributes

The following attributes are additional to a schema's source text:

- Program class
- Country grouping
- Executable schema
- Responsible
- Changes by person responsible only
- Maintenance info

A schema's source text comprises the following elements:

- Line number
- Function
- Parameters (1–4)
- Log control indicator
- Execution of function indicator
- Text

In support of the schema line-editing functions, the auxiliary function allows you to display the documentation for all the functions, subschemas, and personnel calculation rules contained in the schema's source text. Place the cursor on the desired entry and choose F1; F4 displays all the permitted entries for the marked field.

If you mark a rule or subschema and double-click, the subschema's source text is displayed. Selecting Edit>Choose object does the same.

The Sequence function displays all the steps in a navigation path and allows you to retrace the route.

The standard SAP PA system includes a large number of schemas that can be modified according to your requirements. The customer-modified version is the actual working version. The Compare function shows the differences between modified and standard schemas.

Programming and Customizing HR Evaluations

The logical database PNP is used for evaluating HR master data and time data. It enables convenient, high-performance evaluation of the transparent table PA*nnnn*, which holds infotype records.

The logical database consists of the database driver SAPDBPNP. A logical database PN containing report attributes can be maintained along with the application P if you need to create your own evaluations.

To compile a particular report, the logical database loads the personnel data for each employee into the main memory. The entire history of each infotype is loaded, all infotype records from the lowest to highest system date. This data is deleted before the next personnel number is processed.

Checking Employee and Data Authorization

The logical database executes an authorization check for personnel data. Is the user who starts the report authorized to see any data at all on this employee? Is the user authorized for the particular data needed?

The logical database supports the following filtering processes:

- Person selection
- Sorting of the person selection
- Data selection

The person selections define the personnel numbers to be evaluated by using options that include the following (in addition to 30 other selection criteria):

- Personnel number
- Person selection period
- Period defined/payroll area
- Period defined/payroll period
- Period defined/payroll year
- Period defined/indicator

Matchcode IDs can be used to select persons. Standard sorting is ascending according to personnel number or matchcode. The Sort function allows sorting by name or organizational assignment criteria.

Selecting Data

The infotypes that wholly or partially cover the specified data selection period or are selected by a time period determinator are chosen for processing.

The scope of the selection screen is controlled by the assignment of a report to a report class. This class determines the selection criteria and the matchcode and sort functions offered. SAP standard reports are assigned by table T599W; customer report class assignments are maintained in table T599B.

Distinguishing Physical and Logical Views

A physical view of a data record corresponds with the data format as it's stored in the personnel tables and takes account of the validity period. A logical view can take account of the validity periods of several infotype records, such as a career history. A logical view can correctly marshal data for partial periods.

Every time an alteration is made to an infotype, a new record is created and the old one is given a delimited validity period so that it doesn't overlap the new. A join operation processes records from two or more infotypes. The data from these infotypes is provided for a specific partial period.

A projection operation also processes information from several infotypes, but in this case the validity period of individual fields is computed by taking account of which significant fields do and don't change over the period of interest.

The Join and Projection operations provide two logical views of infotype data. These views can be used in combination to select just the fields important to the evaluation. By combining the validity periods of these fields, an overall period can be determined for each value of interest.

By linking a join and a projection, you can read the master data for a specific partial period.

Using Time-Dependent Control Tables

Infotype data is often coded as a key to save time and space. Permanent residence, for example, is keyed as address type 1 in infotype P0006.

As you process infotypes, the texts or attributes of the keys are read from the relevant control tables. Many of these control tables can become out-of-date, so they're assigned a validity period. The following HR areas have time-dependent control tables:

- Work schedules
- Pay scale structures
- Wage types
- Wage type valuation
- Banking data
- Positions
- Payee codes

In these areas, you must be sure to look up the values for the keys from a control table with the correct validity period. The system will use the table record valid for the begin date.

Generalizing a View

A *view* in HR is usually a logical perspective of interval-dependent internal tables because you almost always are interested in the information pertinent to a specific time period. You can use the logical view to edit and output data according to user specifications.

Defining an Infotype in the Data Dictionary

An infotype *nnnn* requires at least two structures and one table:

- Structure PS*nnnn* contains all the infotype data fields.
- Structure P*nnnn* contains infotype key fields and all the data fields from structure PS*nnnn*.
- Transparent table PA*nnnn* is required if you want to use the infotype within Personnel Administration.
- Transparent table PB*nnnn* is required if you want to use an infotype within Recruitment.

The data definitions of these structures and tables are created in the Data Dictionary. In accordance with the distribution of infotype name ranges, objects P9*nnn*, PS9*nnn*, PA9*nnn*, and PB9*nnn* are assigned to the customer name range.

CHAPTER 13

Developing HR Strategy for IT Divisions

In this chapter

Developing a Strategy for a Specific IT Department

A key measurement of the success of a car company's information services division in the 1990s and beyond lies in results attained relative to the opportunities and constraints created by rapid environmental change. A primary way to gain competitive advantage is to manage people more effectively through the acquisition and development of talent and energy that produce superior performance.

To choose a human resource strategy, division managers must define the human resource issues that are important to their business. For the human resource strategy to be implemented successfully, managers, employees, and other stakeholders need to share the business's vision, values, and mission. Ultimately, the strategy needs to be translated into organizational goals and objectives and into specific unit and individual key result areas and objectives.

Furthermore, any new strategy implies changes in the way people manage. This change needs to be introduced effectively in this division to ensure a smooth transition process.

Finally, as conditions in the automotive industry change more rapidly, strategic planning is shaped as a guide to help the division recognize and address important changes and opportunities to manage them effectively. There are key phases in the development of an HR-IT strategy, whereby the management of human resources is aligned with business strategy through defined human resource issues and strategies. The clearer and more focused the issues and strategies, the closer the alignment.

This chapter outlines the alignment of the human resource issues and strategies prevalent in an information services division with the division's business-related issues and larger Dream Car group:

- Divisional issues include those that result from changes in the company and bigger environments that affect the division.
- Human resource issues include people issues that result from the divisional issues and guide toward certain priorities for the strategy.
- The "Human Resource Strategy" section describes an integrated approach and then divides that approach into goals and guidelines for individual human resource systems, based on the human resource issues identified.

Divisional Issues

Several issues are now identifiable in the information services division.

Current Issues

There's an urgent need to prioritize the current technological projects and to address these with high-impact interventions staffed according to the customers' immediate needs.

The division is now being restructured from two operating arms—Information Systems Development and Information Systems Operations—into three teams: Information Services Strategy Consulting, Information Services Technology, and Information Services Availability Services. How are roles and responsibilities affected by this restructuring?

The division will take on a more consultative, project-oriented role than its previous functional one.

The bulk of systems are based on outdated technology and have been developed for administrative purposes, not for manufacturing processes. The batch process environment is also less reliable than online processing. This places increasing pressure on information services to work as an executive partner with the company's operating divisions to enable the shift to world-class technologies that will improve production significantly.

Becoming and remaining a low-cost quality manufacturer is another key objective, implying that continual improvements need to be made through technological solutions. This has to be achieved with a lower head count.

A current constraint on the division is the low operating budget available for the realization of technological improvements and acquiring the skills required to achieve these improvements.

Possibilities that speed development cycle times—outsourcing of certain developments and off-the-shelf solutions—are being researched to ensure rapid response to market changes and customer requirements.

Poor quality assurance is impeding the division's results.

Possible Future Issues

Leading manufacturing companies are increasingly focusing on the introduction of new products and technology. Business strategies require shifts toward shorter product cycles, simultaneous engineering, and the use of expensive new technology such as expert systems, artificial intelligence, fiber optics, computer-aided design and manufacturing, and robotics.

The possibility of the division becoming a profit center puts increasing pressure on the quality, innovation, and cost-effectiveness of the solutions offered to the company. An even further possibility is completely outsourcing IT services.

Increased competition and decreased customer loyalty in the automotive industry will add to pressures on cost-effectiveness and superior service.

Human Resource Issues

Human resource issues are gaps between the current situation and the desired situation. They represent opportunities for improvement or chances for gaining a new competitive advantage. In a negative sense, they are problems or shortcomings that impede performance.

Based on the divisional issues, the following human resource issues emerge:

■ Current high-impact projects need to be put in action to address company crises; this implies short-term staffing according to project needs. In the future, a resourcing mechanism will have to be in place to staff projects in a way that ensures the success of project outcomes.

■ The division's new structure will significantly affect the current roles and responsibilities governing the division's workflow and will necessitate job competence profiles based on the services.

■ Focus is lacking as specialist skills are needed for the three different computer environments: the complex network environment, two database environments, and four programming environments. This leaves very little time for development of new integrated and innovative solutions for the company's needs. Current employees need to be retrained or new talent needs to be recruited to ensure that core competencies are in place.

■ New ideas are lacking, and truly superior technological innovation is needed to ensure that the organization is a leader in cost-effective, quality manufacturing.

■ Currently, the division can't adapt to change quickly, and competence is needed to lead and manage change.

■ Poor coordination can be addressed with a team focus. This will ensure a streamlined operation and support the integration of services and technologies as the division moves to a consulting mode.

■ The division lacks service orientation.

■ The right labor mix needs to be identified for the new kinds of services being offered to customers. This problem is being addressed.

■ Authority needs to be delegated so that employees are empowered to meet client needs quickly.

■ Low employee commitment can impede the changes needed to meet the increasing challenges faced by the division.

■ A local focus needs to be shifted for IT to support Dream Car of DreamLand's becoming a global competitor. The virtual global information services division already creates opportunities for information exchange, improved facilities, and personnel exchange.

■ Poor quality and results necessitate a project and results orientation to keep the focus on important reorganization issues and ensure that quality standards are adhered to.

■ A lack of business skills has resulted in mismatched technological solutions for business needs. This implies the need for an in-depth understanding of the company's business processes and a focus on cost-effectiveness to ensure the financial viability of the technological solutions.

- Low direct labor productivity necessitates that measures of job outputs need to be put in place. This implies a commitment to excellence; timely delivery of systems, products, and services; and cost-effective orientation.

- The lack of a learning culture needs to be addressed so that regular networking and benchmarking can become part of the division's daily operations.

- Excess managers need to be replaced with leaders to ensure the improvement of the competence and commitment of staff through effective coaching and mentorship.

- Current rewards are inadequate; they don't support and enhance good performance.

Human Resource Strategy

The information services human resource strategy evolves around creating the change needed to effectively add value to the organization. The strategic intent is to build a division of qualified, skilled, competent, and motivated IT professionals who can adapt quickly to the opportunities offered by new technology and the challenges of the business environment.

Integrated Human Resources Approach

An integrated human resources strategy is advocated and ensures that all divisional human-related activities result in the realization of excellence in a balanced scorecard system, namely the following:

- Financial—Making profits, cost-effectiveness.
- Customer perspective—Delighted customers, customer needs are met.
- Internal perspective—Operations run smoothly in the division, processes are clearly defined and managed.
- Divisional learning and growth—Individuals develop and grow to their full potential, leadership is effective, people are competent.

Competence profiles are used as the base of the approach. For the division to become competitive, employees should be competent in their jobs and committed to the division and company. The competence profiles are based on current as well as emerging competencies (influenced by the vision and changing environment), and all human resource systems are naturally integrated. It also links information services and other business units in that outputs identified in competence profiles are entirely customer focused.

The company's National Qualifications Forum (NQF) guides the education and training activities by forcing the division to use an outcome-based learning system.

Human Resource Systems

A short description of each human resource system in such an integrated approach follows.

Manpower Forecasting

The ideal result of a manpower forecast is just-in-time talent through a process of matching the available talent supply to projected future requirements. The following guidelines are in place:

- Plan for manpower through a simulation exercise based on the current and future projects of the division. Factor in the following competence drivers:

  Changes in outputs produced   Changes in customer relationships

  Changes in services provided   New capital investments

- In the short term, forecasts must include high-impact projects that need to be put in place. This can be achieved only through partnerships with other business units.

- Base manpower forecasts on the head count prescribed by Dream Car of DreamLand.

Job Evaluation and Description

The goal of job evaluation and description is to develop job profiles that can function in a changing environment. *Job competence profiles* are job profiles that describe work in terms of outputs and competencies. To align with the NQF, a job description must contain the following:

- The value that the job adds to an organization
- Future forces likely to influence the job
- The key roles of the job
- The key receivers of the job's output
- The outputs needed from the job by those key receivers
- The standards of quality that each output must meet
- Evidence of outputs delivered according to standards
- The variables influencing the outputs
- The knowledge, skill, attitudes, and values that people need to be able to produce these outputs in accordance with standards

The current restructured services have to be used as the base for the development of the job profiles by using the services as separate job families.

Recruitment

The goal of recruitment is to select and hire capable and motivated people of high caliber:

- Recruitment should be based on job competence profiles developed in accordance with the NQF guidelines.

- Recruitment needs must be met through external recruiting or redeployment of talent already in the organization. Staffing surpluses relative to needs are addressed by reassigning employees to other jobs, re-creating teams, or moving individuals out of the company (*decruitment*).

- Job competence profiles allow the IT division to select only the best—that is, employees that meet or exceed the competence requirements for the position. To assure the best recruitment, an assessment will have to be made of the knowledge of human resource personnel in Dream Car of DreamLand of the information services industry. If it's found inadequate, an outsourced personnel agency—focusing on the employment of IT personnel—should be contracted to handle recruitment.

- Competence and potential must be assessed with accepted tools that are focused, relevant, and customized.

- Recruitment must be based on the current human resource policies and procedures of Dream Car of DreamLand.

- Follow recruitment with an orientation period through mentorship and socialization programs.

Performance Assessment and Management

The goal here is to ensure that individuals deliver timely, cost-effective, and reliable results required of them:

- Use the balanced scorecard to measure the following:

Customer perspectives	Assess the quality of output delivered by the employee or team by looking at evidence showing that key receivers' requirements were met to their satisfaction.
Internal perspectives	Measure productivity through the achievement (or lack thereof) of project milestones and measurements of function points.
Divisional learning and growth	Assess individual performance as negotiated up front with the individual.
Financial	Assess the realization of solutions in terms of cost-effectiveness.

Don't forget to measure teamwork, as this has been articulated as a core divisional value.

- Enable high performance through learning activities and a supportive culture where coaching is utilized extensively.

- Give regular constructive feedback to employees that will result in performance improvement.

Succession Planning

The goal of succession planning is to fill strategic openings with individuals who have been prepared for possible future assignments or leadership positions, as a result of deliberate career steps taken.

- Because it's difficult to plan ahead effectively in today's changing environment, a less formal approach should be used.

- The easiest way to ensure that targeted employees will be ready for future assignments is to ensure that they are developed in emerging competencies of the position or role to be filled.

Training and Development

The goal of training and development is to establish a learning culture that supports the philosophy and regulations of the National Qualifications Forum. Training and development guidelines are as follows:

- Align all training to the NQF requirements. This entails adherence to standards for the information systems sector to identify the key learning outcomes for employees. It also implies the use of certified trainers and a mix of training and education programs to be put in place for all employees.

- Set up apprenticeship and mentor programs for individuals with aptitude and potential, and retrain poor performers to increase the division's overall skills set.

- Move the responsibility for development to the individual.

- Measure the success of training initiatives.

- Determine whether training can be given in-house or can be met through outside courses and seminars. Focus on relevance to need, timeliness, quality, location, and cost.

- Focus on the training that will enhance future operations, namely immediate technical skills shortages, consulting and business skills, project management skills, team effectiveness, and leadership effectiveness.

- Allocate enough time for training. (The current international standard is a minimum of seven days a year.)

Rewards

Link rewards to performance as communicated through the balanced scorecard and job competence profiles to ensure contingency thereof on behavior and outputs:

- Benchmark regularly to ensure market relation. This is vital when a policy is followed of employing the best.

- Use the most effective mix of financial and non-financial rewards:

Financial, non-contingent reward	Profit sharing
Financial, contingent reward	Achievement award
Non-financial, non-contingent reward	Vacation
Non-financial, contingent reward	Advancement

Career Management

Ensure that employees take responsibility for their own career development:

- Clear competence profiles provide guidelines for individuals on skills, knowledge, and attitudes needed in jobs and are handy tools for self-development.

- Constructive feedback will enable individuals to set realistic improvement targets.

Implementation Strategy

The following steps are needed for the successful implementation of the strategy:

1. Align the expectations of employees to ensure commitment to the strategy (set up a communication plan).
2. Build the structure based on the strategy. (The current proposal is adequate.)
3. Ensure that all the resources affecting performance are adequate and that the resources are reallocated according to the needs of the new focus areas (facilities, technology, budget, time, and so on).
4. Clarify the new roles and responsibilities.
5. Focus on a few high-impact human resources programs in the short term.
6. Develop competence profiles based on the new teams created and measure these against the vision to identify the competence gaps.
7. Implement the integrated human resource approach based on the competence profiles and competence gap.
8. Revisit human resource programs regularly to ensure that it supports the business strategy.

Structure, Roles, and Responsibilities

Almost all type C and type D industries have project management-related structures. The key variable appears to be task complexity. Companies with complex tasks that also operate in a dynamic environment find project management mandatory. Such industries include aerospace, defense, construction, high technology, engineering, computers, and electronic instrumentation.

The structure in Figure 13.1 is intended to enable successful project management in the IT division. There's an important vertical direction in which the senior management is obliged to relate down to the levels of the various consulting specialties. At the same time, there must be a horizontal direction that defines each project so that all various contributing specialists provide their input in the right places and at the right moments in each project. Several new roles are proposed and each is discussed in the following sections, to create an understanding of the shift in responsibilities needed.

Executive Sponsor

The executive must be involved in the following:

- Planning projects and setting objectives
- Resolving conflicts
- Setting priorities
- Serving as project sponsor

Figure 13.1

Project management for an information services division.

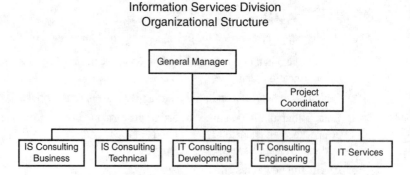

Information Services Division
Organizational Structure

There must be a continuous commitment from senior managers to the projects, and this commitment must be visible.

Strategist

The strategist must implement, develop, and manage the corporate information systems strategy by

- Providing guidance for line-project interrelationships
- Providing an appropriate technical infrastructure
- Providing a support service for the organization's business processes
- Leading the IT division
- Adhering to ISO9002 guidelines
- Setting priorities among projects
- Monitoring performance standards

Data Security Officer and ISO9002 Regulator

This role must advise on and monitor data security and ISO9002 guidelines through the following means:

- Regular interaction with line managers and project managers
- Up-to-date information
- Monitoring needed adjustments

This person is the gateway to quality assurance.

Line Managers

Line managers are responsible for resources in their divisions, including money, manpower, equipment, facilities, materials, and information/technology. They also need to give detailed direction, evaluation, measurement, and control; provide project managers with resources; develop a good relationship with project managers; control an operational budget; and define technical criteria for projects.

The line managers are responsible for decisions regarding promotion, grade, salary, bonus, overtime, responsibility, and future work assignments.

They are expected to work in long time spans, support employees through change processes, and provide a good working environment for employees.

The following skills are expected of line managers:

Team building	Organization
Leadership	Entrepreneurship
Conflict resolution	Resource allocation skills
Technical expertise	Communication skills
Planning	Management skills
Controlling	Time management

Line managers are expected to have the following knowledge:

- Organizational behavior
- IT services
- Industry
- Dream Car business processes
- Latest technology

Finally, line managers need to have these character traits/goals:

Customer service	Persistency
Assertiveness	Consistency
Integrity	Flexibility
Maturity	Energy
Leadership ability	Decision-making ability

N O T E Line managers will identify several roles according to the outputs and competencies needed in their area. The following general positions can be identified:

- Specialists
- Teams with specific focus areas
- Project team members

Project Managers

Project managers serve several functions:

- Request resources from line managers for projects
- Give informal rewards

- Have great responsibility, but little authority
- Provide timely, accurate, and complete data on projects
- Responsibility for coordinating and integrating activities across multiple, functional lines
- Main responsibility is the planning of projects
- A good relationship with line managers
- Ensure that functional units understand their responsibilities
- Control project budget
- Identify problems that may jeopardize project completion
- Manage human relationships
- Make recommendations to line managers on performance of employees
- Define requirements for projects
- Work in short time spans

Project managers need the following knowledge:

- Quantitative tools
- Organizational structures
- Organizational behavior
- Technology
- Project life cycles
- Project management methodologies

They require the following skills:

Communication	Time management
Interpersonal	Interface management
Negotiation	Resource management
Management	Planning and control
Technical	Generalist
Conflict handling	Team-building
Planning	

Finally, project managers need to have these character traits:

Risk-taking	Alertness
Team functioning	Versatility
Commitment	Energy
Honesty	Decision-making ability
Integrity	Toughness

Project Coordinator

The project coordinator is responsible for project administration. As such, he must establish policies, procedures, rules, guidelines, and directives. He also must ensure that these policies, guidelines, and so on conform to overall company policy.

The establishment of project administrative requirements is part of project planning. The project coordinator must work closely with project managers and project leaders during this phase.

The project coordinator also monitors projects affecting all three divisions (outside the Critical Projects division) to ensure quality and timely handovers; monitors effective application of resources; is responsible for budget administration; and manages administrative staff and the project office.

The project coordinator must be knowledgeable about the following:

- Organizational procedures and guidelines
- Project management principles
- Organizational behavior
- Financial systems

The project coordinator also must possess the following skills:

- Administrative
- Organizing
- Planning
- Controlling finances
- Managing resources

Finally, project coordinators need to have these character traits:

- Systematic
- Consistent
- Maturity
- Detail-orientation
- Ability to handle frustrations

Project Team Members

Each member of the project team and office must have a good understanding of the fundamental project requirements, which include the following:

- Customer liaison
- Project direction
- Project planning

- Project control
- Project evaluation
- Project reporting

Occasionally, project leaders are chosen out of team members to run small projects.

Implementing the Change Plan

To implement the new structure, a horizontal and vertical work flow process must be established.

Project management is designed to make better use of existing resources by getting work to flow horizontally as well as vertically within the company. Vertical work flow remains the responsibility of the line managers. Horizontal work flow is the responsibility of the project managers, and their primary effort is to communicate and coordinate activities horizontally between the line divisions. Regular forums are needed between line and project managers.

Setting Up the Staff

A staffing process must be agreed on for projects.

The project manager doesn't staff the project; staffing is a line manager's responsibility. The project manager has the right to request specific resources, but the final decision of what resources will be committed rests with the line managers. Long-term projects that consume resources full time are usually set up as a separate division. The Critical Projects division can meet these requirements.

Establishing a Measurement Process

A measurement process must be set up for projects to include completion

- Within the allocated time period
- Within the budgeted cost
- At the proper performance level
- With user acceptance
- With minimum or mutually agreed on scope changes
- Without disturbing the main workflow
- Without changing the corporate culture

Establishing Support for Individuals

Individuals must be supported through the change process. People have a slower rate of change than business goals, technology, and organizational structures. Employees won't be convinced by training and communication programs, but only after they see the new system in action—and this takes time. It can take up to two years for employee transition.

Identify the Optimum Number of Projects

The optimum number of projects needs to be identified according to

- Resources available
- Priority for resolution of business problems (Critical Projects)
- Level of quality maintained
- Daily work constraints
- Realistic schedules
- Cost constraints

Setting Up a Communication Plan

A formal and informal communication plan must be put in place. It must do the following:

- Inform the IT team of the new structure and vision
- Inform the team of new work methods, roles, and responsibilities
- Give the team a chance to give input into the structure and work methods
- Inform the Dream Car group of the IT division's new structure and work methods

Team-building sessions must be held for the new leadership team and the new functional areas. A competence development program needs to be put in place that gives employees the knowledge, skills, and attitudes needed to work in the new IT structure and with new work methods and technology.

Executive sponsorship must be maintained to ensure the success of the IT team's efforts.

A system development life cycle must be agreed on and formalized to ensure coordination between the various functions and projects.

A formal handover process must be set up to ensure that responsibilities are falling into the "best fit" functional area. This should be done only after the optimum projects and daily activities are identified, to avoid double work.

CHAPTER 14

Seeing HR from a Consultant's Viewpoint

In this chapter

Remembering the HR Highlights

When you're working as a consultant, there is inevitably a concentration on the particular systems and modules that are of most interest to your client. You may not have time to think about much else.

On the other hand, the good and bad things that remain in the consultant's mind long after the system is up and running are probably worth noting for the consideration of others. First the good points—then the bad.

The data transfer between Recruitment and Personnel Administration works very well and is one of the most important processes managed by the module. HR is built from the PA and PD application modules, and there has grown an impression that there's too much record duplication to serve what can be installed as two separated systems. When the transfer functions are running smoothly, the duplication argument fades against the considerable benefits of being able to use the richer structures of PD without losing the rigor of PA's payroll machinery.

Displaying Complex Structures

The Organizational Management functionality is one of the best programs within HR. The flexibility and facility of building a structure are fascinating.

As of release 4.0B, a matrix structure that allows you to control all the functional reports by project, special activity, and so on is available. This matrix system is additional to the formal structure of organizational units, jobs, and positions. The matrix also extends over the reporting structure of manager, subordinate employee, and so on.

The Structural Graphics display of organizational structures is separate from the display of the matrix structure, which again is separate from the reporting structure. As of release 4.5, these three structures can't be displayed together, and there is no easy workaround.

Controlling Authorization Management

Another interesting functionality within SAP HR is the authorization management concept, which uses human resources organizational structures to allow automatic changes in the user's authorizations.

The concept is simple and consists of assigning profiles to organizational structures as organizational units, jobs, and positions. When a person occupies a position, all authorizations of the organizational structure are inherited by the user connected to that person, due to the organizational structure inheritance concept. This integration allows better control of the authorization procedures and of the rights and needs of each area or position. Much of the administration is automatic and entails almost no human intervention or delay.

The Basis Group implementation team saves a lot of time during implementation because the number of profiles is decreased by at least 70 percent. There's also a more accurate control system as a result.

Report RHPROFL0 needs to be run in order to make the authorization profiles valid for each organizational structure change. It's best to plan a schedule to run this report daily.

When building the profiles, create an authorization group that's structured with the help and intense participation of the human resources group. Make sure that all the members of the authorization group understand perfectly the organizational structure concept and its effects.

On top of the standard authorization is the personnel development authorization concept, which controls access to PD objects. These objects include plan versions, organizational structure, evaluation paths, and so on. One function includes very important features that restrict information based on manager relationships (B012) through such functions as HR_GET_MANAGER_ASSIGNMENT.

The PD profiles are connected to the organizational structure as the standard profiles and are passed to users via the same organizational structures concepts and reports. Running report RPUACG00 makes the PD profiles rules valid to the Personnel Administration master data.

Managing Usernames

If you include communication infotype 0105 (subtype 0001) in the hiring event, you can record an employee's username. If you need to, you also can create a dynamic event that prevents particular employee groups from creating individual usernames.

Calling Data Transfer Made Easy

The Data Transfer Made Easy (Tcode SXDA) component is also another very useful tool. It's available not just for the HR module but for all modules within R/3. This transaction allows you to transfer data from a legacy system by using simple flat files that can be created in different programming languages (C, COBOL, P/L, and the like) or even through an Excel spreadsheet.

This is an easy way of transferring data from and to SAP during customization or normal operation. This tool has saved a lot of time during implementations that would have been spent on organizational structures and their properties, including profiles.

Data Transfer Made Easy allows you to transport data from/to an object's infotypes. For example, you can move data from a legacy system to an SAP system. You can send all the organizational structure, cost centers, descriptions, addresses, and so on, without having to build an ABAP data migration program.

In transaction SXDA, you will find a predefined format to each data type you want to transfer—for example, 0555 for master data and 0777 for personnel development records. This transaction also provides a report of the SAP structure definition to each programming language available (C, COBOL, P/L).

A useful reference is *Initial Data Transfer Made Easy* from the simplification group available in the Accelerated SAP CD-ROM or from SAPnet.

Using the Ad Hoc Query Tool

One of the useful new developments as of release 4.0B is the ad hoc query tool in the Human Resources information system, which allows customers to create new reports easily. The ad hoc tool is very simple to configure and easy to use because it doesn't require any programming language knowledge.

This query tool consults the infotypes, meaning that every item of information contained in an infotype can be accessed through it. If you want to access payroll data via an ad hoc query, you need to have created an infotype to store the data you want to access.

N O T E When you configure the ad hoc query tool, only 99 infotypes can be made available to users. ▉

Administering Compensation

As of release 4.0B, the improved functionalities of Compensation Administration are available with supporting data for all countries.

Position Filling with the Desktop Manager

Release 4.5B's Desktop Manager includes the capability to automatically fill positions by using the Career and Succession module. There's a new graphic display for qualification matchup and the new method of evaluation of qualification that applies different scales to different groups of qualifications.

Creating New Infotypes

Infotypes are still very important within the SAP/HR module. As of release 4.0B, you can create your own infotypes easier than before with transaction PM01.

> **CAUTION**
>
> Don't change an infotype's time constraints without the proper information. Each infotype has its own time constraints, and sometimes you can generate an incompatibility in the future. For example, in some countries, more than one salary increase per day needs to be recorded due to legal requirements. This can't be achieved by using Basic Pay infotype 0008 because of its time constraint, but the payroll may not run properly if you change Basic Pay's time constraint. If you need to have an infotype with a different time constraint, it's better to create your own extra infotype.

Remembering the HR Irritations

Perhaps the best way to look on an irritation is to make it the subject for a training session during the implementation phase.

Adapting to the Payroll Functionality

The payroll functionality seams to be very flexible but still isn't user friendly. Many customers have complained about it, and sometimes it takes a long time to make them feel comfortable with it.

The wage types concept is easy to grasp, but schemas and rules look as though they must be very difficult. They tend to scare customers. Despite this, they aren't that difficult. A good plan when implementing the payroll functionality is to make sure that everyone understands very well the standard schema and the personnel calculation rules. To do that, first spend some time trying to read the relevant international schema and some of its rules. After that, read the net payroll material written by SAP; then copy the schema of the country you want to change and change it!

N O T E   Don't forget that the employees need to have cost centers and the wage types need to be assigned to a FI/CO account to make transfers possible. Always check the processing and evaluation classes. ■

Missing the Overseas Benefits Functionality

The major gap within SAP is the Benefits functionality, which is available to the USA and Canada only. Benefits management is one of the functionalities most required by customers. It's not known when it will be available. Users have to develop their own personnel calculation rules by copying and editing an available schema to make it comply with local regulations.

Regretting the Security and Health Control System

The Security and Health control system is also something that SAP needs to improve; in many countries it doesn't address the basic legal requirements. The main control that can be exercised is based on restrictions and examinations by work centers. The recording of internal medical procedures is offered, plus some unimportant functions.

Glossary of HR Terms and Concepts

12th Rule   A rule that a 12th share of the daily allowance shall be paid for each full hour of traveling on one day of a business trip.

14-Hour Rule   Accounting rule according to German wage-tax law. In the case of a trip abroad for more than one day, the lump sum for meals for the day of the return trip is determined according to the last foreign town before the border and the time at which the border was crossed to re-enter the home country. If the border-crossing took place before 14:00, the day of the return trip is calculated with the valid domestic lump sum. Otherwise, the employee receives the country-specific lump sum for the (foreign) border country.

24-Hour Rule   Accounting rule according to German wage tax law. The maximum and lump sum amounts for additional costs for meals are determined according to the country the employee entered last before 24:00 (midnight) local time.

ABAP/4   Advanced Business Application Programming/4, a fourth-generation language in which SAP R/3 application software is written. SAP developed it.

absence quota   Defines an employee's eligibility for limited absence within a given time, which is reduced by every occasion of absence.

account assignment   Specification of accounts open for posting during a business transaction.

account assignment element   Work breakdown structure element to which actual or commitment postings can be made.

active SAP R/3 Repository   The directory now in operational use that contains descriptions of all the application data of an enterprise and their interrelationships, including how they're used in programs and screen forms. During ABAP/4 program development, a separate development repository directory is maintained for versions of the program components undergoing development or modification.

activity input   Transaction to plan the secondary cost quantities on a receiver cost center that uses activity from a sender cost center.

activity logs   Records of all activities in the SAP R/3 system for each transaction and for each user.

activity type   Classification of an activity and the data structure, for example:

- Number of units produced
- Hours
- Machine times
- Production times

actual costs   All the costs accruing to an object in a period.

additional travel expenses   Receipts for which the following categories don't apply:

- Transportation costs
- Meals
- Accommodation

ALE (Application Link Enabling)   An SAP method for using documents to carry messages that control distributed applications while maintaining integration and consistency of business data and processes across many systems.

allocation group   Defines which orders within one controlling area are to be settled together:

- By settlement timing—monthly, weekly, and so on
- By order types—repair, capital spending, and so on
- By settlement receivers—cost center, GL account

allocation receiver   Object to which the costs of a cost center or order are allocated.

APC (Acquisition or Production Costs)   Value of an asset used in some types of depreciation calculation.

API (Application Programming Interface)   Interface to support communication between applications of different systems.

ASCII   American Standard Code for Information Interchange, which associates each readable character or command to an input or output device with a specific pattern of binary numbers.

assembly order   Request to assemble pre-manufactured parts and assemblies to create finished products according to an existing sales order.

asset class   A grouping of fixed assets that are depreciated in a specified manner.

asset under construction   An asset that's still being produced when the balance sheet is prepared.

asynchronous database updating   A method of updating a database separately from the management of the dialog part of the transaction.

attendee type   A grouping of business event attendees with the same characteristics. These attendees can be individual attendees or group attendees.

availability check   Stock or inventory check automatically carried out after every goods movement. This check should prevent the book or available inventory balance of the physical inventory from becoming negative.

availability indicators   Infotype containing information related to the availability of resource types such as the type of resource, any location-dependent factors, the reservation characteristic of the resource (obligatory, single, multiple), the amount available, the resource priority, and the instances.

background process   Non-interactive execution of programs, sometimes using prepared file data to replicate the user dialog box to use the same standard functions.

backward scheduling   Scheduling a network so that the latest start and finish dates for the activities are calculated backward from the basic finish date.

balance correction   Changes time accounts or transfers balances between accounts.

batch (lot)   A subset of the total quantity of a material held in inventory. This subset is managed separately from other subsets of the same material. A batch of material might have to be identified by its date and place of origin. Delivery lots and lots comprising particular quality grades can be differentiated.

billing document   Generic term for invoices, credit memos, debit memos, and cancellation documents. A billing document comprises a header of data that applies to the whole document plus any number of items.

billing element   In a work breakdown structure, a data object to which you can post invoices and revenues.

bill of material (BoM)   A complete, formally structured list of all sub-assemblies, parts, and materials that go into an assembly or product. It includes a description, quantity, and unit of measure for each constituent part.

bill-to party   Person or company that receives the invoice for a delivery or service. The bill-to party receives the bill but isn't necessarily the payer who settles the bill.

block   A mechanism that enables credit controlling personnel to stop a customer from taking part in any transaction.

booking priority   A two-digit numeric value that can be used to give different weightings to various attendance bookings—waiting list, normal booking, and essential booking—to which priority intervals are assigned.

budget   Prescribed and binding approved version of the cost plan for a project or other task over a given period.

business area   A legally independent organizational unit within a client for which internal reporting balance sheets can be created. The boundaries of a business area will normally be determined on the basis of the sales organization or division responsible, or the delivering plant.

business event   A meeting of people for the purposes of information and/or education and training (for example, further education and training events, congresses, conferences, and so on) held within a certain period in a predefined language. Internal business events are the company's responsibility; external business events are organized by another contractor.

business event group   A coherent grouping of business event types with the same characteristics, or a defined collection of such business event groups.

business event hierarchy   A structure representing all business event groups and business event types with their hierarchical interrelationships.

business event type   Grouping or generalization of business events regardless of the dates on which they're held.

business segment   Intersection of criteria defined in a particular controlling area to suit the relevant operating concern—for example:

- Country, U.S.
- Industry, farming
- Product range, animal feeds
- Customer group, wholesale

business segment criterion   Chosen from an SAP proposal list or existing tables or created manually. Comprises a field name and a field value.

business segment value field   Holds a number, code, or string.

business transaction   A recorded data processing step representing a movement of value in a business system, such as cost planning, invoice posting, and movement of goods.

calculated costs   An order's progress toward completion represented in value terms. Two methods determine the calculated costs: calculation on a revenue base and calculation using quantity produced as a base. If planned revenue is more than planned costs for an order, there are two corresponding methods for calculating the (interim) profit realization.

calculated revenue   The revenue that corresponds to the actual costs incurred for an order, which are determined from results analysis as

Actual costs * planned revenue / planned costs

calendar days rule   The evaluation basis used for lump sum accounting of meals is calendar days. Each calendar day of a trip is calculated individually.

Capacity   Infotype containing information on the number of places available in a room and on the number of attendees possible on a business event type or business event: optimum capacity, minimum capacity, and maximum capacity.

capacity planning   A set of procedures for predicting the staffing and production facilities needed to fulfill confirmed or expected orders. The concept includes the following:

- Long-term rough-cut capacity planning (RCCP)
- Medium-term planning
- Short-term detailed planning (CRP)

CCMS   Computing Center Management System, an SAP product designed to provide efficient management of an R/3 system and any associated systems.

characteristic   A property of an object, such as length, color, or weight, used to describe and distinguish the object. Characteristics are also used to differentiate data objects in a database and are therefore used in personnel records.

CIM   Computer Integrated Manufacturing, the concept of controlling a manufacturing plant by a linked network of computers that's elaborated as an SAP product of the same name.

classification   When an object is assigned to a class, values for the object are assigned to characteristics belonging to the class.

client   The highest level in SAP R/3. Within the R/3 system, *client* refers to the highest level in the organizational hierarchy. Each master record in the SAP R/3 database is associated with only one client so that the data cannot be corrupted. The data of one client cannot be accessed by another client. A client can represent a group of related companies. There are often a training client and a testing client, in addition to the client code that represents your group or corporate identity and under which the SAP system runs normal business. Some data is managed at the client level, because everyone in the corporate group of companies will want to refer to exactly the same information and be certain that it has been maintained as up-to-date and correct. Vendor addresses are an example of data managed at the client level.

clock time evaluation rule   In lump sum accounting, the additional expenses for meals are calculated according to the time of day at which the employee was traveling. For example, between 8 and 9 a.m. the employee receives a travel expense rate appropriate for breakfast.

company code   A unit within a client that maintains accounting balances independently and creates the legally required balance sheet and profit-and-loss statement.

compensation key   Defines how overtime is to be compensated within time accounting, as follows:

- Payment
- Bonus paid or time off for basic hours
- Compensation

condition   A data element, term, or rule that defines price, taxes, and output according to user-determined criteria.

condition record   A data record that stores a condition and perhaps refers to condition supplements. Condition records can include the following:

- Prices
- Discounts and surcharges
- Taxes
- Output

contact person   A person at the customer location who deals with the vendor's sales or marketing department.

contingency order   A results analysis object on which the costs of complaints are collected. Reserves are created by results analysis for the expected cost of complaints and are drawn from as costs are incurred.

contract   A long-term agreement with a vendor that's fulfilled by individual release orders that are initiated according to the customer's requirements.

control indicator   Determines, in cost accounting, which application components are active, how certain data is stored, and what types of validation are to take place.

control key   Determines how an activity or activity element is to be processed in such operations as orders, costings, and capacity planning.

controlling activity   Internal or external physical measure of the activity output of a cost center according to activity type.

controlling area   Area within an organization that shares a cost accounting configuration; normally the same as company code. For cross-company cost accounting, one controlling area might be assigned to multiple company codes of one organization.

controlling area currency   Default currency in cost accounting objects, cost centers, orders, and so on.

conversion   Translation from one data format to another, for example, from decimal to binary code.

core time   Time during which employees must be present in the company. Defined in the *day program*.

cost   The expenditure involved in buying or manufacturing a product.

cost accounting capacity   Output of a cost center and activity that's technically possible during a specific period. Differentiated by category and arranged hierarchically.

cost center   Place in which costs are incurred. A unit within a company distinguished by area of responsibility, location, or accounting method.

cost component   A group of cost origins.

cost component layout (product cost accounting and cost center accounting)   Controls how results of a product cost estimate are saved. Assigns cost elements to cost components and determines the following:

- How the costs for raw materials and finished and semi-finished products are rolled into a multilevel assembly structure
- Which portion of the costs is treated as fixed costs
- Which costs are treated as the cost of goods manufactured
- Which are sales and administration costs
- Which are the costs of goods sold

cost element   Mandatory criterion for classifying costs arising in a company code and the name of the balance sheet account to which these costs are assigned. For example

- Direct cost elements for goods and services procured externally. Direct cost elements are maintained in the General Ledger master records.

- Indirect (internal activity) cost elements, which have no counterpart in the financial accounts and are maintained exclusively in cost accounting.

cost element group   A technical term for a conjunction of cost elements used to select records and to define lines and columns in reports. They can be used for planning purposes.

cost element planning   Planning primary and secondary costs on a cost center, order, or project.

cost element type   Classification of cost elements by uses or origin—for example, material cost element, settlement cost elements for orders, and cost elements for internal cost allocations.

cost object   An account assignment term for individual cost objects to which actual data—that is, costs, budgets, and sales revenues—can be assigned. It can consist of individual products, such as product groups, or local situations based on classification criteria, such as shop floor areas.

cost object hierarchy   Structure of cost objects as nodes to which actual data can be assigned.

cost origin   A logical category to which costs can be assigned. Activity types and cost elements are cost origins.

cost planning   Planning the costs to be incurred during a transaction.

cost planning type   Indicates the purpose of a cost planning method. For example

- Rough planning (estimating costs to be incurred for an order or for an element in a work breakdown structure)
- Cost element planning
- Unit costing

cost-of-sales accounting   Form of results analysis. Sales deductions and unit costs are assigned to the sales transaction.

costing   Calculating total production costs of individual product units, which can be a piece, a batch, a lot, or an order, for example. Costing can also take place on the provision of services.

costing type   Technical term used to control unit costing and product costing. The costing type determines the following:

- For which reference object a costing might be used
- Which costing object will be updated

- How the key of the costing file is made up
- Which costing application can use this costing type

costing variant   Technical term to determine criteria for a cost estimate. Comprises mainly the following:

- Costing type
- Valuation variant
- Organizational level
- Quantity structure determination, which includes the date control parameter

costing version   Determines the quantity structure when cost estimates are created. When production alternatives exist, there can be more than one product cost estimate for a material. Cost estimates with different production alternatives are given different version numbers.

CPI-C   Common Programming Interface-Communications, a set of standardized definitions for communications between programs.

critical   Obligatory resource types are assigned this indicator if not enough resources are available for them in a given period.

customer billing document   Statement of payment due as a result of the business transaction referred to in the document.

customer credit group   A group of customers defined by industry sector, by country, or by any characteristic that's useful for credit management. Credit representatives can generate reports for statistical analysis and retrieve information such as credit holds for processing using customer credit groups.

customer delivery   A collection of sales products delivered together.

customer group   A set of customers nominated or specified in any way for the purpose of statistical reporting or other management tasks.

customer hierarchy   A method of representing complex customer structures such as a buying group. Pricing and other information that's valid for all members of a customer hierarchy can be stored in the master record.

customer inquiry   Request from a customer to a sales organization for a price and availability check of in-hand inventory.

customer quotation   An offer submitted by a sales organization to a customer for the delivery of goods or the provision of services according to fixed terms.

customer-material information record   A collection of information and references to be used in specifying material for a particular customer.

customizing   A procedure and an SAP tool provided as part of the SAP R/3 system comprising two components: implementation guides and customizing menus and the associated functions. It doesn't change program coding. This tool provides support for all activities necessary for the following:

- Initial configuration of the SAP system before going into production
- Adjustment of the system during production
- Implementation of additional SAP applications

data element of a field   A description of the contents of a record or field in terms of their business significance.

database interface   A work area to receive data from ABAP/4 Data Dictionary tables and from which any changed data can be passed to the database.

date of next credit review   The date can be entered manually and used to trigger an automatic credit review that will issue a warning or a block if anyone tries to process a sales order after that date.

day program   Defined work rhythm of the day for an employee. Can consist of several day program blocks.

day type   Indicator that distinguishes the following cases:

- Normal weekday
- Public holiday weekday
- Public holiday Saturday
- Public holiday Sunday

DBMS   Database Management System, a software system used to set up and maintain a database. It includes SQL facilities.

debit memo request   A document created because of a discrepancy in price or quantity or as a result of a customer complaint. The debit memo request must be approved before a debit memo can be created.

Decay Meter   In Personnel Planning, the infotype containing information on the period of time after which the value of a qualification is reduced to half of its original value. In Training and Event Management, the infotype containing information on the period of time between attendance of a business event and the need to re-attend the business event.

delta management   System of transferring only data that has changed when using a Remote Function Call (RFC).

determining pairs for planned working time   Pairs must be determined within time accounting for planned working time. This processing type is assigned only if

- The time pairs are marked with the processing type A for an attendance or P for an absence.
- The maximum daily working time wasn't exceeded.

dialog module A group of dialog steps in a program.

direct cost Costs directly and fully identifiable with a reference object according to the costs-by-cause principle. Materials and energy used in production and staff costs for production and inspection are examples of causes.

distribution (controlling) A business transaction used to allocate primary costs. The original cost element is retained on the receiver cost center. Information on the sender and the receiver is documented in the cost accounting document.

distribution channel An organizational unit that determines how a product reaches the customer. A distribution channel indicates how a company generates business and which organizations are involved in distribution activities.

distribution key Contains rules on how costs are to be distributed. It's used for the following:

- Planning to spread costs over the planning period
- Assessment
- Distribution of direct costs to divide the costs of a sender cost center among the receivers

division An organizational unit set up to supervise distribution and monitor a particular product's profitability. Customer-specific arrangements such as partial deliveries, prices, or payment terms can be defined for each division.

DMS Document Management System, a specialized set of functions provided in R/3 for controlling documents of all kinds and recording any changes made to them.

document A printable record of a business transaction in SD-Sales and Distribution processing. SD has three kinds of printed documents:

- Sales documents
- Shipping documents
- Billing documents

document date Date on which the document becomes valid for processing. Each document's date is different in a sales sequence, for example. In the quotation, the document date is the date from which the quotation is valid; in the order, it's the date from which the agreement becomes binding. For example, the order creation date can vary from the date on which the agreement stipulated in the order becomes binding. In such a case, the agreement date would be taken as the document date.

document flow A stored representation of the document sequence necessary for one particular business transaction. For example, a particular document flow could be defined as a quotation, a sales order, a delivery, and an invoice.

dynpro A dynamic program that controls the screen and its associated validation and processing logic to control exactly one dialog step when interacting with the user.

EDI   Electronic Data Interchange, a standardized scheme for exchanging business data between different systems via defined business documents such as invoices and orders.

entity   The smallest possible collection of data that makes sense from a business viewpoint and is represented in the SAP R/3 system.

entity relationship model   Entities can be linked by logical relationships that have business significance. Entities and their interrelations can be used to build static models of the enterprise, which, in turn, are portrayed in the respective computer application with its tables.

environment analyzer   A help program that generates a list of development objects that belong together and the boundaries between development classes.

EPC   Event-driven process chain, which describes the chronological and logical relationship of functions of the R/3 system and business system statuses that initialize the functions or are generated as a result of function execution.

errand   A trip made by the employee in the course of duties to a place less than a certain mileage, including return journey, from his home and place of work.

external activities   Non-stock components or activities in a production order that are produced or performed outside the company.

external credit data   Credit data about a customer from external sources such as Dun & Bradstreet data, which is standard for SAP R/3. You refer to the D&B credit information number (DUNs number) that identifies the customer and append the D&B indicator and rating. You can also enter the date when you last acquired this data.

factory calendar   Derived from a public holiday calendar. Has a period of validity that must be within the scope of the public holiday calendar. The weekdays that are workdays are also to be specified. For example, Monday to Friday are workdays; Saturday, Sunday, and public holidays are days off.

feature   A software control object that can take on different specifications depending on the organizational unit. A feature can control extremely different operations with its specifications.

fill time for flexible time   Difference between the number of working hours without breaks and the core time. Fill time lies between the start and end of working hours prescribed by the company.

fixed holiday   A public holiday that falls on the same date every year, such as Christmas.

float   A time period that allows you to start a network or activity at a later date without incurring a scheduling delay.

follow-up costs   Incurred after the actual manufacturing process is completed—for example, costs of rework and warranties.

forecast   An estimate of future values based on historical data.

forward scheduling   Way of scheduling a network, starting from the basic start date and adding durations to determine the earliest start and finish dates for successive activities.

free float   Time that an activity can be shifted into the future without affecting the earliest start date of the following activity or the end date of the project. Must not be less than zero or greater than the total float.

function module   A program module that has a clearly defined interface and can be used in several programs. The function module library manages all function modules and provides search facilities in the development environment.

function-oriented cost accounting   Assigning costs to a business function for analysis.

general costs activity   General costs incurred during the lifetime of a project are planned via this type of activity in a network. Examples of such planned costs are insurance, travel, consulting fees, and royalties.

goods issue   The decrease of warehouse inventory resulting from a withdrawal of material or delivery to a customer.

goods issue document   A statement that verifies goods movement and contains information for follow-up tasks. A corresponding material document is initiated for the subsequent outflow of material with the goods issue document in the delivery. The material document contains one or more items and can be printed as a goods issue slip for the actual physical movement of goods.

GUI   Graphical user interface. The SAPGUI gives users an ergonomic and attractive means of controlling and using business software.

hours evaluation rule   In lump sum accounting, the additional expenses for meals are calculated according to the length of the trip.

hypertext   Online documentation set up like a network, with active references pointing to additional text and graphics.

IDoc   Intermediate document. The SAP R/3 system *EDI* interface and the *ALE* program link enabling both use standardized intermediate documents to communicate.

IMG   Implementation Guide, a component of the SAP R/3 system that provides detailed steps for configuring and setting applications.

imputed costs   Value changes that don't represent operational expenditure or correspond to expenditures in content or timing—for example, depreciation and interest.

incentive wage   Form of work remuneration for which not only the attendance time in the enterprise is reimbursed but also during which the achievements accomplished are also taken into account. Piecework and premium wages are included in the incentive wage.

income threshold   The limit up to which social insurance contributions are determined by the employee's income.

incompletion log   A list that indicates what information is missing in a document. You can set up conditions to specify the information that has to be included in a document.

indirect costs   Costs for which one single receiving object can't be directly and fully identified according to the costs-by-cause principle. For example

- *Indirect expenses*, such as building insurance
- *Indirect labor cost*, such as supervisor wages
- *Indirect materials cost*, such as coolant cleaning materials

individual statement   Accounting of actual trip expenses substantiated by the employee's receipts.

information type   Carrier of system controlling features such as attributes and time constraint.

infotype   See *information type*.

initial cost split   Cost component split for raw materials procurement showing such details as the following:

- Purchase price
- Freight charges
- Insurance contributions
- Administration costs

inquiry   A customer request to a sales organization for price and on-hand availability.

instance object type   The object type whose objects are used in certain cases instead of the objects assigned in the standard system. Used in the Availability Indicators infotype to determine different resources, such as internal or external instructors.

inventory from which revenue can be generated   The revenue expected in view of already incurred costs can be divided into capitalized costs and capitalized profits. It's calculated as Calculated Revenue minus Actual Revenue. Results analysis calculates the inventory for profit orders.

invoice   Sales and Distribution document used to charge a customer for delivery of goods or for services rendered.

invoice date   Date on which a delivery is due for settlement. In some firms, invoices are processed periodically. All deliveries that become due at the same time can be combined and settled in a collective invoice. As soon as the next billing date determined by the calendar is reached, the orders and deliveries are included in the billing due list and can be billed.

invoice list   Method of billing by combining all billing documents for a specific period for a particular payer. Additional discounts such as factoring discounts can be granted based on the total value of an invoice list. The list might include individual and collective documents.

invoice split   Creation of several billing documents from one reference document such as an order or delivery. The split can be based on materials, for example.

item   Element of a document that carries information on the goods to be delivered or the services to be rendered.

item category   An indicator that defines a document item's characteristics. The following item categories are predefined:

- Items kept in inventory
- Value items
- Text items

The item category controls the following tasks:

- Pricing
- Billing
- Delivery processing
- Stock posting
- Transfer of requirements

job data   Collection of information characteristic of a workplace occupied by an employee—for example, terms of employment, job title, allocation to a cost center, and department.

job order cost accounting   Instrument for the detailed planning and controlling of costs. Serves for the following:

- Collecting
- Analyzing
- Allocating the costs incurred for the internal production of non-capitalized goods

joint products   Made in the same manufacturing process.

Kerberos   A technique for checking user authorizations across open distributed systems.

leave entitlement   By German law, for example, every employee has full claim to at least a number of weekdays' leave annually after six months under the work contract. Collective agreements and individual contracts can provide different leave periods. For shorter work contracts, the claim to 1/12th the annual leave for every full month that the work contract exists is calculated.

library network   Generic network structure that can be used by many projects. Used in project system for repetitive processes or for process planning.

line item   Display of posting according to activity and document number.

logical database   A set of predefined paths for accessing the tables in a specific database system. When defined and coded, they can be used by any report program.

logical system   A system that runs applications integrated on a common database. In SAP terms, this is a *client* in a database.

loop Circular path through activities and their relationships.

lot-size variance Variances between the fixed planned costs and the fixed allocated actual costs that occur because part of the total cost for an order or a cost object doesn't change with output quantity changes. For example, setup costs that don't change no matter how often the operation is carried out.

lump sum accommodation Costs for accommodation are calculated per night with a designated flat rate.

lump sum accounting Payment of an employee's travel expenses by lump sum. Reimbursement doesn't depend on the actual trip expenditures in this case. Three kinds of lump sums must be distinguished:

- Lump sums for transportation costs
- Lump sums for meals
- Lump sums for accommodation

lump sum meals Additional expenses for meals are calculated by lump sum per day with a designated travel expense rate.

lump sum transportation Transportation costs are calculated per kilometer with a designated kilometer flat rate.

LUW Logical Unit of Work, an elementary processing step that's part of an SAP transaction. A logical unit of work is executed entirely or not at all. In particular, database access is always accomplished by separate LUWs, each of which is terminated when the database is updated or when the COMMIT WORK command is entered.

main destination The most important destination on a business trip's itinerary.

make-to-order production Type of production in which a product is normally made only once, although it or a similar product might be made again in the future. The costs of goods manufactured by this type of production are collected on a sales order item or an internal order and settled to profitability analysis.

master data Data relating to individual objects. Remains unchanged for a long time.

matchcode An index key code attached to the original data that can be used to perform quick interactive searches for this data.

material Product, substance, or commodity that's bought or sold commercially or is used, consumed, or created in production. A material master record can also represent a service.

material availability date The date on which a material must be available. On the material availability date, the vendor must start the activities relevant for delivery, such as picking and packing the goods. The material availability date should allow time for the goods to be completely prepared by the loading date.

material determination   The process of conducting an automatic search for a material master record during the creation of SD documents using a key instead of the actual material number. The key can be a customer-specific material number or the EAN number of the material.

material exclusion   A restriction that automatically prevents the sale of specific materials to a particular customer.

material listing   A restriction that controls the sale of specific materials to a customer. Customers can buy only materials included in the material listing assigned to them. The system doesn't allow you to enter in a sales document for particular customer materials not included in the material listing.

material requirements   Generic term for activities involved in creating a production schedule or procurement plan for the materials in a plant, company, or company group.

Material Requirements Planning (MRP)   A set of techniques that uses *bill of material (BoM)*, inventory data, and the master production schedule to calculate material requirements.

material substitution   Automatic replacement by another material for technical reasons or during a sales promotion.

material type   An indicator that subdivides materials into groups, such as raw materials, semi-finished materials, operating supplies, and services, and that also determines the user screen sequence, the numbering in the material master records, the type of inventory management, and the account determination.

maximum amount   The maximum amount that can be reimbursed per day when accounting an individual statement.

maximum amount meals   The limit that the sum of all meals receipts cannot exceed per day.

maximum document value   A specific value that the sales order or delivery cannot exceed. The value is defined in the credit check and is stored in the currency of the credit control area. Checking is initiated by a risk category that's defined specifically for new customers if a credit limit isn't yet specified.

maximum number of dunning levels allowed   The customer's dunning level cannot exceed this specified maximum.

menu painter   An SAP R/3 system tool for developing standardized menus, function keys, and pushbuttons according to the SAP Style Guide.

metadata   Information about data structures used in a program. Examples of metadata are table and field definitions, domains, and descriptions of relationships between tables.

milestone   An operation or task that also confirms the completion of processing of previous tasks. When you confirm a milestone, the system backflushes its component operations to confirm their completion also.

mode   A user interface window in which an activity can be conducted in parallel with other open modes.

modified standard cost estimate A costing type; uses the quantity structure that has changed during the planning period to calculate the cost of goods manufactured for a product.

moving average price Value of the material divided by the quantity in stock. Changes automatically after each goods movement or invoice entry.

negative time recording Method of time recording for determining the attendance and absence times for which only relevant variances from the shift schedule are entered and processed as absences and overtime. It's mostly used for fixed working hours and assumes that the employees generally work according to the allocated shift schedule. Insignificant differences (minutes) aren't normally included.

network In SAP R/3, activity-on-node structure containing instructions on how to carry out activities in a specific order and in a specific time period. Made from activities and relationships.

network type Distinguishes networks by their usage. The network type controls the following:

- Costing variants for plan, target, and actual costs
- Order type
- Number ranges
- Open items
- Status profile
- Authorizations

night shift Working hours in the shift operation reimbursed by a night shift bonus according to a collective agreement.

non-working shift Those days of a shift worker indicated in the shift schedule as work-free in a multiple-shift operation. Can also mean days off, such as bridge days for employees who have accrued them by working in advance.

normal booking A priority assigned if attendance on a business event is guaranteed. It's impossible to make a normal booking if the optimum number of attendees on a business event is already reached.

normal work time An employee's usual working hours. Used within flexible time models when actual times aren't available, as in the case of sick leave.

object currency The currency of the controlling area is the default currency of a cost accounting object, such as cost center, order, and so on.

object dependency Product variants might entail certain combinations of parts and exclude other combinations. If the customer chooses one variant, certain options might not be available for technical or commercial reasons. These reciprocal relationships are represented in the system by object dependency. A special editor is provided in the classification system to maintain the object dependency for characteristics and the characteristic values. You can also store object dependency in a *bill of material (BoM)*. The system uses this information during BoM explosion. Object dependency controls whether all possible components are taken into account in materials planning.

object master data and object dependency Master records for the manufacture of products with many variants. Information on the objects involved and their interrelationships is stored as object master data and object dependency

object master data [...] e variants for a standard product. Bills of [...] structions for combining the individual

[...] play layout—for example, routings, in-

[...] ssigned if their corresponding re-
[...] event is being planned.

OL [...] nology that enables the connection and
inc [...]

one [...] d used to process transactions involving a [...] r a one-time customer, the customer
data [...]

open [...] ot yet reflected in financial accounting, bu [...] tem management provides for
early re [...]

operatin [...] nore controlling areas and company cod [...] re valid for a specific operating
concern. [...] fields are then updated for these
objects. [...]

operating [...] ormance of a cost center for a period—for example, outp [...] time, and machine hours.

operating rate Ratio of actual and planned operating level. Measures the effective usage of a cost center or activity.

operating resources Personnel and material necessary to carry out a project. Can be used once or many times and is defined in value or quantity units. Planned for a period or a point in time. Includes, for example, materials, machines, labor, tools, jigs, fixtures, external services, and work centers.

operational area A company's logical subdivision for accounting or operational reasons and therefore indicated in the EDM (Enterprise Data Model). An operational area is an organizational unit within logistics that subdivides a maintenance site plant according to the responsibility for maintenance.

operations layout   A list, sorted by operations, of costing results from product costing and final costing.

order   An instrument for planning and controlling costs. It describes the work to be done in a company in terms of which task is to be carried out and when, what's needed to carry out this task, and how costs are to be settled.

order category   The SAP application to which the order belongs—SD, for example.

order combination   A combination of complete sales orders, of individual order items from different sales orders, or of partial deliveries of individual order items in a delivery. Order combination in a delivery is possible only when you authorize it for the customer in the customer master record or when you manually authorize it for individual sales orders in the sales order document header.

order group   Technical term for grouping orders into hierarchies. Used to create reports on several orders, combine orders, and create an *order hierarchy*.

order hierarchy   Grouping of orders for processing at the same time as in order planning and order reporting.

order phase   System control instrument for the order master data. Allows and prohibits operations on orders, depending on the phase or stage: opened, released, completed, or closed.

order/project results analysis   Periodic valuation of long-term orders and projects. The order and project results analysis evaluates the ratio between costs and a measure of an order's progress toward completion, such as revenue or the quantity produced. The results analysis data include the following:

- Cost of sales
- Capitalized costs of work in progress
- Capitalized profits
- Reserves for unrealized costs
- Reserves for the cost of complaints and commissions
- Reserves for imminent loss

order settlement   An order's complete or partial crediting. Costs accrued to an order are debited to one or more receivers belonging to financial or cost accounting.

order status   Instrument to control whether an order can be planned or posted to. Reflects the operational progress and the order phase. Determines the following:

- Whether planning documents are created during cost element planning
- The transactions allowed at the moment (phase), such as planning, posting actual costs, and so on
- When an order can be flagged for deletion

order summarization   Allows you to summarize data by putting orders into hierarchies. Also allows you to analyze order costs at a higher level.

order type   Differentiates orders according to their purpose: repair, maintenance, marketing, and capital expenditure, for example.

outline agreement   Generic term for contracts and scheduling agreements. An outline agreement is a long-term agreement with the vendor involving product delivery or rendering of services according to specified requirements. These requirements are valid for a limited time period, a defined total purchase quantity, or a specified total purchase value. A further transaction determines when deliveries and services take place.

output   Information sent to the customer by various media such as mail, EDI, or fax. Examples of output are

■ Printed quotation or order confirmations

■ Order confirmations sent by EDI

■ Shipping notifications sent by fax

overall network   Network resulting from relationships between all existing networks in a company.

overhead   Total cost of indirect expenses, indirect labor, and indirect materials (indirect costs). Allocated to cost objects by means of overhead rates.

overhead cost management   All cost accounting activities for planning and controlling the indirect costs:

■ Responsibility-oriented overhead cost management by cost centers

■ Decision-oriented overhead cost management by action-oriented objects, which are orders and projects

overhead costing   The most common method in product cost accounting:

1. Assign the direct costs to the cost object.
2. Apply the indirect (overhead) costs to the cost object in proportion to the direct costs, expressed as a percentage rate.

overhead group   A key that groups materials to which the same overheads are applied.

overtime   All working hours above the legal, normal work time. The employee has a claim for adequate payment of more than the regular wage (overtime bonus). Extra hours aren't strictly overtime unless the total number of weekly working hours exceeds the legally determined number of hours. Despite this definition, the term *overtime* is commonly used instead of *extra hours*. Therefore, overtime can also be defined more generally as approved, and thus paid, hours above and beyond normal working hours.

PA settlement structure   To settle costs incurred on a sender to various business segments depending on the cost element. The profitability analysis settlement structure is a combination of assignments of cost element groups to profitability segments.

pair formation   To enable evaluation of employee time events entered at the time recording terminal, time pairs must be formed. This is performed by associating those time events that can logically be allocated to the same day.

partner   An individual within or outside your own organization who is of commercial interest and who can be contacted in the course of a business transaction. A partner can be a human being or a legal entity.

payer   Person or company that settles the bill for a delivery of goods or for services rendered. The payer isn't necessarily the *bill-to party*.

period accounting   One basis for profitability analysis. Costs are identified in the period in which they occur, irrespective of the period in which the corresponding revenue occurs.

piecework wage   A form of *incentive wage* in which the output quantity is reimbursed regardless of the working hours required, in contrast to the *time wage*. Piecework occurs in three forms:

- *Money piecework (rare)*. A fixed amount is paid per produced quantity unit.
- *Piecework (rare)*. A quantitative output is specified per unit of time.
- *Time piecework (frequent)*. Remuneration for work performed is proportional to the output quantity, but calculated in relation to a defined standard time for a specified quantity.

plan version   Control parameters for comparative analyses in planning in cost accounting. The plan version determines whether

- Planning changes are documented.
- A beginning balance is to be generated.
- The planning data of another version can be copied or referenced.

planned activity   The planned cost center activity required to meet the demand, measured in the corresponding physical or technical units.

planned delivery time   Number of days required to procure the material via external procurement.

planned time   Product of the quantity produced and the standard time per base quantity.

planned working time   Working hours or times during which an employee *can* be present, not *must*.

planning   Assigning estimates of the costs of all activities that will be required to carry out the business of an organizational unit over the planning period.

planning document   Line item for documenting planning changes.

planning element   *Work Breakdown Structure (WBS)* element on which cost planning can be carried out.

plant The main organizational entity for production planning and control. *Material Requirements Planning (MRP)* and inventory maintenance are often conducted at the plant level.

plant ID card Identification card used for entering a building, workshop, or controlled area.

pooled table A database table used to store control data, such as program parameters or temporary data. Several pooled tables can be combined to form a table pool, which corresponds to a physical table on the database.

positive time recording Method of time recording for calculating attendance times and absence times for which the variances (absences, overtime) from the shift schedule are entered to the minute. Unlike negative time recording, the actual attendance times of the employees are recorded for flexible time processing.

price difference account To record price differences for materials managed under standard prices, or differences between purchase order and billing prices.

price group Grouping of customers for pricing purposes.

price variance Occurs if planned costs are evaluated in one way and the actual costs in another. The planned standard rates for activities might change in the meantime, for example. Can also be the result of exchange rate fluctuations.

pricing element A factor that contributes to pricing. The following can be identified as pricing elements:

- Price
- Discount
- Surcharge
- Freight
- Tax

pricing procedure Definition of the conditions permitted for a particular document and the sequence in which the system takes these conditions into account during pricing.

pricing scale Scale within a condition record where prices, discounts, or surcharges are defined for different customer order quantities or values.

pricing type Controls whether prices are copied from a reference document to a new document or whether they're recalculated in the new document.

primary cost planning By values and as quantities.

primary costs Costs incurred due to the consumption of goods and services supplied from outside the company. Costs for input factors and resources are procured externally, for example:

- Bought-in parts
- Raw materials
- Supplies
- Services

process manufacturing　A production type; continuous manufacturing process from raw materials to finished product.

processing type　Identified and formed during time evaluation and indicated as follows:

S　Planned time

M　Overtime

A　Absence

product costing　Tool for planning costs and setting prices. It calculates the cost of goods manufactured and goods sold for each product unit using data in the PP-Production Planning module. Product costing based on *Bills of Material (BoM)* and routings is used for the following:

- Calculating production costs of an assembly with alternatives for each production version or each material
- Showing the costs of semi-finished products
- Detailed estimate of the cost components down to their lowest production level

product proposal　Product groupings, combinations, and quantities frequently ordered. You can save time by referring to and copying from product proposals. You can also define a product proposal for a particular customer. The system automatically enters the customer-specific product proposal when you create an order for this particular customer.

production costs, total　The costs of finished products bought for resale, or the costs of goods manufactured, plus sales overhead, special direct costs of sales, and administration overhead.

production cycle　A manufacturing process in which the output of the final manufacturing level (or part of it) becomes input for lower manufacturing levels of the same process (recycle).

production order　For the production department to produce a material. It contains operations, material components, production resources and tools, and costing data.

production planning capacity　A work center's capability to perform a specific task. Capacities are differentiated according to category and arranged hierarchically under a work center.

Production Resources and Tools (PRT)　A specification of the objects needed for carrying out operations at work centers. They're assigned to activities for which they are necessary for execution. PRTs include the following:

- Job instructions
- Tools (including general-purpose hand tools and power tools and specific devices used only in particular activities)
- Test equipment
- Numerically controlled programs
- Drawings
- Machinery and fixtures

PRTs are stored in master records, as follows:

- Material master
- Equipment master
- Document master

profit center   Area of responsibility for which an independent operating profit is calculated. It's responsible for its own profitability. Separate divisional result is calculated.

profit order   Order in which planned revenue is greater than planned costs. Results analysis uses the profit percentage rate of a profit order to calculate the inventory from which revenue can be generated and to calculate the cost of sales.

profit percentage rate   Planned revenue divided by planned costs of an order.

profitability analysis   In SAP R/3, by cost-of-sales approach or period accounting.

project definition   Framework laid down for all objects created within a project. The data, such as dates and organizational data, is binding for the entire project.

project management   An organizational structure created just for the life of the project to be responsible for planning, controlling, and monitoring of the project.

project structure   All significant relationships between the elements in a project.

project system activity   An instruction to perform a task within a network in a set period of time. Work, general costs, or external processing can be associated with it.

project system relationship   Link between start and finish points of two activities in a network or library network. In SAP R/3, the relationship types are the following:

SS	Start-start
FF	Finish-finish
SF	Start-finish
FS	Finish-start

project type   Capital spending or customer project, for example.

public holiday calendar   A structured list of public holidays with a scope of validity specified in years. A public holiday calendar groups public holidays. As a result, individually adapted calendars can be created for different countries or federal states.

public holiday class   According to the Public Holiday Loss of Income Law and the collective agreement, public holidays with different valencies attract different rates of remuneration if they're worked. The high-valued holidays, for example, are the so-called high public holidays such as Easter Sunday, further legal public holidays (such as May 1 in Europe and the Russian Federation or October 3 in Germany), or regional public holidays. The system discriminates by referring to the public holiday class assigned to each public holiday.

public holiday type   Classifies public holidays with respect to the following characteristics:

- Falls on the same date every year
- Always has the same interval to Easter
- Falls on a certain day of the week

Q-API   Queue Application Program Interface, which supports asynchronous communication between applications of different systems by using managed queues or waiting lines.

quantity structure   The quantity-related basis for calculating costs. The Bill of Material (BoM) and routing form the quantity structure for product costing and the preliminary costing of a production order.

quantity variance   Difference between the target costs and the actual costs, which results from the difference between the planned and actual quantities of goods or activity used. For example

- More raw materials from stock for a production order
- Fewer activities from a cost center than were planned for

rate of capacity utilization   Ratio of output to capacity. Fixed costs can be divided into used capacity costs and idle time costs.

realized loss   Usage of reserves for imminent loss by results analysis. Loss can be realized when actual costs are incurred or when revenue is received. Results analysis realizes loss as the difference either between the actual costs and the calculated revenue or between the calculated costs and the actual revenue, as follows:

- Actual costs minus calculated revenue
- Calculated costs minus actual revenue

reference date   Using the reference dates and the offsets, the start and finish dates of the sub-operation or the production resource/tool usage are determined. A time within an activity—for example, the start date. Reference dates are used to determine the start and finish dates of sub-operations as well as usage dates for production resources/tools. You can enter time intervals for reference dates.

reference document   Document from which data is copied into another document.

reference model event   A status with business relevance that can trigger an SAP system function or can be the result of such a function.

resource   All work materials and utilities, including instructors, needed to hold a business event.

resource type   Group of resources with the same characteristics, for example, room, PC, instructor, and training materials. A resource type with special characteristics requires extra data, such as room with capacity data and instructor with affiliation details.

resource-usage variance   Occurs if the used resource is different from the planned one—for example, the actual raw material used is different from the planned raw material.

results analysis   Periodic valuation of long-term orders. Results analysis compares the calculated costs and the actual cost of an order as it progresses toward completion. It calculates inventory (if actual costs are greater than calculated costs) or reserves (if actual costs are less than calculated costs).

The data calculated during results analysis is stored in the form of the following:

- Cost of sales
- Capitalized costs
- Capitalized profit
- Reserves for unrealized costs
- Reserves for costs of complaints and commissions
- Reserves for imminent loss

results analysis account   General Ledger account that records the figures calculated during results analysis.

results analysis data   Includes the following:

- Work in progress and capitalized costs
- Reserves
- Cost of sales

results analysis key   Controls valuation of the relationship between costs and the computational base such as revenue or produced quantity as an order progresses toward completion. The results analysis key determines at least the following characteristics:

- Whether revenue-based, quantity-based, or manual
- Whether to use planned or actual results
- How profits are to be realized
- Whether to split inventory, reserves, and cost of sales

results analysis version   Describes the business purpose for which results analysis was carried out. It determines, for example

- Whether in accordance with German and American law
- Whether for financial accounting purposes
- Whether for profitability analysis
- To which results analysis accounts to post the results
- How the life cycle of an object is to be broken down into open and closed periods

revenue   The operational output from an activity, valued at the market price in the corresponding currency for the normal sales quantity unit. The revenue from a single unit multiplied by the number of units sold equals the sales revenue.

revenue account determination   Notifies the revenue accounts to which prices, discounts, and surcharges are to be posted. The system uses predefined conditions to determine the appropriate accounts.

RFC   Remote Function Call. A protocol, written in ABAP/4, for accessing function modules in other computers. RFC-SDK is a kit for integrating PC applications so that they can access SAP R/3 functions.

risk category   Enables the credit manager to classify customers according to commercial risk. Along with the document type, the risk category helps determine which kind of credit check the system automatically carries out. For example, you might decide to carry out stringent checks at order receipt for high risk customers, but waive a credit check for customers with an acceptable payment history.

RPC   Remote Procedure Call, a protocol for accessing procedures residing in other computers from C programming environments. Corresponds to *RFC*.

sales activity   A data record that contains information on interactions with customers, including sales calls, telephone calls, conferences, or presentations.

sales and distribution document   A document that represents a business transaction in the SD module. SD documents include the following:

- Sales documents
- Shipping documents
- Billing documents

Sales and Operations Planning (SOP)   The creation and maintenance of a meaningful sales plan and corresponding operations plan that includes a forecast of future customer demand.

sales area   An organizational unit responsible for three facets:

- Sales-related aspect (sales organization)
- Customer-related aspect (distribution channel)
- Product-related aspect (division)

sales document   A document that represents a business transaction in the sales department. Sales documents include the following:

- Inquiry
- Quotation
- Sales order
- Outline agreement such as contracts and scheduling agreements
- Returns, credit, and debit requests

sales document type   Indicators used to control processing of various SD documents by allowing the system to process different kinds of business transactions, such as standard orders and credit memo requests, in different ways.

sales order Contractual arrangement between a sales organization and a sold-to party concerning goods to be delivered or services to be rendered and an SAP document that contains information about prices, quantities, and dates.

sales organization The division or other organizational unit responsible for negotiating sales and for distributing products and services. Sales organizations can be assigned to subdivisions of the market by geographical or industrial criteria. Each sales transaction is carried out by one sales organization.

sales plan A sales plan is the overall level of sales, usually stated as the monthly rate of sales per product group or product family. The plan is expressed in units identical to the operations plan for planning purposes and represents a commitment by sales and marketing management to take all reasonable steps necessary to achieve actual customer orders that add up to the sales forecast.

sales unit Unit of measure in which a product is sold. If several alternative sales units of measure have been defined for one product, conversion factors are applied by the system to convert them to the base unit of measurement.

Schedule Infotype for time plan of business events. Contains the following information:

- Day number with date, start time and end time, and flag indicating days off
- Duration in days
- Duration in hours
- Number of dates (one date or several dates)
- Start day

Schedule Model Infotype for time plan of business event types. The Schedule Model can include a schedule pattern and can be user defined.

schedule line A subdivision, according to date and quantity, of an item in a sales document. If the total quantity of an item can be delivered only in partial deliveries, the system creates schedule lines corresponding to each partial delivery and determines the appropriate quantities and delivery dates for each schedule line.

schedule pattern A standard specification for the time structure of business events that can be copied. The schedule pattern consists of a sequence of day descriptions, each containing the following information:

- Day number
- Time block ID (consisting of a maximum of three time blocks, each with start and end times)

scheduling The calculation of the start and end dates of orders and of operations within an order. Network scheduling determines earliest and latest start dates for activities and calculates the required capacity, as well as floats.

scheduling agreement A type of outline agreement. The scheduling agreement is a long-term agreement with a vendor or customer that defines the creation and continuous updating of schedules. Schedules specify timing of partial deliveries for each item in schedule lines.

screen painter An ABAP/4 Development Workbench tool that can be used to create, modify, display, and delete *dynpros*.

secondary cost element Cost centers require services from other cost centers to produce activity of their own. These costs are secondary. Planned assessment is used to plan the secondary cost quantities. Activity input is used to plan the secondary cost values.

shift schedule Precise specification of the daily working hours of an employee or employee group over a determined period.

sick pay Paid to the employee from legal health insurance for the period during the work incapacity in which he/she receives no wage or salary from the employer—that is, generally after the period of continued pay expires. The amount of sick pay depends on the amount of remuneration.

simultaneous costing process Displays the actual costs incurred to date for such cost objects as an order. The process describes all costings of an order in the SAP system, including order settlement. These costings come in the form of preliminary costings and actual costings. The values can then be analyzed in final analysis.

skeleton time The time between the beginning and end of *planned working time*.

SQL Structured Query Language, defined by ANSI (American National Standards Institute) as a fourth-generation language for defining and manipulating data.

standard cost estimate Calculates the standard price for semi-finished and finished products. Relevant to the valuation of materials with standard price control. Usually created once for all products at the beginning of the fiscal year or a new season. The most important type of costing in product costing. The basis for profit planning or variance-oriented product cost controlling.

standard hierarchy Tree structure for classifying all data objects of one type. For example, the cost centers belonging to a company from a cost accounting viewpoint are represented by a standard hierarchy copied from the R/3 Reference Model and customized.

standard price Constant price with which a material is evaluated without taking into account goods movements and invoices. It's used for semi-finished and finished products where they are part of product costing.

static credit limit check The customer's credit exposure cannot exceed the established credit limit. The credit exposure is the total combined value of the following:

- Open sales documents
- Open delivery documents
- Open billing documents
- Open items in accounts receivable

The open order value is the value of order items that haven't yet been delivered. The open delivery value is the value of the delivery items that haven't yet been invoiced. The open invoice value is the value of the billing document items that haven't yet been forwarded to accounting. The open items represent documents that have been forwarded to accounting but aren't yet settled by the customer.

status Order items with the category TAK are made to order and have an object status that passes through the following phases:

- *Released.* The system sets this status automatically when the item is created. It indicates that production can be initiated.
- *Revenue Posted.* The system sets this status automatically as soon as revenue is posted for an item for the first time.
- *Fully Invoiced.* This status must be set manually as soon as all revenues are posted for the item.
- *Completed.* This status must be set manually when the procedure is completed.

After the status 3 Fully Invoiced is set, no more revenues can be posted. If the status 4 Completed is set, no further costs can be posted.

stopover A destination other than the main destination during a business trip or errand.

style guide A collection of the SAP design standards for uniform design and consistent operation routines for SAP applications.

sub-item An item in a sales document that refers to a higher level item. Services and rebates in kind can be entered as sub-items belonging to main items.

substitution A temporary revenue for the job of another colleague who, for example, is sick. If a better-remunerated job is occupied, the representing employee must be paid correspondingly higher for the substitution hours worked.

summarization object An object containing data calculated during order summarization, project summarization, or the summarization of a cost object hierarchy. A summarization object can, for example, contain the costs incurred for all orders of a specific order type and a specific responsible cost center.

surcharge Supplement, usually as a percentage, that is used to apply overhead in absorption costing.

target costs Calculated by using the planned costs, along with the following:

- The planned activities divided by the actual activities (for cost centers)
- The planned quantities divided by the actual quantities of goods manufactured (for orders)

target document A document to which the data from a reference document is copied.

task list type Distinguishes task lists according to their functionality. In production planning task lists, for example, a distinction is drawn between routings and reference operation sets.

tax category A code that identifies the condition that the system is to use to determine country-specific taxes automatically during pricing.

tax classification Specification of the method for calculating the tax liability of the customer based on the tax structure of the customer's country.

TCP/IP Transmission Control Protocol/Internet Protocol, the standard network protocol for open systems.

text A system function that provides a note pad in which you can store any related text about the current customer. The system indicates in the credit management status screen whether any text is already available about this customer.

text type A classification for various texts that users can define in master records or in documents. Text types include the following:

- Sales texts
- Shipping texts
- Internal notes

third-party business transaction Commerce in which goods or services are delivered directly from the vendor to the customer.

time data All employee data that has a temporal aspect of some form—for example, sickness period, working hours, vacation, and overtime.

time evaluation The process of evaluating attendance and absence times with the help of a program that generates time types (flextime balance, productive hours) and wage types (extra pay for night work, Sunday work, and public holiday work).

time event A time such as clock-in or clock-out recorded by an identified employee at a time recording terminal.

time indicator Method of identifying time periods by the following codes:

01	Overtime
02	Fill time
03	Core time
04	Break in core time
05	Break in fill time
06	Paid break

time interval Time period between at least two activities linked in a relationship. The relationship type determines how start and finish times are used in the calculation.

time model Groups a number of day programs and is used as the basis for generating shift schedules.

time pair Groups time events that are logically allocated to one day—for example, the clock-in and clock-out times of an employee's daily work schedule. In HR, a time pair might define a very short period, such as a break or a working spell between breaks. The actual times of a time pair can define how breaks are to be paid, which night shift bonus is to be assigned, and so on.

time quota   The specification of a time interval for which the employee can be present or absent under certain circumstances.

time recording   Individual entry of the attendance times of an employee, but also the investigation of actual data about work orders, operating funds, and materials and tools using production data collection, generally via electronic time recording systems.

time recording plant ID card   Identification card that generally has a bar code, magnetic strip, or infrared coding to enable it to mark time events such as coming, going, short business trips, and so on at time recording devices.

time type   During time evaluation, balances are formed from the employee attendance and absence times. These balances are updated in the time type records.

time wage   Form of wages for which the employee's attendance is reimbursed, regardless of the produced benefits. A certain pay rate is paid per unit of time.

total float   Time that an activity can be shifted out into the future, starting from its earliest dates, without affecting the latest dates of its successors or the latest finish date of the network.

transaction   The series of related work steps required to perform a specific task on a business data processing system. One or more screens might be required. From the user's viewpoint, it represents a self-contained unit. In terms of dialog programming, it's a complex object that consists of a module pool, screens, and so on and is called with a transaction code.

transaction currency   Currency in which the actual business transaction was carried out.

travel privileges   Employee-specific parameters for travel expense accounting.

trip destination   Place of stay (town and country) during a business trip. A distinction is made here between main destination and one or more stopovers.

unit costing   Costing method in which Bills of Material (BoM) and routings aren't used. Determines planned costs for assemblies or to support detailed planning of cost accounting objects such as cost centers or orders.

unit of measure   A standard measurement recognized by the SAP R/3 system. The following are examples of units of measure:

- Base unit of measure
- Unit of entry
- Unit of issue
- Order unit
- Sales unit
- Weight group

Grouping, used in delivery processing, refers to the weight of a convenient quantity of a material. The weight group is one factor the system uses to determine the route. It's also used in delivery scheduling to determine the pick/pack time.

usage variance   Difference between planned and actual costs caused by higher usage of material, time, and so on.

user-defined field types   A classification code that interprets the meaning of a user-defined field. For example, a user might designate a specific field as one of the following types:

- General field of 20 characters to be used for codes or text
- Quantity fields with a unit
- Value fields with a unit
- Date fields
- Check boxes

user-defined fields   Entry fields that can be freely defined for an activity or a work breakdown structure element (Project System) or an operation (Production Planning).

user exit   An interface provided by an SAP R/3 application that allows the user company to insert into a standard R/3 component a call to an additional ABAP/4 program that will be integrated with the rest of the application.

valuation date   Date on which materials and internal and external activities are evaluated in a costing.

valuation variant   Determines how the resources used, the external activities, and the overheads are to be valued in a costing (that is, at what prices).

variance category   Distinguishes variances according to their causes:

- Input—Price and usage variances
- Yield—Scrap, mix variances, labor efficiency variances, and schedule variances
- Allocation—Fixed-cost variances, over-absorption variances, and under-absorption variances

variance key   Controls how variances are calculated. Assigning a variance key to an object determines, for example, whether variances are calculated for the object by period or for the life of the object, which can be a cost center, an order, or a cost object identifier (ID).

variance version   Specifies the basis for the calculation of variances:

- How the target costs are calculated
- Which actual data is compared with the target costs
- Which variance categories are calculated

view   A relational method used to generate a cross-section of data stored in a database. A virtual table defined in the ABAP/4 Dictionary can define a view by specifying how and what will be selected from whichever tables are targeted.

volume variance   Cost difference between the fixed costs estimated for the products based on standard capacity and the allocated fixed costs that are too low or too high due to operating below or above capacity.

waiting-list booking   Booking priority assigned if all places on the business event are already booked.

WBS   See *Work Breakdown Structure (WBS)*.

WBS element   A concrete task or a partial task that can be subdivided.

Work Breakdown Structure (WBS)   A model of a project. Represents in a hierarchy the actions and activities to be carried out on a project. Can be displayed according to phase, function, and object.

work in progress   Unfinished products, the costs of which are calculated by subtracting the costs of the order that already are settled from the actual costs incurred for the order or by evaluating the yield confirmed to date.

work order   Generic term for the following order types:

- Production order
- Process order
- Maintenance order
- Inspection order
- Network

work order time   The specified time for the processing of a work order. In contrast to the occupancy time (standard time), the work order time refers to the worker, not to the means of operation.

work process   An SAP R/3 system task that can be assigned independently, for instance, to a dedicated application server—for example, dialog processing, updating a database from change documents, background processing, spooling, and lock management.

workflow management   Tool for automatic transaction processing used in a specific business environment.

workflow management event   A collection of attributes of objects that describes the change in an object's state.

working hours   The time during which an employee must make his labor available to the employer. The working hours are from the time of starting work up to the end of work, without calculation of breaks.

working in advance   Time worked above the agreed working hours because of a discrepancy between plant operating hours and working hours. This is often "reduced" in the form of bridge days or non-working shifts.

workplace   The actual location at which employees fulfill their tasks within the company's internal working system or organizational unit by means of work and work objects set up for the purpose. The workplace is the smallest spatial structural unit of the enterprise.

Index

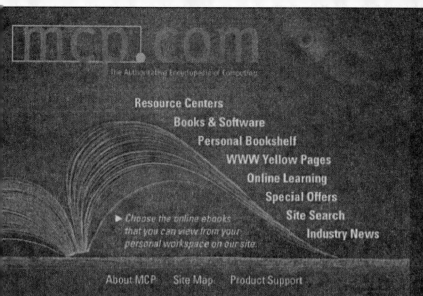

Other Related Titles

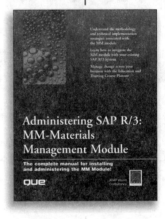
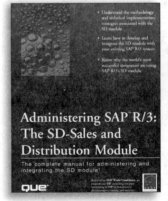

Why Join the ASAP team?

We are a fast growing dynamic group of companies operating globally in an exciting new virtual environment. We have the simple aim to be the best at what we do. We therefore look to recruit the best people on either contract or permanent basis

If you are any of the following, we would like to hear from you.

1. Highly Skilled and Experienced SAP Consultant.

You will have been working with SAP systems for many years and will be a project manager or consultant of standing in the industry. If you are willing to assist in the training and development and perhaps recruitment of your team, then we will be able to offer you exceptional financial rewards and the opportunity of developing the career of your choice.

2. Skilled in Another Area and Looking to Cross Train

You may be a computer expert or a business person with expertise in a particular area, perhaps, logistics, finance, distribution or H.R. etc., and/or with a particular industry knowledge. If you are committed to working with SAP systems in the long term, we will be able to offer you SAP cross training and vital experience. You must have a proven track record in your field and must be prepared to defer financial advancement whilst training and gaining experience. If you have the commitment and the skill you will in time be able to receive from us the high financial rewards and career development choice above.

3. A Person who has worked in a functional job
for an End User Company and who has been involved in all aspects of an SAP project from initial scoping to implementation and post implementation support.
You will have an excellent understanding of the industry or business function you are in. You are likely to have a good degree, ambition, drive, flexibility and the potential to become a top SAP consultant. You will thrive on the prospect of travel and living and working in other countries, jetting off around the world at short notice and working as part of a highly motivated and productive team. You must be committed to a long term career working with SAP. We will be able to offer you an interesting and rewarding career, giving you training and experience in a number of different roles. If you can prove yourself, you can expect rapid career development, with excellent financial rewards. Your only limit is your ability and your aspirations.

How To Contact Us
ASAP World Consultancy, ASAP House, PO Box 4463,
Henley on Thames, Oxfordshire RG9 6YN, UK
Tel:+44 (0)1491 414411   Fax: +44 (0)1491 414412

ASAP - 24 Hour - Virtual Office - New York, USA
Voice Mail: (212) 253 4180 Fax: (212) 253 4180

E-Mail: info@asap-consultancy.co.uk

Web site: http://www.asap-consultancy.co.uk/index.htm

A S A P
WORLD CONSULTANCY™

ASAP Worldwide
Enterprise Applications Resourcing & Recruitment

The company established in July 1997 has ambitious plans to become the world's largest global recruitment company specialising entirely in "the placement of permanent, temporary and contract staff who will be engaged in the implementation, support, training and documentation of systems known as enterprise applications". These include: SAP, BAAN, Peoplesoft, Oracle Applications, System Software Associations, Computer Associates, JD Edwards, Markam, JBA etc.

The company benefits from:

- Detailed knowledge of the market, its requirements and dynamics.

- Use of one of the world's most advanced recruitment systems.

- Access to large databases of candidates.

- A global approach to the staffing problems of a global market.

- Unique and innovative solutions for solving the staffing problems of a high growth market.

- A commitment to offer clients and candidates a professional, efficient and high quality service that is second to none.

- A commitment to the continual development of the services that we offer.

- Reciprocal partnership arrangements with other recruitment companies worldwide.

A S A P
WORLDWIDE™